BLOOD SACRIFICE

Their victims are helpless babies and innocent children. They prey on the weak and confused, using them without mercy for their sick rituals of mutilation and murder. They worship in secret at altars stained with human blood and suffering— often right next door to our homes and our schools.

And their numbers are growing each week.

Now, from the files of *True Detective* Magazine read the dramatic spine-tingling accounts of these CULT KILLERS, America's deadliest threat.

It could save your life.

CULT KILLERS

Edited by
ROSE G. MANDELSBERG

PINNACLE BOOKS
WINDSOR PUBLISHING CORP.

To Raphael whose support continues to guide and inspire me.

The editor wishes to thank the following individuals whose help was instrumental in making this book possible: Sara Heredia-Pearl, Jennifer Sawyer, Detective Don Bond of the Springfield, Oregon Police Department; Inspector Alva Busch, crime scene technician of the Illinois State Police; Detective Nelson Andreu, Miami Police Department; Captain Jerry Miklos and Sergeant Richard Keaton of the Marin County Sheriff's Department.

PINNACLE BOOKS

are published by

Windsor Publishing Corp.
475 Park Avenue South
New York, NY 10016

First Pinnacle Books printing: July, 1991

Printed in the United States of America

TABLE OF CONTENTS

"OCCULT CRIME: TERROR FOR THE INNOCENTS!"

by William K. Beaver

As Richard Ramirez, California's "Night Stalker" murderer, left the courtroom, he raised his left hand, a satanic pentagram drawn on its palm, and said "Hail Satan." In so doing, he joined an infamous group of criminals whose crimes draw inspiration from a belief in satanism and other occult practices.

Crimes linked to the occult vary from child abuse to murder. Police have discovered corpses with satanic pentagrams carved into the chest of the victim. Voodoo and Santeria cults often mutilate and sacrifice animals, leaving the carcasses to be discovered.

This article explores the field of investigating occult-related crimes, with particular attention paid to ritual abuse cases, where children may have been the victims of satanic cults.

It would not be prudent to detail the actual procedures used by police to investigate and gather intelligence on satanic groups and their crimes. Many common methods, such as informants, are readily used. But sometimes additional instruction is needed to teach officers what to look for and how to interpret what they find. This task falls on people such as retired Police Captain Dale Griffis, a nationally recognized expert on occult crime.

Investigating crimes of the occult seldom produces evidence that is easy to understand, interpret or sometimes even to believe. A general class of cases which fits this description are cases now commonly referred to as ritual child abuse.

Jonathan Smith (not his real name) is a young boy whose parents claim he is a victim of ritual child abuse. The parents agreed to talk to *Inside Detective* on the condition they remain anonymous. Their case characterizes the problems faced by law enforcement officials in cases related to occult crime.

Two days after starting kindergarten, Jonathan Smith began making strange, almost unintelligible drawings which frightened his parents. The pictures were dark and foreboding, filled with symbols and shapes, unlike the happy pictures of trees, animals and sunshine which Jonathan had drawn days earlier.

Jonathan also started asking strange questions

about cemeteries, skeletons and dying, formulating "what if" questions, such as the following: "Mom, what if I killed somebody?"

Jonathan's parents became frightened by the change in their son and gently asked him questions, trying to find out why he was so scared and why his attention was focused on such dark subjects. When they asked Jonathan to describe his drawings, he told them about being part of a ritual, about seeing people dressed in robes and being taken from school to a house in the trees."

The house in the trees was only one aspect of Jonathan's story. He also said that he was taken down into the basement at his school and forced to do things with people he called "judges." When asked by his mother how he knew they were judges, Jonathan replied, "Because they were wearing black robes."

Jonathan described the basement in considerable detail, saying that the people there also made him eat little white "puffballs." Doctors who questioned Jonathan about the effect of the "puffballs" surmised that he had been given some sort of LSD.

Jonathan's parents, naturally distraught, went to talk with school officials. After a heated discussion, the school administrators and the parents went to the basement. Sure enough, they saw it was just like the description given by Jonathan, but there was no evidence to support their charges of abuse.

Jonathan's teacher refused to talk without a lawyer present and in the end, did not talk to the boy's parents. According to school personnel, the teacher has been on leave for the past two years and she cannot be reached for comment.

Further investigation by the police and Jonathan's parents was inconclusive. The parents did find a tree house that matched the description given by Jonathan. A crude outline of a child was outlined on the floor and various symbols were spray-painted on the walls.

According to the police, the case is considered open and closed, depending on which detective is asked. The Smiths have had their son in therapy for three years and the school district supplies a private teacher for in-home instruction.

Meanwhile, Mrs. Smith continued her fight, searching for evidence so she can find out exactly what happened to Jonathan. In the process, she discovered several groups which grew from a need to help parents and victims of ritual abuse cases—which the police say are the hardest to substantiate. Over the next three years, Jonathan's parents would discover that he was only one victim of a relatively recent crime phenomenon—the crime of ritual child abuse, a crime with roots in the practice of satanism and the occult.

The subject of ritual child abuse first came to

national attention as the result of the 1983 Mc-Martin Preschool case in California. Several children at the McMartin Preschool complained that they had been sexually abused while there.

The children claimed that several of the preschool workers, including the owner and her son, were among the abusers. While sexual abuse of children was certainly not unheard of in California, several other aspects described by the children shocked even veteran child advocates.

Soon after the initial complaints were filed, parents who had children at the McMartin Preschool received a frightening memorandum from the chief of police in Manhattan Beach which started with the following paragraphs:

Dear Parent:

Department is concluding a criminal investigation involving child molestation (288 P.C.). Ray Buckey, an employee of Virginia McMartin's Preschool, was arrested September 7, 1983, by this department.

The following procedure is obviously an unpleasant one, but to protect the rights of your children, as well as the rights of the accused, this inquiry is necessary for a complete investigation.

Records indicate that your child has been or is currently a student at the preschool. We are asking your assistance in this continuing investigation. Please question your child to see if he or she has been a witness to any crime or he or she has been a victim. Our investigation indicates that possible criminal acts include: oral sex, fondling of genitals, buttocks or chest area, and sodomy, possibly committed under the pretense of "taking the child's temperature." Also, photos may have been taken of children without their clothing . . .

As if the police letter was not enough to completely frighten parents, word soon spread that some of the McMartin Preschool children said that the sexual abuse was accompanied by rituals involving people in long, dark robes, small candles burning all over the room, and constant chanting in a language they could not understand. The children told investigators they were taken from the preschool, driven to an airport, flown to a distant location where the ceremonies and abuse took place and then transported back to the preschool, all in the same day.

Police investigators immediately questioned all the workers at the school. As the public pressure increased, the investigation took on a national priority. Eventually, seven people connected with the school were arrested, including the owner of the school, on a grand jury indictment that listed 323 allegations of child abuse. As a result, the preschool closed in 1984. Since very little of the children's allegations could be confirmed with hard evidence, five of the defendants were released. Investigators relied on the testimony of child psychologists.

Even though little evidence was found to support claims of occult-related activity, the episode produced a nationwide panic. Parents became suspicious of their care employees and almost overnight, more cases of the crime began to appear and it was given a new name—"ritual child abuse."

Believing in episodes of occult-related ritual abuse was not especially difficult for a nation which had been shocked by the "Manson Family," the "Son of Sam," and the suicide of 900 people by request of a preacher wearing sunglasses.

Most of the ritual abuse cases reported across the country shared at least one common denominator with other cases, including:
*Molestation and devil worship in a church or abandoned buildings
*A reference to being in tunnels
*Animals seen in cages
*Burned, stabbed or murdered babies
*Molestations in basements
*Mock marriages
*Nude photography
*Sticking the child with pins or needles
*Foreign objects inserted in the rectum
*Children or molesters wearing robes
*Drinking a pink or red liquid which made them sleepy
*Forcing the victim to have oral sex with others

or animals

Critics who were highly skeptical of the ritual abuse cases claimed that the common factors and the hysteria could all be traced back to a single book called *Michelle Remembers,* about a girl who supposedly remembers under hypnosis being used by her parents in the activities of an occult group. The skeptics also claimed that this approach explained the general lack of evidence in the cases, while the proponents defending the children's stories said the lack of evidence proved the sophistication and cleverness of the child abusers.

In fairness to the skeptics, however, two reporters pointed out in an in-depth study of ritual abuse that of the 36 cases of ritual abuse examined, 95 people were criminally charged, but only 23 at the time of the report had been convicted. Forty-five of those charged had the charges dismissed and 11 were acquitted. Even in the 23 cases of conviction, little evidence was produced to give credence to the idea of satanic connections. On the other hand, children have a hazy time sense and do not make good witnesses.

With the rise in reports of ritual abuse, the general increase in cult activity, the public demands for action and the tremendous amount of media attention paid to all three, it became inevitable that a group of professional police investigators would evolve, a group that concerned itself with, and became experts in, the crimes connected with the occult, satanism and other forms of aberrant, nontraditional criminal behavior.

Dr. Dale Griffis retired from Ohio's Tiffin Police Department after 26 years of service. The last few years of his career gave him an opportunity to become one of the foremost experts on cult activities and nontraditional groups in the United States.

This reporter's interview with Dr. Griffis took place in a small hotel room in Columbia, Ohio. Griffis constantly stayed on the move, his week's itinerary was hectic, to say the least. His week took him from the University of Kansas to Southern Illinois University, then to Bowling Green University in Ohio, an interview with the British Broadcasting Corporation, then finally to Columbus, where he was to lecture on occult crime to a group of students and Human Services personnel at Ohio State University. According to Griffis, it was a typical week.

Dale Griffis is a distinguished-looking gentleman whose calm demeanor belies the horrifying things he had seen, both as a police captain, and as an occult investigator. The crime that made him become involved in the subject of cults and occult crime involved a young boy's suicide. But to hear him tell the story in person reveals the emotion that Griffis felt when he was asked to help investigate the suicide of the young boy who was obviously infatuated with the occult.

"A friend of mine called me from Willard (a city near Tiffin, Ohio) and said that he had a suicide that he wanted me to help investigate. I took my police captain at the time and drove over there," Griffis recalls.

"On the young man's body was written 'Lord Master Satan, I'm coming home.' I had seen suicides before, but this one really affected me, mostly because of the occult-related material connected with the case. I wondered why such a young man had become involved in this type of thing."

Griffis was an experienced detective, having followed in his father's footsteps in the Tiffin Police Department. Tiffin is a medium-sized town about 40 miles southwest of Toledo and different kinds of crime occur there. But occult-related crime was something new for Griffis.

"We tried to apply some solid police techniques to the case, wanting to understand why the kid did it. His parents needed to know. But we came up with zero.

"I remembered hearing about a similar case in California, so I got in touch with Sandy Gallant and she gave me some excellent pointers on how to proceed with the case."

Sandy Gallant is often referred to as the original expert on occult and cult group-related crime. Detective Gallant works for the Intelligence Division of the San Francisco Police Department. Her advice to Griffis made him realize that very soon the problem of cult groups and their related crimes would require special expertise, so he talked his superiors into allowing him to go to California and be trained in the field.

In 1976, Griffis went to California to begin studying the field of occult crime under the tutelage of Sandy Gallant and others.

She showed him around the occult-related places in San Francisco, the occult bookstores and the herbalist stores, where modern-day witches can buy the ingredients necessary for their concoctions.

Griffis went with Gallant to see the home of an ex-lion tamer who started the Church of Satan. They decided not to go up to the door, both because there was a fence around the man's house and because the man supposedly had a live lion living on the premises.

"Besides the fact that I'm not a fool (referring to the lion), I wanted facts, not hoopla," Griffis explains.

In the process of learning about occult crime, Griffis managed to earn college degrees which helped his work. He received a bachelor's degree in psychology. He earned a master's degree by writing a thesis about intelligence gathering for small police departments. His doctoral dissertation was entitled "Mind Control Cults and Their Effects on the Objectives of Law Enforcement."

Although Griffis retired from the police department, he is in constant contact with police agencies and other concerned individuals across the country. He is widely consulted on all aspects of cults and their activities. Over the years, he has built up an impressive database of information concerning cult activities and nontraditional groups.

"The thing just seemed to start growing and now encompasses three computers, five university interns, twenty-two four-drawer filing cabinets of information, and three thousand volumes dealing with the subject.

"I get a lot of calls for information from police departments wanting to know what to look for, which is why I started traveling around the country giving seminars on cult activity. But the majority of my calls are from very frightened and very concerned parents wanting to know what to do about their children, who have somehow come into contact with these cult groups."

The occult groups themselves are not the subject of criminal investigations, but rather the acts they commit. Some groups are especially adept at hiding behind the first amendment of the Constitution, but to investigators like Dale Griffis, the attempt to hide is a farce.

"Under the First Amendment of the Constitution, you have the right to believe anything you want to believe. The practices, though, cannot infringe on the rights of others. I'm interested in aberrant, nontraditional groups who break the law, who use mind control, animal mutilation, illegal drugs and sometimes kidnapping."

When Griffis gives seminars to law enforcement agencies, he tries to teach them what he has learned from experience. There are certain aspects of the satanist's belief system which can make satanic crimes easier to process. The satanist follows a calendar of special holidays so often crimes such as animal sacrifices will occur on those dates.

He also tries to show the police officer how to process the crime scene of an occult-related crime. Satanists will often leave border markings by using colored thread or string. Police often find rocks arranged in certain patterns, or satanic symbols carved into trees.

The hardest part about investigating the satanic crime comes when attention centers on a particular area, which in turn drives the group further underground. Sometimes the police have found it necessary to use clandestine means to gather information against the criminals, such as recording the performance of rituals using infrared and light-gathering night observation equipment. The actual spots of satanic rituals are generally not used again once they are discovered, making the task of finding the group very difficult.

As police investigators become more sophisticated and knowledgeable in dealing with occult-related crime, they continually face new types of situations and changing patterns of occult group activity. The problem becomes even more difficult when the criminal involved is a lone self-styled satanist or someone just experimenting with the occult.

Griffis says the current problem centers not so much on actual occult group activity, but on teenagers and others who are caught up in their interest of the occult.

"Right now, today, we see a lot of problems with the trappings of occultism. Not the American Church of Satan or other groups like that, but kids who are getting involved with the outward occult trappings like books, movies, music and the like."

Griffis' observation supports the results of a Gallup Poll that was conducted in 1988, concerning teenagers' belief in the supernatural. When questioned about various supernatural categories, 58 percent said they believed in astrology and that a person's life could be influenced by the stars and planets, 50 percent believed in the reality of extrasensory perception, 29 percent said they believed in witchcraft, and 22 percent said they believed in ghosts.

If the belief in witchcraft continues to relate to crime, then Griffis says he will continue to pursue his interests, both for himself and for others who need the information.

"Take the McMartin case for example. Whether it turns out to be true or false or whatever, the children are the ones who suffered. There's been a lot of occult-related crime out there. All I'm trying to do is gain some insight for people in trouble," Griffis says.

EDITOR'S NOTE:
Jonathan Smith is not the real name of the person so named in the foregoing story. A fictitious name has been used because there is no reason for public interest in the identity of this person.

"SKINHEADS ON A RAMPAGE."

by William K. Beaver

They have uniquely American acronyms—CASH, WASH, BASH and WAR. They're almost as infamous as the drug-related gangs spreading outward from Los Angeles, but they're only a fraction of a size. The gangs are low in number, but high in profile. They are recognized immediately, their appearance not easily forgotten. They are the skinheads.

The skinheads found in as many as 21 American states and in several foreign countries are not all racist and violent, but the groups who have come to embrace the loose tenets of national socialism, and whose ranks are continually courted by larger American neo-Nazi organizations, create a disproportionate amount of press coverage and fear.

American skinheads are a remnant of the British skinhead punk-rockers who came to life in the 70s. The British skins, as they are sometimes called, have since become quite visible, mainly by causing major disturbances at international soccer matches. The British skinhead ideology moved through other European countries and arrived in the United States in the early 1980s.

Like so many lifestyle imports, good and bad, the skinheads started primarily in New York and California, originally as members of the punk-rock scene. The early punk-rock bands gave rebellion against society as their battle cry, but the fascist groups took the rebellion and added far-right extremism for their own blend of anti-society music.

Several rock bands now in Europe consider themselves united with various national socialist groups, especially Britain's neo-Nazi National Front. The bands, sporting such names as Skrewdriver, Brutal Attack and Skullhead, record music with lyrics which are overtly racist and brutally inflammatory. The neo-Nazi skinhead bands have only recently become known in the United States, as American skinheads have started to import their music and their message.

A group of skinheads in Chicago called Romantic Violence not only tries to promote the British bands like Skrewdriver, but it has also invented its own melange of hate music with a band ominously called Final Solution, after Hitler's program to exterminate the Jews. Most of the skinhead bands tend to alienate the majority of the punks, who think of the skinheads as too far right and too extreme.

Police officials acknowledge that the neo-Nazi skinheads are becoming increasingly more violent and dangerous. They have committed murders, robberies and assaults on blacks, Asians, Pakistanis and other immigrants. Three skinheads in Seattle were charged with the murder of an Ethiopian at a local grocery store after they beat him to death with a baseball bat. A 16-year-old skinhead in Tampa, Florida, received a sentence of life imprisonment for killing a street person, and on the anniversary of *Kristallnacht* in Chicago, several skinheads were arrested for vandalizing a Jewish temple by breaking all the windows and painting swastikas on the wall with red paint.

The skinhead crime rate is especially high near colleges and universities where lifestyles can be found that are both sympathetic to the skinheads and conducive to violence. This locale of skinhead activity corresponds with a recent general statistical rise of racism and racially-inspired harassment and assaults in the nation's colleges.

The rise in racist crime is directly related to a growing ignorance of the state of racism in the United States, according to Mae Owens, a spokesperson for the Center For Democratic Renewal, an Atlanta-based group that monitors racist and far-right-wing activity.

"One of the reasons you see so much violence

from these groups is because they perceive themselves as victims," Owens maintains. "The problem is that young people are presented with a picture by other skinheads and white supremacists that tells them that certain groups, the minorities or perhaps homosexuals, are given too much power. They are told that these groups receive all kinds of special benefits like job preference, but according to the white supremacists, the whites get nothing. So the young people being recruited start to feel as though things are against them and they decide they want to fight back.

"The skinheads often attack minorities and usually they outnumber the victim several times over. The choice of victim comes directly from their ideology which says that the problems they have come from all these other people—the blacks, the Jews, the Asians. Their logic says that if you wipe these people out, then their problems will go away."

Though the primary targets of the neo-Nazi skinheads are usually members of minorities, the hate groups will not hesitate to attack those who they feel are against their cause or who are seen to be sympathetic to non-whites. The skinheads also sometimes commit robberies and assaults for no particular reason.

An incident in New Jersey was videotaped proof of skinhead random crime. A white man with his wife and infant daughter were waiting by a train platform when four skinheads in leather jackets came toward them, yelling racial slurs for no apparent reason. As a struggle between the skinheads and the male victim broke out, a Port Authority Trans-Hudson (PATH) communications specialist saw the fight begin via the videocamera mounted over the platform. The specialist turned on a video-recorder and then called the police. While waiting for the police to arrive, the specialist yelled through the public address system for the assailants to stop. The skinheads were arrested and charged with second-degree robbery and attempted second-degree assault.

Another incident shows what the skinheads are willing to do, even to their own members. A man who started a group called the Aryan Youth Movement-White Student Union fell in love with a woman who he claimed taught him it was wrong to hate. He decided to leave his organization and was found with his horizontally outstretched hands nailed to a six-foot board.

Neo-Nazi skinhead ideology consists of a loosely connected hodgepodge of classic youth rebellion, punk-music intensity, and the political renderings of neo-national socialism. The following excerpt is from a copy of an Aryan Youth Movement-White Student Union recruitment newsletter. It illustrates the violent vein running through the neo-Nazi skinheads.

26

"The AYM-SWU is a voluntary association of white students. On school campuses throughout America, there are Jewish, Black, Chicano, Asian, Indian, Arab, Communist, Socialist, and homosexual Student Unions . . . All of the above groups promote race-mixing, miscegenation, sexual defiance and a liberal platform . . . Whatever solution insures us our rights, we shall utilize it. We assist white students towards this task and awaken within each of them the burning fire of RACISM."

According to the newsletter, donations from various sources allowed them to distribute 50,000 copies of what they called their "revolutionary recruitment issue." The most revealing part of the newsletter describes the tactics adopted by the AYM-WSU which in turn sheds light on many of the skinhead crimes around the country:

"The Aryan Youth Movement utilizes . . . specific new tactics strictly designed for AYM. 1. "Ganging Up" creates a gang-like mentality among young students and non-students alike. 2. Screw with AYM, you get screwed back. This goes for teachers, police and students who get in the way of revolutionary goal. 3. Our goal is complete racial separatism. 4. Confiscating and destroying all non-Aryan literature from our schools and libraries. 5. Putting up white power posters, stickers, and fliers, whenever we want, wherever we want."

The skinheads mentioned in their newsletter that they are different from the original founders of the Aryan Youth Movement; because earlier tactics didn't work, the new ones would. The new Aryan Youth Movement is led by a young man whose family figures prominently in the American hate movement—his father is the head of the White Aryan Resistance, one of the most vocal of the white supremacy groups. Together, Dave Smith and his father Larry have a plan—they want to unite the skinheads under one white supremacist, neo-Nazi umbrella.

Larry Smith has told a *Rolling Stone* magazine reporter, "They're (the skinheads) pissed off at the system . . . they have their place in the movement."

Larry Smith has played in the white supremacist theater for many years and is a former Grand Dragon of the Ku Klux Klan. He lives in a small California town called Fallbrook.

Smith heads a white supremacy organization called the White Aryan Resistance and his name frequently pops up in discussions about white supremacy and organized hatred groups. He says he has contacts with all of the prominent white supremacy groups and claims to have a loyal audience of at least 5,000 people.

According to various sources, the White Aryan

Resistance has been involved in the entire spectrum of white supremacy activities. When the leader and founder of the Aryan Youth Movement decided to leave his fledgling organization, Larry Smith quickly intervened and installed a new president into the reformed and reorganized White Aryan Resistance-Aryan Youth Movement; Smith's son Dave.

Together they have tried to organize the skinheads into a cohesive, politically aware movement. Law enforcement officials and the Smiths themselves say that the result is less than successful.

The measures taken by Smith are high profile, including the attempt to start a white supremacy record label to promote bands in the United States similar in style and message to the British neo-Nazi bands. To stay in communication with his skinhead youth, Smith uses a telephone message machine in the name of the White Aryan Resistance, where members can call for the latest news.

A recent edition of the message started with a wolf cry, over which Smith announces that "this is the cry of the wolf, listen for it as you travel the highways, and byways." The tape continues with a message that says the Los Angeles skinheads are organizing a campaign to call the South African consulates around the country and are expressing support for the white people of

South Africa. Perhaps the most damaging part of the message is the announcement of a person's name, address and telephone number in Florida, with the proclamation that this person "is a sharpie and does not like white racial skins. Ask him why he doesn't like you."

The message continues by saying that Jesse Jackson should stay away from protesting at the Aryan Nation's Congress in Idaho because, "unlike the conservatives, they (the skinheads) bite back. Besides there are hundreds of these meetings going on around the country and you can't protest them all."

What makes Smith so dangerous, according to his critics, is that he goes after young people, often as young as 12 or 13, and tries to indoctrinate them into the white supremacist ideology. The methods used to appeal to the youth are tailored to target youth—usually white, suburban upper and middle-class young people who need and want to belong to something.

"The leadership of these hate groups try to bring youth into groups they can identify with. They want the youth for their cause because the older people have already dealt with the black/white issue and some people refuse to acknowledge that any sort of racist problem still exists in the United States," argues Mae Owens.

"What this does is create a kind of national blanket of silence. The supremacist groups convince the youth that something is wrong in our country, for example the blacks are gaining too much power, and then they say that only their white group is doing anything to stop them."

Mixed with a refusal by some people to see anything wrong with racism is the disproportionate amount of press coverage the skinheads receive. One extremely visible example was an episode of Geraldo Rivera's talk show, which he called "Young Hate Mongers."

Rivera scheduled several members of the neo-Nazi skinheads to appear, including Dave Smith, representing the White Aryan Resistance; the skinhead leader of the American Front, and the leader of the Skinheads of National Resistance. To argue against them was Roy Innis, chairman of the Congress of Racial Equality.

Halfway through the taping of the now famous episode, Smith announced that he "was sick and tired of Uncle Tom here (meaning Innis) sucking up and trying to be a white man." Innis jumped up and started choking Smith. Suddenly, several skinheads came out of the audience as a brawl broke out, and in the melee, Rivera was hit with a chair and wound up with a broken nose. For the next several days, Rivera and the skinheads received a wealth of publicity from the incident.

To date, most of the skinhead groups have not responded to Smith's attempts at unity, keeping instead only a loose association with each other.

When the skinheads do respond, the results produced by only a few members can disrupt a city and in some cases, raise constitutional questions.

The Ohio town of Cincinnati is, by any definition, a conservative town. Nowhere in the city can adult materials—books or videos—be purchased. Attempting to curb violent crime, Cincinnati recently passed an ordinance requiring purchasers of handguns to wait for a two-week period. So when two local skinhead groups started advertising for members and spreading hate messages on local television channels, the city's conservatism quickly faced a challenge.

Two neo-Nazi skinhead groups, one called the "White American Skinheads" (WASH), and the other called the "SS Action Group" began by recruiting members from the Cincinnati suburbs and from across the Ohio River in Kentucky. Recruiters passed out fliers and leaflets in Cincinnati which read:

. . . *we are part of a worldwide white nationalist movement of youth. We of WASH are proud to be white, gentile and American. We would prefer to smash the present anti-white, Zionist (Jew), puppet-run government with a healthy, new white man's order! Band with us today, white man! Hail victory!*

The skinhead groups began in August 1987, putting recruiting messages on the public access channel in the Cincinnati suburb of Norwood.

The 17-second advertisements called for people to "join the American Nazis and smash red, Jew and black power."

Several residents raised complaints about messages, but representatives from the cable television company replied with public announcements stating that the groups were within their constitutional rights to air the advertisements.

One area businessman privately conducted a poll and then held a news conference to try and stop the messages from appearing. The plan was unsuccessful, but when a member of the Cincinnati Citizen's Cable Board resigned because the message was still being played, the case came to national attention, through the entertainment weekly *Variety*.

The Cincinnati mayor suggested in October 1987 that the public access channels be suspended until a solution could be found. One of the leaders of the skinheads told reporters that the skinheads would try to distribute videotapes of Larry Smith's television neo-Nazi talk show, "Race and Reason," which they claimed was already being aired in 12 states.

The shows never materialized and eventually the recruiting messages stopped. The skinheads became less visible until December 1988, when a fight broke out between racist and non-racist skinheads during a Cincinnati anti-racism march.

Cincinnati Police Sergeant Dave Hall was responsible for keeping intelligence on youth gang activity in Cincinnati.

"The skinheads that were in Cincinnati were very transient, almost moving as the weather changes. One of their leaders was from the skinhead group in Chicago, and the leader of the SS—Action Group chapter here in Cincinnati was from Detroit," he says.

"Even though the skinheads got a lot of press from the incident with the television stations, they were never that big in Cincinnati. Their membership was estimated to be about forty people at their peak. But the majority of the group left Cincinnati in 1988."

Sergeant Hall feels that because the phenomenon of skinhead gangs is recent, not a great deal is known about them. The skinhead members and their crimes tend to receive tremendous amounts of press coverage, but the national membership of skinheads in all the various groups is only estimated to be about 2,000.

According to Sergeant Hall, effective police work brings the youth gangs under scrutiny and often control. Eventually the gang members just leave the city for somewhere less difficult. The key factor in the Cincinnati police program against the youth gang activity is to always treat all crimes as simply crime and not attach any notoriety to the situation.

Cincinnati is not the only community that has

fought back against the hatred ideology of the neo-Nazi skinheads. A community in California's Napa Valley decided to confront the neo-Nazis when a group tried to organize an "Aryan Woodstock."

On the northeast side of San Pablo Bay lies Vallejo, a city of roughly 100,000 only 45 miles north of San Francisco. Vallejo sits at the edge of California's Napa Valley region, known internationally for its wine industry. On March 4, 1989, it also became known for the attempted white supremacy rock concert. Larry Smith of the White Aryan Resistance and the chairman of the neo-Nazi skinhead group, the American Front, organized the concert with the intent of recruiting new members using the ageless, youth-oriented medium of music.

The bands they attracted to participate represented the frontline of America white supremacy music. The scheduled appearance by the Boot Boys of Tulsa, Hammerhead from Wisconsin, and New Glory from Philadelphia was billed as an "Aryan Woodstock."

The organizers rented some acres of land from a Vallejo doctor who later said the group represented themselves as the Environmental Action Group. According to the organizers, they hoped to attract nearly 1,500 people.

When the local community found out what was planned, local and county officials searched for a way to stop the concert, fearing wide out-breaks of violence. A hearing was held at the Napa County Board of Supervisors, where Smith argued that the officials were trying to prevent Smith's group from freely expressing their political views.

Officials from the combined interests of Napa and Salone Counties argued that the group was violating a 1971 county ordinance which required that all organizers for outdoor concert events must obtain proper permits from the county. The county claimed the purpose of the permits was to insure that the groups responsible for any concert event provided portable restrooms, running water and measures for organized crowd control and parking facilities.

The day before the planned event, a Napa County Superior Court judge ruled for the county. He issued a restraining order which denied the group's plans for a concert, but the judge also ordered that the group could still have a meeting if they wished. The message on WAR's machine said "it is on . . . the party's on, boys."

"On the day of the meeting, most of the law enforcement people in the area were very concerned about the potential for violence, knowing the reputation of these groups," said Lieutenant Clare Sallede of the Vallejo Police.

The day of the meeting brought weather hardly outstanding for an outdoor gathering. Because of the continuous rain, only about 100-200 skinheads actually came to the event. But there were far more protesters against the skinheads. There were members from such anti-racist groups as the Jewish Defense League, the Marxist-Leninist Party, the John Brown Anti-Klan Committee, and an Ad Hoc Committee to Oppose the Nazi Skinheads.

"It was very strange there. There were only a few actual skinheads. There were far more protesters. And there were actually more law enforcement people there than both groups combined," said Lieutenant Sallede.

There were an estimated 450 police officers on duty or nearby the event, with several hundred more on alert in neighboring areas and cities.

There were only minor scuffles and shouting between the groups who were kept separated by police. The protesters started leaving around 2:00 p.m. and by 4:30 even the skinheads were gone. But from the point of view of the skinheads, the event was a success. The event received extensive coverage in *The Christian Science Monitor,* the San Francisco newspapers and *The New York Times.* "I think in our area (Vallejo), no one really cared who these guys (skinheads) were until this event took place. They got far more press coverage than was needed. I think they feed off the media," said Lieutenant Sallede.

The event at Vallejo is only a partial clue to the measures the large neo-Nazi, white supremacy groups are taking to encourage white youths to join the skinhead organizations, now considered to be the so-called fighting arm of the white supremacists. The national groups announced plans to have a skinhead gathering as part of the annual Aryan Nation's Congress in Hayden Lake, Idaho, in April 1989.

The problem with the skinheads will only grow worse, according to a 1989 report published by the Southern Poverty Law Center and similar report from the Anti-Defamation League of the B'nai B'rith. Both reports state that the skinheads are starting to increase their alliance with the far-right white supremacy groups, posing considerable danger.

The Southern Poverty Law Center warns that "not since the height of Klan activity during the civil rights era has there been a white supremacist group so obsessed with violence."

As the spokeswoman of the Center for Democratic Renewal sees it, the skinheads are the most dangerous of the white supremacists.

"They are becoming the white supremacist's warriors, their own army of street fighters."

EDITOR'S NOTE:
Mae Owens, Larry and Dave Smith are not the

real names of the persons so named in the foregoing story. Fictitious names have been used because there is no reason for public interest in the identities of these persons.

"ONE SOUL SACRIFICED AT AN ALTAR OF EVIL!"

by Bruce Gibney

In the Fall of 1988, NBC aired a two-hour special on Satanism in America. Produced by Geraldo Rivera, the sensational documentary jolted complacent viewers as it unrolled gruesome footage of Satanic rituals and human sacrifices intercut with a panel discussion composed of real-life witches and warlocks.

Critics wrote it off as tabloid sleaze, but millions watched—and wondered—their concern going beyond curiosity. In the nine months following the documentary, newspapers around the country carried stories of devil sacrifices.

Among the most shocking:

—In San Francisco, a former waiter was sentenced to life in prison for the kidnap, rape and murder of a Skid Row drifter. According to testimony, the victim had been tied to a bed, gang-raped, then murdered in a Satanic ritual in which his blood was drained and a pentagram was carved into his chest.

—In the small town of Carl Junction, Missouri, five teenagers, all admitted disciples of Satan, confessed to murdering a 19-year-old classmate. They told police they did it because they wanted to perform a human sacrifice and because, according to the Satanic bible, "it was all right to kill someone if the person deserved it."

—In Tampa, Florida, a 19-year-old confessed to stabbing his mother 40 times in an insane act of devotion to Satan. On the day of the murder, the deranged son wrote a "things to do" note that read: "Go to school. Leave at 11:45. Drive to Mom's house. Say hello. Stab her dead."

Arrested, the youth showed police a Satanic poem he had read over his mother's corpse that read, "Lord Satan, I have stricken this woman from the Earth. I have slain the womb from which I was born."

By May 1989, concern over Satanic cults reached such a point that a weekly tabloid published a cover story, "How To Tell If Your Kid Worships Satan." It advised parents to be on the lookout if their teenage children lost their sense of humor, dressed in black and were fascinated with bizarre symbols and heavy metal music.

It sold over one million copies.

The story quoted a Satanic expert who said there had been estimates that as many as 50,000 youths are killed each year during Satanic rituals in America.

One of those murders took place in Douglas County, Georgia. Until last year, the black arts and red devil were subjects best left to tabloid talk show hosts and ministers in Douglas' many fundamentalist churches.

After events in early 1988, Satanic cults were the hot topic of conversation in this small rural country west of Atlanta, Georgia and a source of concern.

On January 27, 1988, a detective with the Gonzales, Louisiana Police Department contacted the Douglas County Sheriff's Office. He told Major Phil Miller that he had information about the murder of a young woman in his county.

In the early morning hours of January 26, 1988, a patrol officer was cruising the downtown business district of Gonzales when he spotted a van with a Georgia license plate driving in a suspicious manner.

Wondering what the out-of-state van was doing in that part of town at that hour, the officer followed for several blocks, then pulled the van over when it did not make a complete stop at a stop sign.

Inside the vehicle were Terry Belcher and Robert McIntyre, both 16, and Malisa Earnest, 17. All three were from Douglasville, Georgia.

Belcher said they had left Douglasville for a

vacation in New Orleans. A license plate check, however, showed the van had been reported stolen by McIntyre's parents. The trio was booked into the Gonzales jail in connection with the reported theft of the van.

Later that morning, Sergeant Bill Landry of the Gonzales Police Department was contacted at his home and told that a female informant at the county jail had asked to speak to him.

The 23-year-old woman had been picked up for loitering and was due to be released. She insisted, however, on first talking to Landry. Landry knew the woman; she had helped solve several cases.

But what could be so important that she would want to drag him to the jail?

Curious, he went to find out.

The inmate was brought to an interrogation room. Visibly upset, she said she had shared the same jail cell with Malisa Earnest, who told her a wild story involving a Satanic cult and the murder of a young woman.

According to her story, Earnest and another teenager had been picked up by two teenagers who took them to a farmhouse near Douglasville.

There, Earnest said, according to the informant, they smoked marijuana, listened to heavy metal music and conducted Satanic rites that included reading from the Satanic bible and drinking blood.

Earnest further related, the inmate said, that they murdered her hitchhiking companion in an effort to conjure up Satan, then buried the body.

The informant said her blood went ice-cold as the teen described the Satanic rituals and the grisly murder of the hitchhiker.

She said she had met a lot of tough, violent characters on the street, but this one with the pretty, wistful smile and her story of human sacrifice was by far the scariest.

"I really believe she did all those things she said she did," the inmate said.

She told Landry she was so scared that she did not press for the name of the victim or where the body was buried. Only after the inmate was let go, did she summon the courage to contact Landry.

Landry said he had no way of knowing if Malisa Earnest was telling the truth, but he did trust the inmate, who called him to the jail.

"She was damn scared," he said. "I know she wasn't making it up."

Major Phil Miller didn't know what to make of it. His detectives kept close tabs on things going on in the county and he had heard nothing about human sacrifices. One detective had investigated a report of strangers gathering at an abandoned church but determined that it was just a bunch of kids getting together to drink beer.

Miller checked Missing Persons. There was nothing on a teenage girl such as the one who was supposed to have been sacrificed on the farm.

A crime check on the three suspects did not turn up anything to indicate that they were mixed up in anything as gruesome as witchcraft and human sacrifice.

Belcher had been arrested on a few misdemeanor charges. McIntyre and Earnest were both clean. Their most serious offense was the stolen-car rap — which wasn't all that serious, since the van belong to McIntyre's parents.

Major Miller reported his findings to Sheriff Earl Lee. "Where are they now?" the sheriff asked.

Miller said Belcher and McIntyre were being held in the Gonzales jail on the stolen car warrant. Malisa Earnest claimed she had only been a passenger in the van and had been released.

"All this stuff about Satanism and human sacrifices sounds pretty far out," the sheriff admitted. "Any idea who the victim is?"

Miller shook his head negatively. "We will check it out. You never know these days."

Police learned that Malisa Earnest lived with her parents in eastern Douglas County but had recently been sent to a juvenile home for troubled kids.

Things got interesting after police called the juvenile home and learned that Malisa and three other girls had left the facility and were listed as runaways.

Two of the girls had returned. Still missing was Theresa Simmons, 17.

The group-home supervisor said the teen was deeply troubled when admitted but had been making progress in dealing with her problems.

"It surprised me that she ran away," she said. "She was very bright and had made a great deal of improvement."

The supervisor said the juvenile home was not a prison or detention facility and it was not uncommon for girls new to the system to run away. Often they returned in a few days and stayed to work out their problems.

"I expected Theresa to be back," the supervisor said. "I was really surprised when we didn't hear from her."

In questioning friends, police learned that Theresa had contacted a girl who had been at the juvenile facility, but the girl had since returned home.

The girl said she had heard from Theresa several days after she ran away. "She told me that she and another girl ran off just to see what it was like," the girl explained. "She said they had gotten picked up by some teenagers hitchhiking and were living in a big farmhouse."

The girlfriend related that Theresa did not

sound happy and said she felt like a prisoner at the farmhouse and wanted to go home.

"She seemed real unhappy," the girlfriend said.

The last time she heard from Theresa was Friday, January 22nd. Theresa told her she didn't like the teen boys who had picked her up and was thinking about returning to the juvenile home to complete therapy.

Instead, she simply disappeared.

Investigators contacted the parents of the missing girl and the teens locked up in the Gonzales jail. No one had seen the pretty teen or knew where she was.

The statements created a troubling verbal picture: a young woman runs away from a group home on impulse only to regret her action. She calls her best friend from a farmhouse where she feels like a prisoner and says she is thinking of going back.

Then she drops out of sight.

Police didn't know where she was but suspected that the key to solving the mystery lay with the van-driving trio arrested in Gonzales, Louisiana.

Malisa Earnest had not been charged in connection with the stolen van and had been released on her own recognizance. Robert McIntyre and Terry Belcher were still in jail. They were flown back to Atlanta, Georgia. Deputies hustled them to the sheriff's station where they were questioned about the missing girl. Belcher admitted that he picked up a girl hitchhiking but claimed that he had let her out and didn't know what happened to her afterwards.

McIntyre was equally reticent.

After an hour of questioning, investigators met outside the interrogation rooms, and discussed what they had learned.

Which, as it turned out, wasn't much.

Sheriff Lee then hit on a plan that might make the teens more talkative. He went back into the interrogation room and asked Belcher if he knew anything about black magic or Satanic cults.

Belcher broke into a smile. He explained that he had been a member of a Satanic cult for about a year. There were nine in the cult. They had all accepted Satan as their savior and he had given them divine power.

Acting surprised, the sheriff said he knew little about Satanic cults and asked Belcher how he became a high priest and what it involved.

Belcher, who had been tight-lipped since arriving at the airport, became animated when talking about his favorite subject.

The teen's descent into witchcraft and Satanism was a shocking story and became the talk of the town and the subject of national news stories.

By his own admission, Belcher was just an average high school Joe with a taste for beer and pretty coeds. His life changed after he met a Douglasville woman who claimed to be a witch.

Belcher said they talked about Satanism and she asked if he liked heavy metal music. He said he did, and two of his favorite groups were Ozzie Osbourne and Judas Priest.

He said she told him that many of his favorite heavy metal bands were practicing Satanists who wrote of Satanic rituals in their songs.

Belcher said he didn't know anything about that; he just liked the music. He knew the titles of a bunch of songs but never listened closely to the lyrics.

The lyrics, the woman insisted, were important and contained lots of Satanic messages.

Belcher said he was stunned by some of those messages. First he had met a real live witch. Next he discovered that the guys he and his pals envied were writing music about the devil.

Belcher said he met regularly with the witch. They played heavy metal music and they read from the Satanic bible. After he became a convert, they conducted Satanic rituals which included the evisceration of animals and the drinking of their blood.

Belcher said he progressed from follower to high priest and began his own cult, attracting his own followers.

"It was neat," he boasted. "It gave me power."

He said McIntyre and Earnest were both followers and participated in Satanic rituals. When asked about Theresa Simmons, however, he grew quiet.

The sheriff said that they knew the 17-year-old was dead and that Belcher and McIntyre had information about her murder.

"I didn't kill anyone!" Belcher snapped.

Pressed for information, however, he admitted that she was dead.

"You know that for a fact?" he was asked.

"Yes."

"Who killed her?"

Sheriff Lee was stunned by the response.

"Malisa Earnest," Belcher said.

Belcher said he and McIntyre picked up the girls hitchhiking and took them to his aunt and uncle's home outside Douglasville. He said his relatives were elderly and were hardly aware of what was going on.

He said they stayed at the farmhouse and partied every night. Malisa got into the black magic but Theresa was stand-offish.

"I don't think she was into it," Belcher said.

He said after a night of drugs and heavy metal music, he and McIntyre walked out of the bedroom, leaving Malisa and Theresa behind.

When they returned, Malisa was sitting on top of Theresa with her hands around her throat.

"We pulled her off," Belcher said. "But Theresa was dead."

He said they panicked and instead of calling police, they buried the body in the woods behind the farmhouse.

Belcher admitted it was wrong not to call police but insisted he and McIntyre had not participated in the murder.

Belcher didn't know why Malisa did it—perhaps jealousy. The sheriff left the interview room convinced Belcher was lying. He was also convinced that the devil-worshipping teen knew what had happened to the pretty young runaway—if only he could get Belcher to talk.

During the break, the sheriff learned that Malisa Earnest had been arrested at the bus station and was at the sheriff's station ready to be questioned.

The sheriff went back into the interrogation room and gave Belcher the bad news.

The smug teen said the he wasn't worried, that the runaway was under his powers of persuasion and would do what he said.

"Frankly, I don't believe you have such powers," the sheriff scoffed.

Belcher shrugged. "Suit yourself."

Malisa Earnest was brought into the interrogation room. With the meeting secretly videotaped, Belcher read from the Satanic bible and told the teen that he had power over her soul.

But arrested and facing a murder rap, Malisa had different ideas. She told Belcher that he didn't own her and she could do what she wanted.

So much for Satanic powers.

The sheriff entered the room and told him that the demonstration proved Belcher was only a mere mortal and did not possess Satanic power over anyone.

Deflated, Belcher agreed. Asked if he wanted to make a statement, he nodded. "I will tell you how it really happened," he said.

He repeated the story about picking up the two girls and taking them to the farmhouse. Over the weekend, they smoked grass, drank beer and listened to heavy metal music.

Belcher said he was delighted to discover that Malisa had dabbled in Satanism and accepted him as a high priest. They had sex almost immediately.

Belcher said he and McIntyre were ardent Satanists and had performed animal sacrifices and blood rituals. They had discussed human sacrifices but could not find the right subject.

Over the weekend, they decided they had found one—Theresa Simmons.

In a way, she was perfect. She was a runaway, no one had spotted them picking her up, and no one knew where she was.

Belcher said they discussed the idea of a human sacrifice with Malisa and she went along with it. Over more grass and heavy metal music, they discussed how they were going to conduct the ritual. They decided knives and guns were too messy and agreed on strangulation.

That evening, the three teenage Satanists and a reluctant Theresa Simmons gathered in the upstairs bedroom. They worked themselves into a frenzy on grass, heavy metal music, and Satanic scripture, before they looped a leather shoelace around Theresa's neck.

"We all took turns tightening the lace," Belcher said.

Afterward, they hauled the body behind the house and buried it in a shallow grave.

Belcher described the makeshift grave and drew a crude map of the location. Deputies hurried to the house and had little trouble finding the shallow grave. Underneath a thin layer of dirt lay the body of Theresa Simmons. She was fully clothed with a shoelace still knotted around her neck.

Terry Belcher, Robert McIntyre and Malisa Earnest were arrested and charged with first-degree murder.

The sheriff's department formed a Satanic task force to look into Belcher's allegations that a cult was operating in Douglas County and might be responsible for more crimes.

Although Belcher widely exaggerated the problem, police did find evidence of cult activity, mostly among Doulgas County teenagers.

One teen told detectives he was introduced to Satanism after he was approached in high school and asked if he wanted to go to a party. He was promised that there would be plenty of pretty women and drugs, but when he arrived he was the only guest.

He said they smoked grass, listened to heavy metal music and talked about the meaning of the lyrics. At other meetings, they drank blood from freshly slaughtered dogs and cats.

Most of the teenagers, however, said they had little interest in Satanic cults and went to the meetings because of the drugs, beer and heavy metal music they enjoyed.

To parents, however, it sounded like their worst nightmares come true.

Reporters and photographers arrived in Douglasville to record the grim story. A camera crew from Geraldo Rivera's production team, also appeared. A snip of their coverage was featured in the controversial NBC special on Satanic worship.

Terry Belcher went on trial in May 1988. In yet another twist, while in jail the self-proclaimed high priest renounced the teachings of Satan and adopted Jesus Christ as his savior.

Wearing a cross around his neck, Belcher pleaded guilty to murder, received an automatic life sentence and agreed to testify against his former Satanic slave, Robert McIntyre.

Before a packed courtroom, Belcher gleefully recounted his months as a devil worshipper when he and nine of his bloodthirsty followers butchered dogs, cats and chickens, all in the name of Satan.

"We ate their eyeballs and innards and drank their blood," Belcher said. "We toasted the devil by drinking the blood."

"Why did you do it?" he was asked.

Though he had renounced the Devil's teachings, Belcher sounded almost giddy in recalling old times. "The rituals were performed for power, the taste of blood," he testified. "I got money, power, sex, drugs, anything I wanted. It was easy to get. It was like Satan helped you get them."

He confessed to participating in the murder of Theresa Simmons and hiding her body in the shallow grave.

He then appeared as the chief witness against former friend Robert McIntyre. The slight, introverted McIntyre was portrayed as a follower who had been pushed around by his dominating, Hell-raising buddy.

Belcher, however, testified that McIntyre was a devoted follower of Satan and was eager to commit the human sacrifice they had talked about.

He described how they got psyched up for the grisly event by smoking pot and listening to heavy metal rock music of Ozzie Osbourne.

He testified that the noted British rocker was one of their favorites because he sang about Satan and nuclear bombs.

In a bizarre reenactment, Belcher stepped from

the witness stand and, along with prosecutor David McDade, knelt in front of the jury to demonstrate how they strangled Teresa Simmons with the shoelace.

The witness elicited gasps of disbelief when he testified that McIntyre attempted to have sex with the victim's body after she was murdered. He said he and Malisa Earnest left the bedroom for a minute and when they returned they saw McIntyre with his pants down attempting intercourse with the body.

He said they chanted over the corpse in hopes of summoning the devil and later buried the body behind the house.

McIntyre was convicted of first degree murder on June 10th. Both he and his former friend, Belcher, were sentenced to life terms.

Malisa Earnest was found guilty of being an accessory to murder and sentenced to three years in prison.

All three are currently serving their prison terms in the Georgia prison system.

"THE DEADLIEST CULT IN AMERICA!"

by Channing Corbin

When Alan Berg, 50, bought it on the night of Monday, June 18, 1984 at approximately 9:30 p.m., he was given the whole nine yards or, in other words, his killer who'd lain patiently in ambush had calmly pumped between 10 to 12 rounds of heavy .45-caliber bullets into Berg's body. This factor alone denoted a considerable degree of raw, naked hatred in a classic case of overkill.

It was difficult to ascertain exactly how many times the Denver talk-show host was shot because of the number of gunshot wounds. Some of them were entry wounds; others might have been caused by exiting slugs. It all came down in the victim's driveway located in front of his posh townhouse in eastern Denver, Colorado as he stepped out of his Volkswagen after dining with his ex-wife. Eight minutes after the shooting, Denver police received a call to the effect that there may have been a mugging at Berg's address.

Two Denver policewomen, Nina Orton and Diane Brookshire, were the first to arrive at the scene at about 9:41 p.m., a scant minute or so after an ambulance and a team of paramedics had swung up into the driveway of the swank condominium. They found Berg sprawled grotesquely on the concrete ramp near his black Volkswagen convertible with one leg partially beneath the car, obviously dead.

Ironically, the first of a multitude of mysterious aspects to later become an integral aspect of the crime was the true identity of the caller who'd reported a "man down" and a possible mugging and Berg's address. Crime scene technicians had later recovered in the victim's car with another four or five located in the closed garage door beyond the black V/W.

Top priority was accorded the task of photographing the ghastly scene from every conceivable angle. Berg's body lay in a welter of blood. He clutched a small paper sack which was later found to contain a can of dog food for his beloved Airdale, Fred. The victim was pronounced dead at 9:45 p.m. His assassination style execution promptly became Denver's most sensational crime of the decade for multiple reasons.

Initially, Alan Berg was a highly controversial local celebrity possessed of a unique personality. Occasionally, he would remark, "I'm a man who people love to hate." Enigmatically his cryptic comment held a measure of truth in view of the unbridled violence involved in his murder.

Alan Berg had a host of staunch friends who'd viewed him as being a warm, witty and caring man. Many others classified him as being an extremely talented actor who pretended to be something he wasn't in order to earn the handsome salary paid to him by Denver's radio station KOA. Berg worked the 9 a.m. to 1 p.m. shift, during which he hosted a talk show. Many things he said and did while on the air earned him the reputation of being obnoxious.

So renowned was his status as a master of acrimonious conduct while on the air that he'd recently been featured on TV's "60 Minutes." He often told callers they were stupid and frequently hung up on them.

By Tuesday morning, Berg's body and his black V/W had been removed and the news of the slaying had hit the national wire service. Already, 46 Denver police officers, plus 14 FBI agents and Denver County D.A. investigators, had been formed into a massive 60-member task force. The nature of the crime coupled with the prominent reputation of Alan Berg singled out the murder as being an act which demanded a swift solution. Crime scene experts had excised five copper-jacketed .45-caliber slugs from the garage door and triangulated the exact location of the profusion of ejected shell cartridge cases which littered the crime scene.

Due to the lethal hail of fire-power involved, it was already a foregone conclusion that a conventional type of weapon was not utilized in the ambush style slaying. Berg was literally cut in half by a weapon commonly referred to as a sub-machine gun. Federal regulations make it difficult but not impossible to legally purchase a clip-fed, gas-operated fully automatic pistol. Such weapons which are not fully automatic when purchased can be easily converted with slight modifications.

Ballistics experts of the Colorado Bureau of Investigation (CBI) stated that a total of 22 such sub-machine guns manufactured internationally basically met the specifications of the murder weapon. This field was reduced to nine and then to but one. The lightweight, combat type firearm is known as the M-10, and can easily be converted to a fully automatic weapon. Most assuredly, it is not conventional type of hunting gun. That is, unless your quarry is human.

After Denver police had processed the crime scene and removed their barriers, an almost constant stream of traffic commenced to move slowly past the scene of the crime. Numerous people stopped to pin clusters of flowers and sympathy notes to the garage door. It was irrefutable that despite his caustic disposition, the victim enjoyed an immense popularity. His talk show was credited with raising the ratings of Radio Station KOA tremendously. Berg's reputed salary was pegged at a cool $100,000 yearly.

In his role as an erratic, sometimes downright vulgar talk show host, Berg had previously received considerable hate mail and these and some telephone calls had contained death threats, the most recent of which he'd received in January, 1984. He was, among other things, a staunch advocate of strict gun control. Coincidentally, gun control was to have been his principal topic of discussion on his talk show for Tuesday. If anyone desires to stir up heated emotions in most of the west, all he needs to do is to come down on the side of gun control. Privately, Denver police were inclined to view Berg's callous execution to this facet of his radio personality. They and the FBI knew full well of the existence of extreme right-wing organizations dedicated to protecting their claimed right to own and bear arms, even to the point of violence.

The real motive for the shocking crime, however, might even lie much further back in Berg's past. Of Jewish extraction and a law school graduate, he'd once been a practicing attorney in Chicago, where he'd purportedly represented some quite prominent underworld hoodlums. Was it possible that he'd once lost a case and his former client had come to Denver to even the score? Alan Berg left the windy city and moved to Denver in 1969 with a severe drinking problem. His wife had left him and he was on the skids.

He'd managed to get the "big monkey" off of his back and taken a job at $65 a week selling shoes. Being an enterprising individual, he'd soon opened up a custom shirt shop and later a quality store called the Boot Broker. His venture into the exotic field of radio came about when a friend invited Berg to appear on a KWBZ talk show as an invited guest. Like most of us, Alan Berg enjoyed being the center of attraction and he loved it. In 1971, his friend quit his position with the radio and Berg was offered the opportunity to fill his vacancy. He accepted with alacrity and was thus launched on an entirely new career.

Berg adapted his roguish personality early on in his career. In November, 1979 while on the air with radio station KWBZ, the head of the Colorado Ku Klux Klan burst into the studios and allegedly threatened to kill Berg right in the middle of his broadcast. The KKK leader was calmed down, arrested and charged, and Alan Berg made the front page of the Denver newspapers. Berg told reporters that the Kluxer had been pointing a pistol at him when he'd threatened him with instant death. The Klansman denied this and the entire case was resolved out of court.

Berg later took a position at Denver KHOW, where he attained the highest ratings ever accorded a talk show host. He was later fired from that station in 1979 and re-joined KWBZ for a short while before being offered a lucrative position with KOA. Instinctively, as a born showman, he realized that radio listeners would simply not tune in to a dull, mundane talk show. They wanted audible action. They enjoyed stinging verbosity and an audacious host who was adept and perfectly capable of slugging it out with the most opinionated caller in the area. Radio station KOA knew by the rash of fan mail they received lauding vilifying Berg that he'd drastically elevated their ratings and that he was worth every cent of his annual salary of $100,000.

Alan Berg owned two other cars besides his black V/W. They were a rare Bricklin and a De Lorean sports car. His friends and neighbors described him as a flashy dresser. Besides being on good terms with his ex-wife, he had a girlfriend. Everyone who personally knew Alan Berg had nothing but praise for him. Evidently, only during his four-hour talk show was he the provocative, caustic personality with a vast audience of listeners who either loved and admired him or else detested him with a passion.

On the day after Berg's murder, Radio Station KOA posted a $10,000 reward for any information leading to the arrest and conviction of his slayers. They located one who reported having seen a white car speeding down a dark alley after the burst of gunfire. That's all, just a white car traveling at a high speed in a dark alley. Numerous others were located who'd heard the gunfire. Their estimates of the number of shots fired ranged from two on up to nine.

Actually, the staccato hail of rapid gunfire would have been impossible to count. This is why such paramilitary combat weapons are frequently called "burp" guns. The M-10 is this country's answer to Israeli's Uzi pistol, only much more powerful. Don Mulnix, Chief of Detectives, Denver City Police Department, was designated as one of several lead coordinators heading up the 60-man task force now assisted by agents from the U.S. Bureau of Alcohol, Tobacco and Firearms.

The government agency would undertake to locate and review every single transaction involving the purchase of an M-10 semi-automatic, clip-fed weapon. Each and every purchaser would be contacted and their weapon examined to ascertain if it was modified to convert it to a full-automatic firearm. Denver police had roughed up a tenuous lead relative to an eyewitness to the wanton murder of Alan Berg. His name was known and at first, he could not be located. When he was, it was determined that he'd not witnessed the shooting.

Station KCNC TV added another $10,000 to the reward fund. Tips poured into the Denver PD, and all were thoroughly checked out with negative results. Police listened to all tapes of Berg's recent talk shows several of which contained death threats. In some instances, the callers had identified themselves. In others, they remained anonymous. Each and every lead, regardless of how nebulous it was, was traced out with negative results.

Among many other things, Alan Berg had been an arch-liberal. This was his personal choice. He seemed to have developed an uncanny knack of identifying a conservative caller within but a few sentences of a conversation. However, he was every bit as ascerbic with moderates and liberals as he was with those to the right of the spectrum.

One TV news announcer remarked that he'd adopted the habit of checking out his yard and garage before leaving his car at night. This aura of dread was normal. It was entirely possible that some nut out there somewhere had launched a vendetta against members of the news media and that Alan Berg had been the first to be decimated.

Lawmen close to the massive probe, however, were disinclined to give this thesis any credence. They were convinced that the solution to the perplexing atrocity lay somewhere in the victim's lifestyle, celebrity status and background. Investigators had re-constructed Berg's last day on this earth with considerable care. His topic for his talk show that day was the Pope's recent pronunciations on sex and its role in the Catholic sphere. He also taped a commercial for the American Cancer Society. He dined with his exwife and took her car, saying he was going home. He'd stopped and bought a can of dog food for Fred. At about 9:30 p.m., he'd been mowed down by his cold-blooded murderer, who'd been awaiting his arrival in ambush in the inky darkness, awaiting his chance to strike.

As the probe became more coordinated and with the basic preliminaries accomplished, police found themselves stymied by an absolute dearth of leads. A note found pinned to the victim's garage door bore a printed message, "I was here." At first the missive was viewed as a clue. It was later determined that the note was left there by Berg's ex-wife during a previous visit. Most assuredly, the expended .45-caliber shell casings, the slugs dug out of the garage door and those removed from the victim's body during the ensuing autopsy were all vital items of evidence. But they were useless until the death weapon was located.

The use of a heavy-caliber, fully automatic weapon bespoke much about the killer. He was far from being the common, run-of-the-mill murderer as evinced by his choice of the heavy duty, combat type M-10. He was a man consumed by a roiling hatred who meant to convey a message when he cut down his victim in a blazing hail of lead. Police felt certain that Berg's slayer had jousted with his victim via the telephone during the course of one of the victim's controversial four-hour talk shows. But as detectives reviewed the talk show tapes, they were unsuccessful in establishing any viable links which would provide them with a much needed connection.

After the Denver County Coroner's Office had completed a totally exacting postmortem of the decedent's body, his remains were released for final rites and burial. A co-employee had closed out Alan Berg's talk show. Many Denverites clamored for a solution to Berg's slaying. Police both sustained and accelerated their probe.

Alan Berg was laid to rest on Thursday, June 21, 1984 in a plot next to his father's in Waldheim Cemetery, Free Sons of Israel Section near Chicago. It was a very private 15-minute ritual attended by only five mourners including his former wife.

In Denver, police sought a local KKK activist for questioning. They'd also learned that Berg and his girlfriend of nine months had engaged in a heated argument just days before his death. The victim's paramour had denied the allegation and it was eventually deemed to be unfounded.

Every known right-wing extremist and neo-Nazi fanatic in Colorado was subjected to close scrutiny. The more that police delved into Berg's recent past the more convinced they became that his killer was of this ilk. The general public was amazed to learn that it's perfectly legal to own a machine gun if the owner has paid a $200 transfer tax to the U.S. Department of Treasury and if the weapon is purchased from a registered dealer. However, numerous such weapons were smuggled into the U.S. during the Vietnam era illegally.

Investigators carefully screened all of the victim's telephone records in an effort to establish a link between Berg and 25 potential suspects, many of whom lived out of state. They met with negative results. The FBI was playing a vital role in the massive probe. They'd successfully infiltrated most of the extremist groups comprising professional hate-mongers. Major records checks were conducted by computers. Despite the vast amount of effort applied, all hints as to the identity of the assassin continued to elude them completely.

Several Denver radio and TV stations beefed up their security measures. Alan Berg's horrific murder had a tremendous impact on many elements on Denver's society. Many news media sources had come to view it as the act of a terrorist group. Seven days subsequent to Berg's murder, police were obliged to admit publicly that all avenues of the investigation had been fully exploited and that they were stymied by a lack of leads. The original task force of 60 was scaled down to 35 sleuths, then to twenty and finally reduced to two.

Captain Doug White, Commander of the Crimes Against Persons Bureau, was designated to supervise Detectives Ervin Haynes and Ray Estrada while they collected all accrued data. White stressed that the investigation was not confined to paramilitary groups. Among a multitude of other possibilities, police were checking out an angle that smacked of a professional "hit" over gambling debts. Chief Mulnix indicated that it was entirely possible that Berg's murder had international implications, and that the FBI was in touch with Interpol.

On July 10th, Denver lawmen reiterated that they were still searching for a militant local Klan member in connection with the vicious slaying of Alan Berg. Police declared that the Klansman was not classified as a suspect but was wanted for questioning as a potential witness. A reputed Klan arsenal in Denver was raided on a tip from an informant. Searched with a warrant, the rental shed was barren.

Understandably, police investigating a homicide case never release everything they've developed during the probe. Frequently, news releases are somewhat distorted. This pacifies the media and the public and doesn't spook potential suspects into fleeing the area. There were so many agencies involved in the Berg murder probe that considerable confusion ensued. The reason that the metro Denver task force was drastically scaled down was primarily due to the fact that some irrefutable leads were developed early on in the probe which indicated that prime suspects had left Denver.

In reiteration, all tapes of Berg's caustic talk shows were carefully reviewed, along with hate mail, some of which included death threats. Roughly 25 names were accrued of potential suspects in this manner. Also, the tip that witnesses had seen a car occupied by two well-dressed males parked in front of Berg's home prior to his murder proved to have been a solid one. Several persons provided precise descriptions of the duo and the car which had vanished after the killing. Investigators had noted that Alan Berg derived considerable delight in taunting members of right-wing extremist groups such as the KKK and the Minute Men.

It was also determined that he'd verbally crossed swords and jousted with several members of the far right on his talk show and that the extremists had come out second best. Leads relative to gambling debts, a reputed argument with a lawyer and with his girlfriend had been checked out and been proved to be unfounded. Twenty-four individuals with whom he'd locked horns were also cleared of all suspicion during the course of 300 interviews. The 25 remaining suspects were mostly ultra-conservatives and militant right wingers, most of whom could not be located. Denver police expressed confidence on June 23rd that the case would eventually be solved and released a statement to the news media to that effect.

The fact that they went public with this declaration meant that they knew much more than they were willing to tell. It meant that they'd developed viable suspects and when they were located and arrested, the Berg murder case would be solved. On June 29th, they released another statement to the effect that Alan Berg's death wasn't a murder but an assassination, defined as meaning the murder of a public personality for political reasons.

They alleged that the crime was committed by a terrorist group. The first suspect in the case was named on about July 10th. He was 45-year-old David Lane, who was identified as a Klansman. Lane was not a KKK member, however, but a neo-Nazi and a member of the Aryan Nations based in Hayden Lake, Idaho.

Lane was also wanted for bombing a synagogue in Boise, Idaho on April 29, 1984. Subsequent to winding down the intensive probe in Denver, the FBI had formed up crack task forces in Idaho, Washington and Montana. These units worked on a 24-hour basis, using airplanes and other sophisticated equipment in their attempts to ferret out dozens of suspects in a host of diverse crimes and to break the back of the New Order and the White American Bastion, splinter groups of the Aryan Nations.

Gary Yarbrough of Sandpoint, Idaho was also named as a suspect in the Berg case after he was involved in a shootout with FBI agents on October 18, 1984 and subsequently arrested and held without bond. A search of his residence turned up a virtual arsenal including 100 sticks of dynamite, hand grenades and $15,000 worth of firearms including a MAC 10 machine pistol, which was ballistically proven to be the weapon used to kill Alan Berg. Yarbrough was lodged in the Ada County Jail in Boise, Idaho to be held for trial.

Without exception, neo-Nazis pride themselves on being hardcase and a law unto themselves. They view their role as being comparable to that of soldiers involved in a holy war and they'd sworn to rid the U.S. of Jews and blacks by whatever means. They delighted in burning crosses on their "enemy's" lawns. In the Berg case, they'd purportedly been so incensed that they'd elected to liquidate the man who taunted and humiliated them. Police now described the caper as having been executed by a five-man hit squad using two cars. They elaborated on this theory, saying it might well have been a ritualistic, bizarre initiation operation, intended to qualify members of the New Order as suitable candidates as neo-Nazis.

Denver police traveled to Boise, Idaho to interview Yarbrough, who refused to even talk to them. In reiteration, the wicked looking MAC 10 automatic pistol had positively been identified as the gun used to slay Berg. Yarbrough told the press that the gun was not the death weapon. He was quite loquacious during interviews with the news media.

A brief resume of the history of the Aryan Nations white supremacist group follows. It was initially founded in 1976 by a man named Richard Butler on a 20-acre compound located near picturesque Hayden Lake, Idaho. The organization was originally based near Lancaster, California, where lawmen had confiscated five tons of munitions from a bunker built by the group. They'd decided that northern Idaho offered a more lax atmosphere. In August, 1983, a neo-Nazi was sentenced to death for the murders of two blacks and a white man mistaken for a Jew. On April 23, 1984, six members of the Aryan Nations were indicted for the robbery of an armored car holdup in Seattle, Washington which netted them a net total of $500,000. On April 29, 1984, the synagogue in Boise, Idaho was bombed, allegedly by Yarbrough. In June, Alan Berg was unmercifully executed, purportedly by a 5-man-hit squad made up of members of the noe-Nazi's New Order. In July, 1984 an armored car was halted and robbed in Ukiah, California of $3.6 million. In the days prior to the heist, Gary Yarbrough was an impoverished dishwasher. The day after the holdup, he allegedly was a man of affluence, flashing huge rolls of crisp $20 bills.

He was a prime suspect in this caper. Some of the stolen money was recovered subsequent to his arrest. Armored car robberies allegedly were the neo-Nazis' favorite means of raising funds to subsidize their so-called holy war. Much of the loot was thought to have been spent on arms, grenades, explosives and other nefarious devices required to sustain their violent objectives.

It was on November 18, 1984 that Yarbrough was arrested after he'd made the foolish mistake of opening fire on FBI agents who were watching his house, located 10 miles north of Sandpoint, Idaho. Search warrants were drafted subsequent to his apprehension, which led to the location of the automatic machine-pistol used to kill Berg, and other incriminating evidence. The crime was actually committed on October 18th and Yarbrough's arrest took place in Portland, Oregon during a second shoot-out with the FBI at a motel there. Robert Jay Mathews, 31, a cohort of Yarbrough, was wounded during the fire-fight and escaped.

During the first week of December, 1984, sealed indictments were handed down against Yarbrough, Mathews and four other neo-Nazis for their alleged involvement in the Seattle armored car robbery. That same week, Mathews was run to the ground by a contingent of federal agents in Puget Sound, Washington. Mathews again elected to engage the FBI in a gun battle which lasted for 34 hours, after which he was killed when flares fired into the house he was in caused an explosion. It was on December 14, 1984 that Denver police identified Yarbrough as a prime suspect in the Alan Berg slaying.

Thus we have a thumbnail sketch of the faction deemed responsible for the atrocious Denver homicide of the caustic, controversial KOA talk show host. Oddly enough, the neo-Nazis had operated with comparative impunity since 1976, when the Feds declared open season on them subsequent to developing suspects in their ranks thought to be responsible for Berg's assassination. Their total number remained unknown, although it was learned that they had chapters scattered all over the U.S. Almost without exception, all members were staunchly dedicated to their beliefs and willing to die for their cause if necessary. They strictly adhered to their oaths and their activities were cloaked in an inviolate shroud of secrecy.

Six months after Berg's death, David Lane still remained at large. He was still classified by the news media as a prime suspect in the Berg killing. A very detailed article was published in a major Denver newspaper about this enigmatic personality on December 23, 1984. He was said to be in "deep hiding" in a right-wing safe-house. He was described as a dedicated man to whom "silence was golden."

It was Lane who'd verbally sparred with Berg on the talk show. He'd written a letter in August denying any involvement in Berg's murder, which he circulated among right-wing fringe groups. The news media asked, essentially, if Lane was innocent, why hadn't he come forward with an alibi?

Robert Jay Mathews had demonstrated traits similar to Lane's when he held 100 FBI agents at bay for 34 hours before dying in an inferno. Oddly enough, no warrants had been issued for Lane's arrest by any law enforcement agency. Yarbrough, still awaiting trial, now stated the death gun was given to him by a friend whom he declined to identify. Despite the fact that this highly incriminating piece of evidence was found in his home, he was not formally charged in the Berg case, although he was repeatedly termed a prime suspect.

KUSA-TV in Denver reported that they had developed information from an informant to the effect that Lane had told another individual of his intention to liquidate Berg after having verbally clashed with the talk show host numerous times, usually coming off second best and humiliated beyond description. The informant was an inmate in a California jail where he was being held on unrelated charges.

In December, Lane was named in a criminal complaint out of Philadelphia on counterfeiting charges. It had also been established that the New Order had used computers to collate information on numerous Jews in the U.S. marked for future attention.

In January, 1985, Republican Senator Packwood of Oregon received a death threat from a member of the New Order. Packwood, an arch-liberal, and his family, were accorded top priority protection by the FBI, who took the threat seriously. They were now fully cognizant of the unbridled viciousness of the neo-Nazis. Nothing further developed as a result of the threat. Yarbrough's attorney, a public defender, had asked for and received a month's extension on the accused's upcoming trial. Two more suspects in the Ukiah armored car caper were arrested during the first week of January.

On the other side of the coin, Jewish militants were organizing to protect their places of worship with "shoot-to-kill orders" to be exercised against the neo-Nazis, if necessary. It now truly smacked of a real war as the magnitude of the intensive probe continued to mount. What was at first thought to have been the diabolical handiwork of a chagrined Denver conservative had by now mushroomed into a national criminal investigation. FBI agents continued to pursue their quarry, members of the New Order.

It was learned that Gary Yarbrough and his brother were well known in Pima County, Arizona where they'd formerly lived. They'd been arrested there for burglary and strongarm robberies and were described as being "Dillinger" types. Yarbrough's brother had been arrested by now in

Nashville, Tenn. Two more suspects in the Ukiah armored car holdup were nabbed in a poker parlor in Montana, bringing the number of arrests to 10 within two months in the massive probe. A 13 count indictment was handed down against Gary Yarbrough by an Idaho grand jury. Loot from the $3.6 million robbery was known to have been divided up in Boise, Idaho between numerous neo-Nazis, including several women.

David Lane remained at large. He was wanted in Philadelphia for counterfeiting $10 bills as a part of a scheme to disrupt the U.S. economy as well as to finance a takeover of the U.S. government. No one knew why they weren't expediting the plan by counterfeiting bills of large denominations. Police named Robert J. Mathews, now deceased, and Bruce Carroll Pierce as also being key suspects in Berg's murder. They (the police) still retained their hit-squad theory, claiming now that the FBI believed that from two to six killers had ambushed the victim.

Two Brinks employees were arrested in San Francisco and charged with providing the neo-Nazis with crucial inside information. A $30 million robbery had been in the planning stage when the feds launched their probe. That sum would have financed a hell of a lot of violence. Yarbrough shocked federal prosecutors when he abruptly pleaded guilty to 11 counts of illegal gun possession counts prior to his trial. He still faced charges of firing at an FBI agent. He remained mum about the Berg case, however, refusing all offers to plea-bargain with a confession.

By late March, 1985, it would not be stretching the truth to say that by now every FBI agent in the U.S. had been involved to one degree or another in the massive crackdown on the neo-Nazi factions. They had made tremendous headway and were thinning the ranks of the New Order through numerous arrests. During the last week of March, 1985, two car loads of federal agents roared into the small town of Belen, New Mexico on a tip that Bruce Pierce was in hiding there. The information proved to be false and Pierce, one of a number of named suspects in the Berg murder, was not found. They'd earlier staged a similar raid in Troy, Montana hoping to arrest Pierce there, but he'd eluded them.

The scope of such an investigation defies description. The feds were using every resource at their disposal including thousands of informants. It left the accused and the suspects no place to hide. Most had police records. Their relatives were contacted and often placed under surveillance, as were known friends and associates. Safe-houses were located and watched. Every lead was followed up on. Favors were granted to reliable informants who provided valid information. Even at that, it was time consuming, expensive and often frustrating, but the various task forces remained hard at it.

Pierce was known to have been in Ogden, Utah on January 28, 1985, when he had all of his upper teeth extracted by a dentist there. He was using the alias of Mike Roberts at the time. This factor was typical of the care employed in the FBI's search for this one suspect in the Berg murder case. The name of the dentist was developed. He described the suspect as a pleasant man who paid for his services in cash.

Aryan Busters T-shirts became a big seller in Idaho after a real estate agent had them printed and placed on the market. The FBI developed information indicating that a member of the New Order named Walter Earl West, 42, may have been executed by his comrades after he'd commenced shooting off his mouth about neo-Nazi activities. He'd turned up missing and no trace of him could be found.

It was also learned that the neo-Nazis were training guerrillas in northern Idaho and Montana. It was established that Bruce Pierce was traveling with his pregnant wife and three children in a white Toyota Land Cruiser. The feds remained just one step behind him throughout his flight. It was known that Pierce would not hesitate to engage the federal agents in a shoot-out if given the opportunity.

At 7:41 p.m. on March 26, 1985, Pierce walked into an AAA office located in Rossville, Ga. Minutes later, he was rushed by 40 FBI agents and local police officers who threw him to the floor and relieved him of the derringer and several pistols he was packing. The feds had been tipped off that he was headed for Rossville and had tailed him once he'd entered town. Pierce was driving a van at the time loaded with weapons and explosives. Lawmen feared the vehicle was booby-trapped, but a careful check disclosed that it wasn't.

Pierce was now identified as the most wanted suspect in the Berg homicide case. Denver authorities claimed they lacked sufficient evidence to formally charge him. He was booked in Georgia on several federal charges including counterfeiting and armed robbery. A Denver prosecutor and two detectives flew to Atlanta to interview Pierce, who'd already begun to serve a two-year term in the federal pen for passing bogus $50 bills. Pierce, in keeping with the code of the New Order, declined to talk to the Denver authorities about the Berg case.

Yarbrough had stood trial for assaulting federal officers and was given 25 years in prison when found guilty, as well as having pleaded guilty to the 11 gun counts. He described himself as a "frontline Aryan warrior." In any event, he was now a neutralized warrior. He and four other New

Order members remained classified as prime suspects in Berg's death. On Saturday, March 30, 1985, FBI agents arrested the much-sought-after David Lane in Winston-Salem, North Carolina at 11:45 a.m. at a shopping plaza. As was the case in Pierce's apprehension, they hadn't given Lane the slightest edge. His arrest was carried out without incident after he'd been tailed for two days by the FBI. Oddly enough, Lane was unarmed when six agents took him into custody. He was accompanied by two Ku Klux Klan sympathizers at the time. Only one other Berg murder suspect now remained at large.

He was identified by the FBI as being a neo-Nazi named Richard Scutari, a resident of Port Salerno, Florida. Although Denver lawmen and the FBI continued to refer to Lane as one of five prime suspects in Berg's murder, no formal charges were filed against him subsequent to his arrest, although he was held on other criminal counts including the counterfeiting of $50 bills. By now, a vast amount of publicity had been generated about this totally fascinating case. Numerous individuals who followed all developments were prompted to ponder several salient implications.

One was, how had it been possible for the neo-Nazis to operate for so long with brazen impunity? They'd occupied armed and para-military compounds all over the U.S. with warehouses crammed chock full of arms and explosives. Why had it taken Berg's murder to precipitate a solution to two armored car robberies? In April, 1985 an FBI agent testified in Winston-Salem, N.C. that David Lane was present when Berg was riddled with .45 caliber slugs. Why wasn't he charged by Colorado authorities? The only plausible answer to these and other puzzlers was that the FBI knew many deep, dark secrets about this fantastic case that the general public didn't. Also, the vast probe was far from being completed.

Lane was a bitter man subsequent to his apprehension, claiming he'd been betrayed by fellow extremists. He had. This was how the FBI had traced him to North Carolina. He was later transported to Idaho to face charges involving the Ukiah armored car caper. He'd emphatically denied any involvement in Berg's demise. The search for Scutari was intensified. His arrest, too, was now but a matter of time. Throughout the entire lengthy, massive investigation, Berg's murder was the crux of the probe. All other developments were more or less extraneous. Despite his controversial personality, Alan Berg had enjoyed a wide following of admirers.

In mid-April, 1985, the FBI unveiled a massive federal racketeering indictment against numerous members of the New Order. At this point, 28 individuals had been arrested in 13 states on a diverse variety of criminal counts. Berg's murder was the core of the indictment, which also included sedition, counterfeiting and armed robbery. Astonishingly enough, one of the major breaks in the probe had occurred in Philadelphia when an admitted neo-Nazi tried to buy a lottery ticket with a bogus $10 bill. The FBI had trailed him from a beer store to his home and arrested him, after which he was cultivated as an informant providing a wealth of invaluable information, some of which had led to David Lane's arrest.

The informant was given three years probation in return for his cooperation. He went underground for the feds and managed to develop additional information. He became a marked man in the eyes of his former associates, and for this reason will not be further identified or described herein. Out of the 24 neo-Nazis named in the indictment, five were named as suspects in Berg's murder. They were Bruce Carroll Pierce, David Lane, Robert Jay Mathews, Richard E. Scutari and Jean M. Craig. Mathews was dead. Scutari remained at large at the time of the indictment.

Federal authorities declared that they would share their findings with Denver authorities, which they did. The investigation continued. A government prosecutor declared that the massive probe had neutralized the New Order and broken the back of the nefarious neo-Nazis. The federal indictment was the first time that suspects were formally implicated in the Berg homicide. Denver authorities still refrained from filing any official charges. Colorado criminal statutes are exceedingly liberal, and perhaps Denver prosecutors felt that the U.S. government could deal with the suspects more severely. This is a purely speculative theory. The racketeering indictment itself carried maximum sentences of 20 years upon conviction.

In mid-April near Branson, Missouri, a neo-Nazi named David Charles Tate, 22, of Athol, Idaho allegedly gunned down a state trooper who'd stopped his van for a minor traffic violation near the Arkansas state line. Trooper Jimmie Linegar, 31, was shot four times. His companion, Officer Allen Hines, was struck three times and critically injured. An intensive manhunt was promptly launched for Tate, who'd fled after the shooting.

Tate was one of the individuals charged in the federal racketeering indictment. He was now sought throughout the Ozarks as a murder suspect as well. A cohort of Tate who was present at the time the two troopers were shot was arrested 60 miles from the scene of the crime and released to the FBI in Ft. Smith, Arkansas. Jean M. Craig, one of the five suspects formally named as having participated in Alan Berg's death, had been taken into custody. She stated that she wanted nothing more to do with the neo-Nazis faction. Craig, 52, was a resident of Laramie, Wyoming.

She was ordered held without bond pending her transfer to Seattle, Washington. Richard Scutari still managed to elude capture. Seattle had been selected as a holding area for all arrested suspects and it appeared that all future trials would be prosecuted there. Police located a major neo-Nazi compound near Three Brothers, Arkansas during their search for Tate, who was arrested on April 20th, 50 miles from the remote encampment which was placed under close surveillance. Lawmen sought for a search warrant which would allow for them to search every building inside the compound. State police packing high powered semi-automatic rifles surrounded the para-military encampment and manned roadblocks pending the issuance of two search warrants.

They suspected that the structures inside the compound contained land mines, explosives, arms, and other weaponry. They wished to avoid a direct confrontation, if possible, with the neo-Nazis, whom they knew to be well trained in combat tactics. The encampment encompassed 224 square acres. State police endeavored to negotiate the surrender of the camp's commander, Jim Ellison. He'd declared that God had instructed him not to surrender. Police moved in and took over one-third of the compound without a major incident. Four women and 13 children voluntarily left the encampment and they were relocated by lawmen.

Tate was held without bond in Springfield, Missouri where a crowd of cheering residents screamed, "Kill him! Kill him!" as they milled about in front of the Greene County Jail. The Order was now described as being a humbled supremacy, as the search for Scutari continued. The neo-Nazis were described now as a cult comprised of paranoiacs and other assorted "crazies." Nevertheless, the danger they posed was inescapable to even the most casual observer. They had garnered an awesome amount of power. On about April 23rd, two neo-Nazis named in warrants gave up to lawmen, having tired of living the life of fugitives without a place to hide. This left only the elusive Scutari still at large. He was now thought to be in hiding somewhere near the encampment outside Three Brothers, Arkansas.

The huge neo-Nazi fortress had now been totally taken over by the authorities, who were conducting searches of all structures. Extreme caution was exercised after it was rumored that the compound was booby-trapped with land mines. One huge cave on the premises could be entered only by an under-water route. It was thought to contain a large cache of arms. Fifty-five occupants of the camp had surrendered to the FBI. A fire fight had been avoided by the host of lawmen charged with taking over the fortress.

In Seattle, Bruce Carroll Pierce had pleaded innocent to all charges lodged against him, including any involvement in Berg's murder. He was arraigned during a two-hour hearing held in the U.S. Courthouse there. He'd reputedly taken over the leadership of the New Order after the death of Robert Mathews during the 34-hour standoff with the feds on December 8, 1984 in Puget Sound, Washington. Gary Yarbrough was also scheduled to be arraigned within days, as were other suspects. Scutari had not been located. It was thought possible that he'd been slain by his comrades to seal his lips.

On about April 25, 1985, a most shocking bit of information was released by the FBI in Little Rock, Arkansas relative to the search of the compound near Three Brothers. Unsealed documents linked the neo-Nazi factions with harboring kidnapped children, many of whom were found in the camp. Details surrounding this development were unclear. Also, it was disclosed that 30 gallons of cyanide and an arsenal of weapons were discovered during the search. Thirty gallons of cyanide would poison a lot of water destined for human consumption. A quantity of polychlorinated biphenyl, a carcinogen, was also found as well as 155 ounces of gold and Krugerrands, which were buried. A bullet-pocked target of a policeman was discovered at a shooting range.

On March 13, 1985, the body of a woman named Jean Carrigan was discovered along an Oklahoma highway with her throat slashed from ear to ear. It was now established that she'd been slain by a neo-Nazi to insure her silence. Jim Ellison, commander of the 224-acre compound, had finally agreed to surrender to police and had been ordered to be held under a $150,000 bond. Gary Yarbrough, whose nickname was "Yosemite Sam," had pleaded innocent to all charges against him in Seattle.

It will be recalled that Yarbrough had already been sentenced to 25 years in prison in Idaho. The FBI had established that all participants in the Ukiah armored car heist had each received from $10,000 to $40,000 when the loot was split up in Idaho. By now, there was very little about the Order's activities that they didn't know about. In reiteration, much of their success was due to the owner of the beer store who'd taken the license number of a car driven by a man who'd twice tried to buy a 50-cent lottery ticket with a bogus $10 bill.

That individual's cooperation later proved to be priceless after he'd provided the feds with a wealth of invaluable, valid information about numerous neo-Nazis. On about April 23, 1985 a 6-man, 6-woman jury in Salt Lake City, Utah had convicted a neo-Nazi of having harbored the still missing Richard Joseph Scutari. The 25-year-old man now faced a 10-year prison term for his offense. A number of other suspects in the case had commenced to soften up and to discuss plea bargaining deals in exchange for their cooperation. This development helped federal prosecutors tremendously.

The FBI had entered the Berg murder probe within days after its occurrence. In reality, they were far better capable and qualified to conduct the massive, lengthy probe, which had escalated into one of national scope, than any other agency in the U.S. They possessed the necessary know-how, the resources, the contacts and the finances to correlate the highly complex probe. As of the time of this writing, it is apparent that through their efforts they have paved the way for the ultimate prosecution of everyone involved in Alan Berg's murder.

In all probability, those prosecutions will be held by Colorado authorities sometime in the near future. The brutal death of a man who was shot down as he emerged from his car carrying a can of dog food for his beloved pet had always been the crux of the intensive investigation. The most fascinating facet of this crime was that at the time of its commission, the basic theories were that it had been a one-man caper committed by a disgruntled local talk show listener, a Mafia member, or some other type of a homicidal kook. No one dreamt that the murder was the work of a huge band of neo-Nazi terrorists bent on the overthrow of our government and who had made such tremendous strides in pursuit of their avowed intentions.

We can rest assured that the FBI would not have made any of the allegations which they have, or named suspects, all of whom have been indicted, unless they were able to sustain the contentions. Their credibility is at stake. It is impossible to lavish enough praise for a job well done by the Federal Bureau of Investigation in what had formerly been a seemingly unsolvable crime. In keeping with the mores of our land, it must be remembered that all suspects named in this factual narration must be considered as being innocent of the crimes with which they are currently charged unless and until they are duly convicted in a court of law.

"WAS A PAGAN ALTAR USED FOR HUMAN SACRIFICE?"

by Bob Ford

When her mom kissed Lashonda good night, she had no way of knowing she was giving the little girl a last goodbye kiss. Within a few hours her 3-year-old daughter would be snatched from her bed and murdered. A pathologist's report would later show that the child was sexually assaulted after being killed—a deviate behavior called necrophilia.

Lashonda Randolph was one of five children, all pre-school age. The family of seven lived in a three-bedroom apartment on Jaggers Terrace, a housing project in Columbia, South Carolina.

At around nine o'clock on Monday night, March 23, 1987, the mother tucked the children in bed. First she said goodnight to the twins and the little boy, then to Lashonda and her older sister.

In the quiet of that night, the parents watched television until ten o'clock, then locked up and went to bed. Tomorrow was a workday—they would be getting up at six.

Tomorrow was Tuesday, March 24th, a day the couple would never forget.

The mother was startled that morning when she walked into the kitchen and saw the back door standing wide open. The father noticed that two packs of Kool cigarettes and a pair of red-rimmed sunglasses were missing from the coffee table in front of the TV set.

The woman was fearful as she ran upstairs to check on the children.

Lashonda was gone!

The couple telephoned a social worker they knew to get advice. They were told, "Call the police."

The Columbia Police Department was notified at 6:30 a.m. The patrol officers who responded to the complaint then called for a detective and an evidence technician.

Investigator Harold R. Chambers was the first detective to arrive. Friends call the 21-year police veteran "Chub." He's a member of the Detective Bureau's elite Major Crime Squad.

After a few words with the parents, Chambers and his partner, Investigator Tommy Thomas, requested bloodhounds from the State Law Enforcement Division (SLED). Captain J. R. "Randy" Tate, chief of the Investigative Bureau, called out the SRT (Special Response Team) to secure the area while detectives looked for clues to the disappearance of the little girl. Tate also ordered in off-duty detectives. More than 35 law enforcement officers were soon involved in the search.

It was suggested that perhaps the little girl just wandered off. That was a possibility, of course, but Detective Chambers didn't think so. There'd been a burglary. There was a print of a man's workshoe in the dirt just outside the kitchen window. And the child's mother said that Lashonda always played close to the house. She'd been kidnapped; Chambers was sure of that.

Standing in the doorway at the back of the apartment, Chambers looked toward the edge of a steep embankment. A path led down the hill to a set of railroad tracks, then back up the other side.

Investigators Chambers and Thomas wanted to keep the area around the apartment from being contaminated by fresh footprints until the bloodhounds arrived. Keeping people back was difficult. Neighbors were curious and there were lots of school kids; the family lived next door to an elementary school. By 7:30, children were all over the neighborhood; many of them used the path across the tracks as a shortcut.

Uniformed officers were stationed beside the embankment path and along the railroad tracks hoping to preserve any fresh scent left by the missing child. The bloodhounds arrived at 8:15, but the dogs were unable to "strike a trail," Chambers said.

Captain Tate organized a canvass of the neighborhood, while Chambers and other detectives began interviewing possible witnesses.

At 10:40 a.m., Chambers climbed into a South Carolina Wildlife Department helicopter. The pilot flew a grid pattern starting at the apartment. Chambers used binoculars and a walkie-talkie to coordinate ground-search teams. "We looked for anything out of the ordinary," Chambers said later. "We didn't see anything that looked suspicious—zero." The helicopter search was called off at 3:00 p.m.

The child's mother had given a snapshot to Linda Marsh, head of SLED's Missing Persons Information Center. By mid-afternoon, black and white posters with a picture and physical description of the 3-foot-tall, 40-pound victim were distributed to hundreds of convenience stores, gas stations, and businesses within a six-mile radius of the crime scene.

By noon, Jaggers Terrace was crowded with spectators curious about police activity. The perimeter had been lined off with crime-scene tape. Camera crews from four television stations, radio station newspeople, and reporters and photographers from both daily newspapers worked their way through the crowd to police officials.

Reporters demanded to know what was going on. Police Chief Robert A. Wilbur had little to report. A child was missing, presumably kidnapped. Officers were doing everything they could to find her. At that point, there were no details to give.

"We moved the family in with a neighbor then used their apartment for interviews," Detective Chambers said. About a dozen people were driven to headquarters, where they gave voluntary written statements.

"We talked to everybody who thought they'd seen or heard anything," Investigator Thomas said. "We checked out all the telephone tips — every possible lead. You'd think there would have been something. None of it was concrete."

Detectives worked through the night and into the next morning. Still nothing!

On Wednesday, March 25th, at 11:50 a.m., a mail carrier telephoned the police. He said that a woman told him she'd seen what looked like a "hand sticking out from a pile of cloth" in a vacant field in Valley Park near Five Points.

Five Points is a fashionable shopping district near the University of South Carolina's downtown campus.

As reported, there was indeed a hand — a small hand sticking out from under a dark blue cloth. The medium dark-skinned child's hand had turned a bluish-gray. Detectives peeled back a flag of cloth and knew they'd found Lashonda Randolph.

The forensic team arrived minutes later. They

video-taped everything. Still photographs were taken. The victim's body was near a dirt path used for a short-cut between two side streets behind one of the Five Points shopping centers.

After the evidence technicians packed up, paramedics put the victim in a body bag and zippered it closed. The small body occupied only a fraction of the space in the plastic bag. The medics gently loaded Lashonda's body onto the ambulance as a hushed crowd pressed against the crime-scene tape.

Chambers said later that the body had been in the field since late Tuesday or early Wednesday. It had rained hard Wednesday morning, but the ground underneath the victim was dry.

The cloth wrapped around the victim was removed at the morgue. It was a dark blue minister's robe with red piping, the first real clue in the bizarre case, but its significance was a mystery. Under the robe, the little girl was wearing the light-blue button-up shirt she'd wore to bed Monday night. Her underpants were missing.

Investigator Chambers, the case officer, and his partner, Tommy Thomas, were present during the postmortem examination conducted by Dr. William R. Anderson, a pathologist. The preliminary autopsy report revealed "acute brain swelling with congestion and edema . . . consistent with suffocation. Manner of death: homicide."

"She'd been smothered to death," Chambers

said. Results of the microscopic and body fluids examination would come later with the complete autopsy report.

On Wednesday evening, six or seven hours after the child's body was found, Patrolman Heyward Douglas was dispatched to the Gonzales Gardens Apartments to take a stolen vehicle report. Douglas didn't know that the seemingly unrelated report he was about to take would lead to a major breakthrough in the kidnapping and murder investigation.

The complainant, Ralph March, told Douglas that his 1979 light blue Pontiac Gran LeMans was stolen around midnight on Tuesday. He said he met the man who stole his car at a night club on Gervais Street on Tuesday night. The stranger was drinking beer and told Marsh that his little girl had died. Marsh said he felt sorry for the man and suggested that they drive up to Kershaw County for a "weekend retreat."

Along the way, Marsh stopped at a convenience store to use the restroom. He left the keys in the ignition. No sooner had he stepped out of the car than the stranger jumped behind the wheel and drove off.

Patrolman Douglas knew the report of a stolen motor vehicle should be made in Kershaw County where the crime occurred. But, "just on a hunch," he decided to "look around for a little bit."

He started checking near the night club where

Marsh had said he'd met the stranger. The search took less than 15 minutes. Parked on Stark Street near the corner of Oak was the light-blue Pontiac with paper dealer tags. The sergeant and another detective headed Douglas's way when they heard the officer call in a "recovered 10-71 motor vehicle."

A pack of Kool cigarettes and a pair of red-rimmed sunglasses were on the front seat, although their presence meant nothing at that moment.

While Douglas stood on the corner discussing the car with the two detectives, he noticed something strange. A young man across the street was walking rapidly back and forth, never taking his eyes off the officers clustered near the stolen blue automobile.

When police beckoned to the curious young man, he bolted up a driveway, then ran left behind the house. When the officers reached the back of the house, Douglas said later, "he'd totally disappeared. I shined my light around the back yard, but he was gone. The closest thing was a garage."

Officer Douglas turned his light on the partially opened garage door. Each time he turned his light off he heard a "squeak." When the light flashed back on again the noise would stop. "I finally snapped the light off and back on and caught the gleam of a pair of eyes peering out from behind the garage door," Douglas recalled.

Quickly all three officers drew their revolvers. Douglas called out, "Police! You in the garage— come out slowly with your hands behind your head!"

An instant later the man walked out of the garage with his fingers clasped behind his head. He assured the officers that he was alone.

Investigator Jacob W. Farrow and Detective Sergeant Norman Cladwell entered the garage slowly. There were cardboard boxes on the left and a couple of tires leaning against the wall at the back. Halfway down on the right, a curtained doorway led to another room in the L-shaped building.

A dim light flickered through the flimsy curtain. The officers peeked into the room. A single candle sat on top of a chest resembling a makeshift altar. An American flag hung upside down covering the only window. On a nail beside the flag hung a minister's robe—white with wide red trim on the front. Religious banners and recognition plaques hung on the walls. On the "altar" were six Sunday school ushers' badges with purple ribbon and gold fringe. In the far corner of the small room was an unmade bed.

Investigator Chambers said everybody had a gut feeling that "this has got to be it—this is where he brought the child."

Captain Tate had the SRT secure the area around the garage. Evidence technicians processing the room found a child's underpants on the floor underneath the bed.

The man from the garage told detectives that the car parked near the corner was left there by his younger brother, Larry Donnell Williams, 23. He said that Larry stayed at the garage behind his mother's house, but he had been rushed to the hospital in an ambulance about five o'clock on Wednesday morning for an emergency operation.

Chambers checked with the hospital. It was true. The youth had been operated on for a bleeding stomach ulcer early that morning. It was now 10:00 p.m. and he was in the hospital recovery room.

By 8:15 Thursday morning, all evidence from the garage had been tagged and transferred to the property room at police headquarters. Chambers said that detectives wanted to interview Larry Williams, but since he'd just had major surgery, they decided to wait. "We had enough to charge him with the stolen car. There was an armed guard outside his room, so we knew he wasn't going anywhere."

Early on Thursday afternoon, Investigator Farrow went to Jaggers Terrace with the red-rimmed sunglasses and the child's underpants. "The mother recognized the panties right away," Chambers said. "They were fairly new. Shonda had worn them once or twice." The red-rimmed sun glasses were identified by the father.

On Thursday afternoon, March 26th, Investigator Dorsey M. Taylor uncovered a burglary that would further link the suspect in the hospital to the case. Taylor was trying to find out where the ministerial robes and other religious paraphernalia had come from. He systematically checked churches in the neighborhood to see if there'd been an unreported burglary.

Taylor found an open bathroom window at the Jones Tabernacle Fire-Baptized Holiness Church, an old wooden building on Laurens Street, 10 blocks from the Williams' garage.

The minister came to the church to inventory property. Several robes and a recognition plaque were missing. The preacher later identified the blue robe used to wrap up the victim, and the white robe which police found in the garage.

Evidence technicians dusting for fingerprints found a latent print on an orange juice carton in the minster's office. Police obtained the suspect's fingerprint card on file from a previous arrest. Investigator Chambers said that the prints matched. Both sets belonged to Larry Donnell Williams.

"That's when it all came together," Chambers said. "We'd placed him in the stolen car with the red-rimmed sunglasses. The car was parked across the street from the garage. The blue robe the child was wrapped in and the white robe from the garage both came from the church where we found his fingerprints. The real clincher was the child's panties, which was found under the bed."

It was time to talk to the suspect. But police were cautious. Captain Tate had been in contact with FBI psychologists, who advised against an adversarial interview. They recommended that, because the suspect was a black man, it would be best to have a black officer interview him.

Investigator Jake Farrow was assigned to go up to the seventh-floor hospital room and talk to Williams. Farrow arrived there on Friday at 8:45 p.m. Williams was seated in a wheelchair with I.V. tubes in his arm. Farrow identified himself as a Columbia police officer and gave Williams the required Miranda warning. Then they just talked.

The matter of Lashonda Randolph was never discussed during the hour-and-ten-minute interview. "All they did was chitchat," Chambers said. "There was no confrontation. The investigation wasn't even mentioned. Basically it was like a social call. He (Williams) didn't even ask why there was a uniformed police officer outside his door."

At about 10:00 p.m., Farrow left the hospital, having sown the seeds of a clever plan. Would the technique bear fruit?

Lashonda Randolph's funeral was at 3:00 p.m. on Saturday at the Zion Benevolent Baptist Church in rural Richland County. The church was packed. Police videotaped everybody at the funeral, in case a suspect attended ceremonies.

The little girl was dressed n a white lace Easter dress and a double strand of pearls, with flowers in her hair. The church choir sang "Onward Christian Soldiers."

Meanwhile, the autopsy report was released; reporters learned that there was evidence of rape. Media reports speculated that the little girl may have been killed on a pagan altar as a human sacrifice. One so-called source, whom reporters failed to identify, claimed that Shonda died "in some kind of weird religious ritual."

Television and newspaper reports also claimed that there were bloodstains on the makeshift altar, which laboratory analysis revealed as the blood of a hog. Police steadfastly denied all media claims of a ritualistic slaying.

On Friday, John David Spade, public information officer for the City of Columbia, had said at a press briefing, "We're not trying to panic the public, but there is a criminal element in the community. We urge you to use utmost caution with the safety of children — especially younger children."

Television stations interviewed mothers of young children in Jaggers Terrace and Valley Park. Several women told reporters they were locking their doors and windows because they were afraid a child-killer was stalking their neighborhood.

Shortly before 3:30 p.m. on Saturday, while

Shonda's funeral was still going on, a nurse called Columbia police and said that Williams wanted to see Jake Farrow, the detective he'd talked to earlier. Investigators were anxious. Was the plan working? Was Williams ready to confess? They'd soon know. Arrangements were made to meet with Williams in an office on the seventh-floor of the hospital.

Ever since Thursday, Williams had been without pain medication. Investigator Chambers said they'd delayed interviews because they didn't want the suspect to recant any statements he might make, claiming he'd been under the influence of painkillers.

At 4:55 p.m., Detective Jake Farrow met Larry Donnell Williams in an office at Richland Memorial Hospital. Farrow again made cheerful conversation, but still gave the required Miranda warning, explaining that Williams was not required to say anything or answer any questions and that he had the right to a lawyer if he wanted one. Williams told Farrow that he understood the warnings but wanted to continue.

During the next two hours, Williams admitted to burglarizing the little girl's home on March 23rd. He said he did it because he needed money. While he was upstairs the little girl woke up and saw him. Williams said he was afraid she'd cry out, so he picked her up and "toted" her all the way back to the garage, where he kept her until she died the following day. Jaggers Terrace is about two miles from Williams' garage in Valley Park.

Williams said he fed Shonda a hot dog on Tuesday morning at about ten o'clock, but she started crying. He said he put his hand over her mouth so she'd be quiet. Williams told Farrow he held his right hand over her mouth for about five minutes. "I didn't know I was pressing on her nose too hard," he said. When Williams removed his hand from her face the child had stopped breathing.

Williams said he wrapped a minister's robe around the dead girl at around 7:00 p.m. on Tuesday. Then he carried her several blocks to the open field, where he put her down "so somebody would find her."

Williams said that after he disposed of the body, he went to the night club, where he met the man who offered to take him to Camden. He admitted stealing the man's car when they stopped at a convenience store. He drove back to the night club, but developed stomach cramps, so he drove home, parked the car in front of his mother's house, and called an ambulance.

Williams had given an oral confession. The "easy does it" interview plan had succeeded beyond all expectations. Williams had admitted everything.

Farrow wanted to get Williams' confession down on paper, but it was visiting hours, and people were coming in and out of rooms. The noise was distracting. The two men agreed to get together again after visiting hours were over. That would also give Williams extra time to think things over, so there'd be no doubt about what he wanted to do. Farrow left the hospital at 6:45 p.m.

As agreed, Investigator Farrow returned at 9:30 p.m. He went to the hospital's seventh-floor office as before. Williams said he was ready to put the whole incredible story down in black and white.

Farrow again gave Williams his rights; the suspect again confessed to everything. This time it was in writing, sworn to and witnessed. That was the way Larry Donnell Williams wanted it.

Chambers said that all of the essentials were contained in the five-page document—the burglary of the church and the home, the kidnapping, the murder, and the auto theft. It was all there in black and white and Williams signed it. Dorsey Taylor, the detective who discovered the church break-in, witnessed Williams' confession.

In spite of the confession, it was still too early to announce an arrest. Police wanted to review the statement point-by-point to be certain beyond all doubt that they had their man. Only then would they ask for warrants. Williams was in the hospital under armed guard. "He wasn't going anywhere," Chambers said. In response to a reporter's inquiry late Saturday, Chief Wilbur said, "An arrest is imminent."

On Monday morning, March 30th, Chambers countersigned the warrants formally charging Larry Donnell Williams with kidnapping, murder, two counts of burglary, and grand larceny. He'd already been charged with possession of a stolen motor vehicle. Now the armed guard was moved inside Williams' hospital room.

News of the arrest was announced soon after the warrants were served, but details of the confession were withheld. Fifth Circuit Solicitor James C. Anders hoped to avoid a change of venue because of too much pre-trial publicity.

There'd already been a lot of speculation, and the media were making an issue of the autopsy report which said the child had been raped. Reporters were asking why Williams wasn't charged with rape. Choosing not to defend the prosecution's position, Anders said only, "I refuse to comment. This is a matter for the courts, not the newspaper."

Larry Williams was released from the hospital on April 1st and immediately jailed without bond. He was quickly transferred "for safekeeping" to a maximum security section of the state's Central Correctional Institution (CCI).

Less than a week later, on April 7th, Williams disavowed his confession in a handwritten letter to his mother. Columbia's local NBC television station, WIS-TV 10, broadcast the story using quotes from the letter turned over to the media by the suspect's mother.

Williams wrote, in part, "I know I did a lot of wrong things in my life, but murder no way. I don't have the heart to kill a dog . . . talk about killing a human being."

The Solicitor's office was not impressed. The following day, Anders filed notice with Williams' lawyers that he'd seek the death penalty.

Circuit Judge Ralph King Anderson signed a "gag order" prohibiting police and the prosecutor's office from making any comment about the Williams case out of court.

At a pre-trial hearing on April 13th, Judge Anderson ordered reporters and spectators out of the courtroom. A secret hearing was ordered so that prosecutors could present evidence they'd collected. The court ordered the defendant to surrender samples of his hair, blood, and saliva so that evidence technicians could compare it with samples from the crime scene.

In the face of criticism as he cleared the courtroom, Judge Anderson said that he feared too much pre-trial publicity, and that what he was doing was a "balance of Constitutional rights."

The issue became moot a month later. On May 18th, Judge Anderson ruled in favor of a defense motion to move the trial to Spartanburg County in the western part of South Carolina. Trial was set for July 20th.

On April 24th, the Richland County grand jury

indicted Larry Donnell Williams on all the charges filed by the Columbia Police Department, plus one more—first-degree criminal sexual conduct, the legal term for rape in South Carolina.

Lashonda Randolph's autopsy report indicated that the microscopic examination of the victim's anal and vaginal orifices showed the presence of sperm. Earlier, the coroner had said that the child was raped, but the matter of bringing the sexual misconduct charge was deferred to the grand jury.

The court was notified that the defendant was mentally able to stand trial. "There is no question about his competency to stand trial," Columbia Attorney Cameron Currie said. "He (Williams) understands the charges against him."

On Tuesday, July 21st, Larry Donnell Williams stood up in General Sessions Court in Spartanburg County as the clerk read formal charges of kidnapping, murder, and criminal sexual conduct, two counts of burglary, grand larceny, and auto theft. In front of 40 potential jurors, the 23-year-old defendant claimed that he was innocent on all counts. Twelve jurors and two alternates would be selected to hear the death penalty case expected to begin the next day.

By Wednesday morning a jury had been selected and the death penalty trial was ready to begin. But overnight, there had been dramatic charges in the plans of both the defense and the prosecution.

Solicitor Jim Anders learned only the night before of new testimony which, because of a quirk in the law, would most likely prevent Williams from being sentenced to die in the electric chair. So the prosecution decided to allow Williams to plead guilty to all of the charges in exchange for his life.

Judge Ralph King Anderson asked the defendant: "Mr. Williams, did you, on March 24, 1987, in Richland County, murder Lashonda Randolph?"

The 23-year-old defendant answered in a whisper, "Yes, sir," then dropped his head. Judge Anderson again asked Williams if he committed the murder. William again answered, "Yes," then looked down at the floor. Court observers said that Judge Anderson asked Williams at least 50 times if he was certain he wanted to plead guilty to the charges. Williams answered repeatedly that he was sure.

Only then did Judge Anderson pass sentence. For the confessed crime of murder, Williams was sentenced to life in prison. For the other charges to which he'd confessed including kidnapping, two counts of burglary, first-degree criminal sexual conduct, grand larceny, and possession of a stolen motor vehicle, the defendant was sentenced to a second life term plus 60 years. The combined sentences amount to two consecutive life terms plus 60 years.

Under South Carolina law, Williams will not be

eligible for parole for a minimum of 30 years. He'll be 53 years old then. Anders said that's "the most serious punishment you can give someone except the electric chair," in South Carolina.

Anders said he abandoned his plans to seek the death penalty when he learned the night before the trial began that the state's pathologist would testify that the little girl was raped after she died. "Under South Carolina law, necrophilia, having sex with the dead, is technically not criminal sexual conduct—rape," Anders explained. Rape was the aggravating circumstance that would have enabled the state to seek the death penalty.

Questions about religious paraphernalia found in Williams' living quarters and reports of bloodstains on a makeshift altar remain unexplained.

EDITOR'S NOTE:
Ralph Marsh is not the real name of the person so named in the foregoing story. A fictitious name has been used because there is no reason for public interest in the identity of this person.

"SATANISTS OFFERED A HUMAN SACRIFICE."

by Jack G. Heise

On Monday, December 8, 1987, Deputy Mike Randolph walked into the Jasper County Sheriff's Office in Carthage, Missouri, with a puzzled look on his face. "What's up?" Sheriff Leland Boatwright asked.

"Have you ever heard about devil worshipping and satanism?" Randolph asked.

"Sure," Boatwright responded. "I've read about it, like those Manson kooks in California and I read something about a black church they've got in San Francisco in which people go to worship the devil just like other people go to church to worship God."

Nodding, Randolph said, "That's what I mean. I read that just a while back they had a case in Houston, Texas, where some kids, including a girl, took another kid to a cemetery, carved symbols on his body and set his hair on fire before they ate him to death. Do you suppose anything like that could happen around here?"

With a broad smile, Sheriff Boatwright answered, "Man, we're country folks. People around here are too busy taking care of their cattle or farms to go in for that goofy stuff. What makes you ask?"

Randolph related that he had been on patrol in the morning when the dispatcher had contacted him. He was told that a woman living in a rural area outside Carl Junction had called in to report her 19-year-old son mysteriously missing.

Randolph had stopped by the woman's house to get additional information. The woman had told him that her son Steven Newberry was an overweight high school student who had a learning disability, but was a good boy. He worked nights at a restaurant in the Carl Junction area as a dishwasher.

On Sunday afternoon, some teenaged boys in a car had stopped in front of the house and honked the car horn. Steven had gone out to talk to them and then had come back inside and had excitedly called to his mother, "Hey, Mom, I'm going out with the guys for a while."

Mrs. Newberry told Deputy Randolph that her son had picked up his baseball bat and hurried back to where his friends were waiting. She said she had been pleased that Steven had made some friends because he hadn't been accepted by boys of his own age because of his learning disability and

114

inability to play most games with them.

She told Randolph that she had started to worry when he had not returned for dinner. Later, she called the restaurant where he worked and learned Steven had not shown up there. She said she did not know the boys in the car who had picked up Steven. In the morning, when he had still not returned, she had called the sheriff's office.

"You know, a nineteen-year-old kid away from home overnight wouldn't be a big deal," Randolph said. "But after talking to the woman I was pretty well convinced that something may have happened to him."

Randolph said he had stopped by the school where officials had told him that Steven had not come to class. That was unusual, they told Randolph, because although Steven was a slow learner, he was an avid pupil who was eager to learn and anxious to be accepted by his peers.

"What about the kids who picked him up on Sunday?" Sheriff Boatwright asked.

Randolph said he had talked to a number of young persons at the school but had not found anyone who would admit to having visited the missing youth's house or to knowing who might have been in the car.

"What's this got to do with devil worshipping and satanism?" Boatwright queried.

"I'm coming to that," Randolph responded.

He explained that in talking to some of the students they had made vague references to a group of teenagers who had gotten into satanism. They had some books on the subject and were into heavy metal music with lyrics that extolled devil worship, torture and sacrifices. There was talk that they had a meeting place they called a "coven" where they had sacrificed animals in their rituals.

"You aren't thinking that these punks into satanism could have picked up the Newberry boy for a human sacrifice?" Boatwright asked.

Scowling as he answered, Randolph said, "I know it sounds weird, but look at the facts. These kids came by to pick him up. His mother said that was strange because he didn't have any friends and now he's missing."

Sheriff Boatwright called in Chief Deputy Larry Parrill and Deputies Joe Fort and Ray Youngblood. Deputy Randolph went over the information that he had already given Boatwright.

"What do you guys think?" Boatwright asked them.

The deputies were unsure. Youngblood asked Randolph, "Are you sure it was high school students who picked up the Newberry boy, or could they have been people he met at the restaurant where he worked?"

Randolph said he did not know. Newberry's mother had told him that she had not recognized the youths in the car. She thought there were three of them about the same age as her son.

The conversation turned to satanism. Parrill commented that high school kids sometimes get into all kinds of things, like smoking marijuana, but he thought it highly unlikely they would be involved in devil worship and human sacrifices.

"The kid is missing," Boatwright said. "And apparently something happened to him. But I don't think there is much we can do about it until morning; then we can start checking and find out who it was who picked him up and what happened."

However, they did not have to wait until morning.

In the early evening, a woman, red-eyed from crying, came in with a young man. She told the desk clerk that her son had something to tell the police. Asked what it was, the woman said it concerned Steven Newberry.

The alert quickly brought in Sheriff Boatwright and the deputies. Taken into an office, the woman, in a voice shaken by emotion, told the officers, "My son has something he wants to tell you."

"Yes?" Parrill asked.

The youth hesitated for several moments and then replied, "I don't want my mother to hear all of it."

The woman agreed to leave the room.

With a tape recorder turned on, the youth identified himself as 17-year-old Theron Roland. Advised of his legal rights, Roland said he understood them and was making the statement

117

voluntarily.

"Where should I start?" Roland asked.

"Why not from the beginning," Parrill advised him. "That's usually the best place."

Roland began by relating that he and two of his high school friends, Roland Clements and James Hardy, both 17, had become interested in satanism when Clements had obtained a copy of a satanic bible and began reading to them. They thought it might be cool to start a devil worship club and sent away for some satanic paraphernalia, such as black candles, a baphomet (which is a medallion that has the head of a goat) and pentacles (the inverted Star of David). They also bought some heavy black metal music.

Roland related that they wanted to tattoo themselves with some of the satanic symbols, but were fearful their parents would question them about it, so instead they used washable paint to put the devil's sign of "666" on their knuckles.

They looked for a place to have a coven for their meetings and found a spot by an abandoned chemical plant near the Missouri-Kansas border where there was a well. They used spray paint for some satanic symbols and would gather there to play their heavy metal music and chant phrases from the satanic bible.

They progressed to the point that they wanted to have a satanic sacrifice and brought a cat with them. They used baseball bats to beat the cat to death while they sang the words of their heavy metal music and chanted phrases from the satanic bible.

Roland claimed that it was Clements' idea to have a real human sacrifice so they selected Steven Newberry to be the person they would sacrifice to Satan.

"Why Newberry?" Parrill questioned.

Roland explained that according to the satanic bible on human sacrifices, the only time a satanist would perform a human sacrifice would be to serve a two-fold purpose: To release the magician's wrath in throwing a curse and, more importantly, to dispose of an obnoxious individual. They had selected Steven Newberry because he was mentally slow, overweight and awkward; they felt he was inferior and his death would be of no importance.

Continuing with his statement, Roland related that he, Clements and Hardy, had gone to Newberry's home on Sunday afternoon and asked him if he wanted to join their club. They told him to bring along his baseball bat and they were going to a meeting.

They drove out to the well where they had their coven. They had a cat with them and, after playing their heavy metal music and chanting from the satanic bible, they used the baseball bats to club the cat to death and dropped it into the well.

Suddenly, Clements hit Newberry on the head with his baseball bat. Newberry looked at him and asked, "Why me?"

Clements urged the others to join in on the sacrifice and they beat Newberry until he resembled the Black Friday lyrics, "I mangle their faces till no feature remains." With Newberry dead, the trio dumped his body in the well along with the sacrificed cats.

The deputies listening to the grisly account could scarcely believe what they had heard. Chief Deputy Parrill asked, "Why have you come in to tell us about this?"

Roland said that, after Newberry was killed, he began to recognize that it was the wrong thing to have done. He was unable to sleep Sunday night thinking about it and when he came home from school on Monday, he had gone to his room and began to cry. His mother finally persuaded him to tell her what was wrong. Then he told her that he and two of his school friends had killed Steven Newberry, she insisted that they go to the police.

Theron Roland concluded his statement by saying that he would lead the officers to the well. Jasper County Prosecutor David Dally was called in and given Roland's statement. They all left to go to the well. En route, Roland told the officials that when they sacrificed the cats, they had drunk some of the blood, according to the satanic bible ritual. But Roland said he had been unable to drink the blood of Newberry after he had been killed.

It was 11 o'clock at night when the groups reached the well. Using portable lights, the deputies were able to bring Newberry's corpse out of the cistern. A postmortem conducted later revealed that the victim's battered body had been struck at least 50 times with the baseball bats.

Prosecutor Dally issued warrants charging Ronald Clements and James Hardy with murder. The youths were taken into custody.

When the small town of Carl Junction learned the bizarre and gruesome details of the crime, they were shocked and reluctant to believe it had taken place. All three youths charged with the murder were honor students at the school and James Hardy had been president of the senior class.

Attorneys for the youths entered innocent pleas on the grounds of mental disease or defects.

James Hardy was scheduled to go on trial first. In a change of venue from Jasper County to Camden County before Judge James Franklin, Hardy entered a guilty plea in exchange for a promise from Prosecutor Dally that he would not ask for the death penalty.

In an unemotional statement to the court, Hardy related how he and the others had beaten Newberry to death while performing the ritual of human sacrifice according to the ordinances of the satanic bible.

He concluded his statement by saying, "I think there may have been something wrong with me to have carried it out, but I was of sound mind to have planned it."

Ronald Clements decided to go on trial with a plea of innocent by reason of insanity before Judge Herbert Casteel in Carthage. following the hearing of testimony by Theron Roland and James Hardy and statements by psychiatrists that they considered Clements to be sane enough to determine right from wrong, the jury returned a guilty verdict, with the recommendation that he be sentenced to life in prison. Theron Roland was the last of the trio to go on trial. Like Clements, he pleaded innocent by reason of insanity, but was found guilty with a recommendation that he spend the rest of his natural life in prison.

With the trials completed, the judges in each of the cases handed down the sentences and Roland, Clements and Hardy are all in prison.

At the conclusion of the case, Prosecutor Dally was quoted as saying that, as bizarre as it may seem that three intelligent youths could have become involved in satanism, it was not unique to Jasper County. He quoted a report given by the director of the Institute of Humanities at Colorado University in Denver in which he said, "The paranoid fantasy is becoming a major national social problem. If you are not looking for it, you don't see the evidence. But when you are looking for it, you see it everywhere."

"THE DARK SIDE OF OUTLAW BIKERS."

by Bob Loeffelbein

In May 1985, in 50 locations in 11 states—including the cities of Phoenix, Arizona, New Haven, Connecticut, Boston, Massachusetts, Cleveland, Ohio, Omaha, Nebraska, and Charlotte, North Carolina—over 1,000 law enforcement agents from local, state and federal police organizations simultaneously rounded up and arrested more than 100 Hell's Angels. This was the first all-out attempt to crush this crime "family" that allegedly made millions from drug dealing, extortion, bribery, harboring fugitives and even contract murder. It was the culmination of a three-year undercover and infiltration operation, and followed a similar multi-state raid in February 1985 that had corralled about 90 members of another cycle gang, the Bandidos.

In spite of a fearsome arsenal of weapons found—ranging from UZI submachine guns to anti-tank weapons—most Angels surrendered peaceably. The only casualty was a state trooper in Connecticut, shot in the hip. The reputed head of the national organization of Hell's Angels was ignominiously captured in front of 500 people and TV cameras as he tried to flee down a fire escape ladder, while police, backed by a helicopter, an armored van and attack dogs, battered in the doors of the gang's regional headquarters in the East Village section of Manhattan with sledgehammers.

"We're just a bunch of happy-go-lucky guys trying to make it in this world," said the head of the notorious Hell's Angels motorcycle gang.

But that was back in 1982, with a national law enforcement focus directed more and more toward criminal violence, where outlaw motorcycle gangs were gaining increasing national attention by the media and the police.

According to Pennsylvania Congressman Robert Walker, "The problem of motorcycle gangs is pervasive and growing. They pose a serious threat to our society . . ."

FBI investigations have confirmed a deepening gang involvement in narcotics manufacturing and distribution, prostitution, weapons-related violations, extortion, arson-for-hire, pornography, protection rackets, loan sharking, interstate transportation of stolen motor vehicles, insurance fraud, and murder.

According to a member of the Angels ". . .

club structure was easily adapted to drug trafficking. All essential jobs could be filled with members—distributors, dealers, enforcers, transporters." Yet many of the outlaw groups started as recreational groups, with the Angels probably changing first.

Hunter Thompson, who has written much about the Hell's Angels, traced the beginning of the gang to groups like the POBOBs (Pissed Off Bastards of Bloomington) and and the Market Street Commandos. Originally both were said to include persons drawn together in loosely-knit groups of individuals sharing a common, but as yet relatively rare, interest in motorcycles. The Hell's Angels was only one of several active offshoots between the late 1940s and the 1960s, and it was several media events that brought them to public attention and provided the media boost that propelled them toward a national reputation.

In the summer of 1947, in Hollister, California, thousands of cyclists started gathering for motorcycle runs. Later they were held at Riverside, California. They soon got out of control, with rioting, destruction of property and, eventually, two deaths, but the movie, "The Wild Ones," starring Marlon Brando, was made from these confrontations and portrayed the bikers as modern-day Robin Hoods seeking revenge on a world that did them wrong. It was followed by another film, "Easyrider," starring Peter Fonda, and even one featuring Elvis Presley. They romanticized cycle club behavior and drew more people to memberships. Through the 1950s and early 1960s, police problems were limited primarily to controlling large gatherings, however.

Then, in July 1965, an alleged gang rape by the Hell's Angels, during an annual rally at Bass Lake in California, provided an orgy of publicity over a six-month period that went to gang members' heads.

As the members matured — many are now in their mid-30s — gang problems also changed for the police, branching out to include community fear, territorial battles among rival clubs, rivalry for control of narcotics trade and vice traffic, and crime conspiracies.

More recently, according to police departments, the Angels have started using more subtle big-crime tricks like investing and laundering money through legitimate businesses, and using computer hookups for administration of business. Working relationships with other criminal groups have also surfaced, with reports of Angels accepting murder contracts, strong-arming business competitors, and enforcing collections on gambling debts.

In order to be more effective in gang investigations now, law enforcement agencies have found they must have a deeper knowledge of group behavior in the gangs, as well as their structure and characteristics. There is a need for specific police intelligence-gathering activities just to keep track of the frequent migrations of gang members, and to identify fugitives occasionally connected with some groups.

A more pervasive problem is the perception citizens have of the dangers posed by gangs in their communities. Though their presence is a legitimate cause for anxiety, if no incidents are triggered, there is little the police can do except furnish a presence.

Another continuing problem is inter-gang warfare, establishing rights to operate in various regions. Gang deaths have resulted in battles in parking lots, attacks on gang clubhouses and firebomb and shotgun raids on homes. Frequently, of course, outsiders are also injured. In New York, for example, five people were killed and 22 injured in such a vengeance war. Because of reluctance by gang members to cooperate with police, it is often impossible to understand the motivations for such violence.

In some cases, though, the causes are known. Some gangland execution-style slayings in Charlotte, North Carolina, involving Hell's Angels, Outlaws and other gangs, were tied to a struggle for dominance of the area's lucrative vice and narcotics trade. Incidents there could be read by police and an intensified law enforcement effort introduced.

In the 1970s, another problem surfaced indicating gang involvement in criminal activity. An interstate network of one-time rebel groups was formed, providing links for more sophisticated criminal activities. Crime territories were determined, and fixed roles and ways of doing business were evolved.

The high degree of mobility of these far-flung gangs, in attending everything from rallies to funerals, has made it extremely difficult for police to identify and keep track of individuals of police interest.

Such gatherings between members of diverse gangs extend not only to their social networks, but are used to perpetuate and extend the flow of contraband and further other criminal activity. Some gangs, in fact, have found such mobility to be so advantageous they have formed "nomad" chapters, where members don't belong to any area-based club but become "permanent transients."

A code of silence evolved which made this brotherhood extremely difficult to penetrate by undercover police. One Hell's Angel member stated it like this, "The Hell's Angels is an honor society, man. We live by some of the strictest rules going and, if you break one, you might not have the chance to break another."

Another member-turned-government-witness provided evidence of this code by describing the killing of two probationary members over the mere suggestion that one was a police informer.

Witness intimidation by gang members is an extension of this code, and a problem police frequently faced in building cases against gangs. The Margo Compton case is an example. She testified against Hell's Angels, but following her court disclosure about a club member's involvement in drugs and prostitution, her twin six-year-old daughters and the 19-year-old son of her boyfriend were killed. Later she also was slain.

Police officers have often been targeted for gang violence. A detective from Solano County, California, was crippled by a bomb blast in 1977 during his investigation of the Hell's Angels. A Maryland deputy sheriff was shot and killed when he interrupted a Pagan gang duo in a burglary. In Portland, Oregon, an officer was killed in a raid on the Outsiders gang headquarters. And in Garden Grove, California, a gang member shot his way out of a bar, killing one policeman and wounding four others.

Gangs now practice extensive security precautions; even using police-band radio scanners and surveillance of police officers and prosecutors. Instances of attempted infiltration of government and law enforcement agencies by gang members has been reported, along with cases of gang efforts to obtain information from law enforcement agency employees.

Motorcycle gangs constitute a bizarre subculture in the U.S. and Canada, but, for some reason, it has not been dignified for study by serious social scientists. Yet, in dealing with emergent problem groups like this, which develop special characteristics that set them apart from all others, group behavior is important to understand.

The cycle gang subculture is based upon a number of common factors in addition to mutual interest in motorcycles—regional characteristics, common social and psychological traits, like occupations and/or interests, and probably certain styles of dress and behavior.

Outlaw gang members challenge dominant features of American and Canadian society, not only with their criminal behavior but with overt actions intended to shock. Randal Montgomery, who has written much about this subculture in Canadian criminology journals, states: "Observations of outlaw motorcycle clubs leave the impression that club members are striving for adult masculine status, often overcompensating for real or felt deficiencies. In addition, outlaw bikers practice many of the rites used by youths to confer adulthood on themselves (e.g., self-adornment, acquisition of new name and language, seclusion from women, break from home, sexual ambivalence, hazing, economic profit from older members, education for new roles, fertility themes, and death and rebirth myths)."

A sexual fertility theme is consistently present among outlaw bikers. Sex rituals are occasionally included as part of the initiation ceremony, club meeting or cycle run. Sexual "achievements" by members are rewarded by the group, often formally depicted by various colored jacket patches, denoting "witnessed" sex acts, rather like merit badges for deviant acts.

Initially attracted because of the excitement gang life offers, many women are later held involuntarily or remain out of fear. They are usually not gang members. They may be the "property" of one member or used by several. But the female role is that of a servant. They are looked on as objects to be used.

Because of fear and a relatively low level of self-esteem, and often simply because she has no place to go, the gang "mama" feels unable to break away. She develops a strong dependency. Not unlike some battered women, she may even accept responsibility for being abused and may feel guilty for not living up to a gang member's expectations. For many, sex becomes a means to establish intimacy, becoming confused with affection.

The sociopathic group member often has little tolerance for frustration. He externalizes life's pressures by blaming others for his problems.

This is combined with an impulsiveness that produces an individual who fails to think through the consequences and irrationality of his crimes. He does not learn from bad past experiences because he gives them little thought; he is simply reactive. It follows then, that such a gang member will often have a police record listing a variety of crimes often motivated by impulse.

An incident in Houston, Texas, exemplifies the danger of such impulsiveness. A member of the Conquistadors gang, reacting to the discovery of an 11-year-old boy fishing in a pond on gang property, fired an M-2 machine gun into the boy's home, injuring him.

Gang members' language is saturated with vulgarity and terminology with double meanings understood only by them.

As one social scientist explained, value orientations differ among varying groups of people because the views and beliefs people have are the products of learning and past group relationships. Most members of outlaw gangs are from lower or lower-middle class levels of society and, as such, bring with them their class-associated behaviors. However, there are a few middle-class virtues bikers accept, such as cultivation of personality and high value placement on skills.

Gang members, according to writer Montgomery, tend to caricature or exaggerate even minor personality quirks since they receive positive reinforcement from other members. Often such quirks or mannerisms result in new names for an individual—Flapper, Spider, Greaser, Loser, Roach, Wild Man, Zit—and these become the only names they are known by in the organization.

Several "skills" highly esteemed by outlaw bikers are fighting, highway vandalism, cycle theft and stripping, shoplifting, reckless riding, conning, technical practical jokes (like wiring a fellow member who has passed out to an electrical outlet, soaking his jeans with beer, then plugging him in) and, unaccountably, poetry.

The gang member has to constantly prove himself through such bizarre or criminal behavior. He is characterized by a lack of guile or remorse. The group allows him an excuse to become deviant, to impress brother gang members.

But this type of person is also self-centered and has difficulty with interpersonal relationships. Even within the group he has difficulty keeping close friends because of his irresponsible and cynical nature. His real commitment is to himself.

As individuals with like values become more involved with each other, as in cycle gangs, certain values become reinforced and accentuated as accepted group behavior. One common finding is that the outlaw biker believes the world wants to like him—it is everyone else who is out of step.

Initiations for memberships are carried out with that idea in mind. Membership is gained after a process of "testing" to see if the "probate" will fit in. This probate is required to submit to the desires of gang members, wait on them and run errands. Some gangs require that the probate commit a crime, witnessed by a member, which effectively filters out potential police informers and gives the group an effective hold over the new member.

The initiation includes some sort of symbolic attachment to the group—the putting on of the "colors" (club jacket) and perhaps including tattooing the club name or logo on arm or back.

Social scientists have established a relationship between tattoos and maladjustment, showing that persons with many tattoos tend to be more deviant, hostile, impulsive and sociopathic than persons without.

The initiation may also include some revilement, such as having initiates lie on the ground while members pour oil or pig urine over them, or they urinate, defecate or vomit on them.

One class-level characteristic attributed to gang members is hopelessness. Members have little hope of succeeding in society in terms of living up to societal expectations that require achievement and education. One Hell's Angel-turned-government-witness identified the strong connection between his psychological needs and his gang association when he said, "My self-esteem and my deepest friendships were bolted to my motorcycle."

Mutual support combats the feeling of hopelessness and provides for some individual security needs.

By the late 1960s, being a Hell's Angel had become a full-time job for many and at least one income supplement for most, according to an ex-member's testimony. Such income had burgeoned over the years. When 11 members of Hell's Angels were indicted in San Francisco more recently, they were able to raise $3 million in bail money and, when freed, drove off in a limousine.

"THE LETHAL CARESS OF A DEVIL WORSHIPPER?"

by Gary C. King

The date was June 1, 1988. Summer was just around the corner. All indications were that it was going to be a hot one in the Pacific Northwest, particularly in Oregon's Willamette Valley, where the cities of Eugene and Springfield are located. With temperatures in the mid-to-upper-80s, the magnolias and roses were already beginning to show their varied colors along the busy streets, in residential yard , and especially around public buildings.

It was just such peaceful scene that several members of the Springfield Police Department were dispatched to later that same day, except that it was on lower ground near a water-filtration plant. They weren't there, however, to listen to the treetops stirring with the whisper of a cooling breeze. They had been called there to investigate the unnerving discovery of a young woman's body, and their presence soon created movement from the curious transients in the nearby forest camps.

Captain Jerry Smith, who headed the investigation under the direction of Springfield Police Chief Rob DeuPree, was among the first to arrive. He briefly observed the body, noted that the woman was probably in her late teens, then directed officers from his department to cordon off a large area around the corpse. He, along with other investigators, then set about determining the dimensions of the crime scene.

The woman, observed Smith, was only partially clad. Her clothing was nowhere to be found. She wasn't wearing any jewelry, which seemed odd for a woman of that age, and there was no purse or wallet on or near the corpse, another oddity.

A gut feeling told him that this wasn't a sexual assault; it just didn't look like one. But, he couldn't help asking, why was the victim only partially clad and where were the missing clothes? Why would the perpetrator take them? Although he didn't really expect to find the missing clothes, Smith nonetheless instructed a couple of officers to search beyond the perimeters of the crime scene just in case the killer or killers had left any items behind. They were also told to flush out and question any hoboes living in the area.

After photographs of the victim were taken, a Lane County deputy medical examiner made his preliminary observations. Among the things he noted was that the victim bore marks and abrasions on her neck. He suspected that the hyoid bone was fractured or crushed, often an indication of strangulation. He also observed discoloration of the neck and face, as well as a swollen protruding tongue, which also supported his theory as to the cause of death.

Postmortem lividity on the undermost portions of the victim's body indicated that she had been killed where she was found. He agreed with Smith's opinion that it didn't appear she had been sexually assaulted. He said, however, that laboratory tests would have to be conducted to make certain.

After Oregon State Police (OSP) crime lab technicians completed their examination of the victim's body, the corpse was placed inside the body bag and transported to the Lane County Morgue in Eugene.

Although they had conducted a grid search of the area and were fairly certain that they hadn't missed anything, the probers went over the designated crime scene again just to be sure. But night soon drew down on the investigators like a black cowl and, they packed up their gear and called it a day.

The next day was almost as hectic. The lawmen rounded up what few hoboes they could find for questioning, but the cops quickly decided that none of those questioned knew anything about the homicide.

Following another search of the crime scene, the probers decided that any additional effort in this area would only be futile. It appeared that there was nothing in the woods which could point them toward a suspect, and no one associated with the investigation would say what evidence, if any, had been found.

Meanwhile, an autopsy of the victim's body by Dr. Frank Ratti, Lane County Medical Examiner, revealed that she did in fact die from strangulation. It appeared, said the report, that she had been choked, and at some point a thin, solid item had been pressed against her throat with great pressure. Ratti did not speculate on what that item may have been. A published newspaper account reported that she had also been struck in the head by a heavy object.

Usually, Jane (or John) Doe cases are the hardest to solve because the sleuths don't have a satisfactory place to begin their probe, specifically a name upon which they can lay their foundation and begin building a case. But to the surprise of the investigators, significant progress was soon made along those lines.

By the following day the homicide probers had made at least a tentative identification of the forest victim after inquiries were made by concerned relatives of Melissa Ann Meyer, 19, from Seattle. The age and physical description provided by the inquiries certainly fit that of the victim prompting Lane County authorities to request that Meyer's dental records be sent to them.

Shortly after the records arrived, a positive identification was made. With the woman's identity the probers now, at least, had their first significant lead. From this simple discovery they could begin tracing the young woman's movements during the last hours of her life by contacting those who knew her, and from that, with any luck, they were hopeful they could eventually focus on a suspect.

The Springfield investigators soon learned that Melissa, adopted as a child, had moved to Eugene, a college town (home of the University of Oregon), from Seattle in February 1988. She was not employed anywhere, however, and detectives could find nothing to indicate that she was attending college. Her last known address was an apartment located on West Eighth Avenue in Eugene. She was last seen on May 30th in the downtown area.

Prior to her relocation, the detectives learned, she had enrolled in a drug treatment program in Seattle. By interviewing Meyer's acquaintances, the detectives soon determined that she often visited Eugene's downtown mall in the months prior to her death.

The mall was known to be frequented by prostitutes and was a favorite hangout for drug addicts and pushers. This could be where she met the person or persons who killed her, theorized the detectives. But Melissa Meyer, police learned, had no arrest record and no known involvement in criminal activity. So why did she regularly go to the mall? Just a people-watcher?

As news of the murder spread through the community, a chilling question surged to the forefront. Could she have been a victim of the Green River Killer? It was a question pondered by many, especially lawmen. Like many of the 40 women (mostly prostitutes) killed by the Northwest's worst serial murderer, Meyer was found in a heavily wooded area. And since four of the killer's known victims had been found in Oregon, it was a distinct possibility that had to be considered.

"We don't have any evidence that leads us to believe she was a prostitute or engaged in anything of that nature," said Captain Smith, in an apparent reference to the possibility that she had become a victim of the serial killer. "There are a lot of things we don't know about her right now."

Three days later, on Friday, June 3rd, a close relative of 17-year-old Candice Michelle Roy contacted Eugene police and reported the teenager as missing. Normally police wait anywhere from 24 to 72 hours before initiating action on a missing-person report, time enough for a person who left of their own free will to return home. But because of the discovery of Melissa Meyer's murdered body, police waived the waiting period and promptly began investigating Candice Roy's disappearance.

In their quest for information about the girl, investigators first began by questioning her relatives. Among the things they learned was that she lived near the community of Santa Clara, just north of Eugene's city limits, in a rural wooded area.

Like Meyer, Candice Roy had no arrest record and no known involvement in criminal activity. She had just graduated from the Eugene School District's alternative high school, police were told.

Over that weekend, Candice's closest friends and relatives were questioned by investigators in the hope that someone might be able to shed some light on her whereabouts. However, nobody had seen her or had any idea where she might be.

On Monday afternoon the search was over. Candice's partially clad body was found beneath a cluster of fir and cottonwood trees barely four blocks from her home. The location was another wooded area, approximately five miles from where Melissa Meyer's body was found.

The relative who reported Candice missing provided police with a positive identification. Declining to release details, Dr. Ratti, Lane County Medical Examiner, would only say the girl's death was a homicide. Lane County Deputy District Attorney Brian Barnes, however, said the victim bore signs of "obvious trauma," and a police source close to the investigation said she had been strangled only a relatively short time before her body was found.

But what did "a relatively short time" mean? Did it mean that she was killed shortly after her disappearance, or did it mean that she had been alive over the weekend? If she had been alive over the weekend, where had she been? Was it possible that she'd been held captive somewhere until her killer decided to do her in? If that had been the case, why was her body found so close to home? Had she been held in the area all that time?

The investigators knew from experience that the answers to those questions, as well as many others that would arise before this case was cleared, wouldn't come easy, if they came at all.

Was the same killer responsible for both Melissa Meyer's and Candice Roy's deaths? The public, naturally, wanted to know, and so did the cops. Moving cautiously, assistant D.A. Barnes confirmed that the two cases bore "certain similarities."

"We have females of a similar age found in wooded areas," said Barnes. "But beyond that, the investigation is incomplete." He added that the Springfield police and OSP were working practically around the clock comparing evidence collected from the two crime scenes.

"The only common link we have is strangulation, and yet that's a relatively common means used to kill people," said Springfield Police Captain Smith. "Other than that, we really have nothing substantial at this point to say the cases may or may not be related."

Smith did say, however, that members of the Green River Task Force in Seattle had been contacted. They had subsequently asked for specific information about the two deaths to help them determine what similarities, if any, existed between the Lane County victims and those attributed to the Green River Killer.

Later in the week, Dick Larson, spokesman for the Green River Task Force, dispelled rumors that the infamous serial killer may have been involved.

"There are young women found dead all over this country and we aren't naive enough to believe that the Green River Killer is the only person who murders young females and leaves them outside," said Larson. "There is nothing at this point to link the murder or murders in Oregon with our investigations. There would be absolutely no reason for us to send anyone down there . . . to cut past all the blue smoke and mirrors, we're just not interested unless something else turns up."

Meanwhile, telephone calls poured into the district attorney's office, as well as the Springfield and Eugene police departments, from concerned citizens, some of whom claimed to know who killed Candice Roy. Whether they did or not remained to be seen, but at least investigators had some leads to run down in her case.

One such lead placed them in contact with two young women who said they knew who had killed Melissa Ann Meyer. The women told police that the murder had been committed by their boy-friends, Jason Wayne Rose, 20, and John Ray Jones, 17.

According to the information, Meyer had met Rose and Jones in Eugene's downtown mall where she had last been seen on May 30th. For reasons unknown, Meyer accompanied Rose and Jones to a camp at a wooded site where the two men had been staying. After killing Meyer, said the witnesses, Rose and Jones removed several articles of clothing and jewelry from her body.

The investigators knew that their witnesses were being truthful. Certain information they provided was consistent with the investigation, some of which had not been released to the public. Thus, they were granted a search warrant for a mobile home in which Jones had recently resided.

When they arrived at the mobile home, neither Jones nor Rose was there. Nevertheless, the prob-ers executed the search warrant and literally turned the place inside out. By the time they fin-ished, investigators had several items of potential evidence in their possession, including an occult "spell book" which was supposed to enable its user to communicate with the dead.

As the case continued to unfold, the detectives learned that Rose and Jones were heavily involved with the occult, and possibly satanic worship. Along those lines they collected additional evidence, including a pair of dice-like stones which had unfamiliar markings, books for communicating with the dead and for summoning ancient gods of evil, as well as several symbolic handscrawled items.

At first the Lane County authorities didn't know what to make of the occult items or even how or whether they could relate them to Meyer's slaying. Admitting that they were relatively uneducated in satanic activity, the investigators decided to contact Sandi Gallant, a San Francisco policewoman who has made investigating crimes related to the occult her specialty.

Gallant helped identify the dice-like objects as "rune stones," which she said are used by occultists to predict the future.

"She told us it looked as if the attackers killed this girl for a human sacrifice," said Deputy D.A. Brian Barnes of Lane County. "It turned out to be a mess of belief systems tossed into one very lethal one . . . how the heck do you go about selling that to a jury of sensible people?"

Said one Oregon official about the general lack of knowledge of police officers in matters involving satanic activity, "Law enforcement is only now educating itself to the reality of what's been going on for some time."

"Many of us who now accept satanic abuse as real learned first to accept the impossible through exposure to child sexual abuse," said an authority on satanic activity. "It's the same awareness-building process taking place all over again."

As the Lane County authorities continued to investigate the Meyer case, they learned more and more about satanic activity. Among the things they learned was that satanism can generally be broken down into four categories: religious satanists; dabblers; generational satanists; and self-styled satanists.

Religious satanists such as Anton LaVey, who founded the Church of Satan in San Francisco in 1966, publicly condemn criminal activity and stress that membership is not open to everyone. This group is commonly known to be fond of placing nude women on the altar.

An Oregon member of the controversial church recently said that membership is open "only to those with exemplary public and private lives. No individuals of criminal, pathological, or otherwise unstable characters are permitted to affiliate."

Most of those who practice deviant behavior, including ritual sacrifice, he said, have no discernible philosophy and usually congregate in loosely formed groups.

"They merely believe in evil as opposed to good, in Satan instead of God," he said. "They believe if you appease evil, you will get something in return. Most of them have read very little philosophy and understand little about occultism."

Dabblers, the detectives learned, consist mostly of teenagers who have some interest in the occult. Often these teens adopt symbols associated with satanism and get involved with games such as "Dungeons and Dragons," and heavy metal music with satanic themes. Dabblers, the sleuths learned, sometimes progress through several stages, many times leading to criminal sacrificial rites.

Generational Satanists consist of families, linked together, who have been involved with satanic worship for generations. Primarily kept in a particular family or practiced through networks of participating families, Generational Satanists are generally more secret about their worship rituals than the other satanic groups.

Self-styled Satanists include the likes of Charles Manson, Richard Ramirez (L.A.'s "Night Stalker" killer), and Adolfo de Jesus Constanzo, who led the band of devil-worshipping narcotics traffickers believed responsible for 15 ritual murders in Matamoros, Mexico. It was this group, Lane County detectives believed, that Jason Wayne Rose and John Ray Jones fit in, prompting authorities to agree that Melissa Meyer may have been killed during a ritualistic human sacrifice!

Meanwhile, investigators developed a lead

which indicated that Rose and Jones had fled the state. Following up on the lead, detectives had reason to believe that they had gone to Arizona. They updated a previously issued APB, circulated the suspects' photos, and requested assistance from Arizona authorities in tracking them down.

On Monday, June 13th, Rose and Jones were traced to Show Low, Arizona, a remote mountain town located in the eastern portion of the state near the Fort Apache Indian Reservation. Two Springfield officers flew to Phoenix and were at the location within hours.

With help from local authorities, the investigators quietly moved in on the suspects at a small motel where they were believed to be staying. Just minutes before 8:00 p.m. the lawmen flushed Rose and Jones out of the motel and arrested them for suspicion of murder.

The following day Rose and Jones were arraigned on an extradition warrant in Phoenix. The two suspects chose not to contest extradition and were returned to Oregon on Friday, June 17th. They were taken directly to the Springfield Police Department where they underwent intensive grilling by detectives after agreeing to answer their questions. The investigators did not provide any details of the interrogation.

On Monday, June 20th, Jason Wayne Rose appeared in Lane County District court before Judge Frank Alderson for his arraignment. After reading the charges, the judge told the suspect that it was his constitutional right to make no statements about the case before consulting an attorney.

However, Rose took the courtroom officials by surprise when he readily admitted that he had taken part in the strangulation murder of Melissa Meyer.

After the brief court appearance, Deputy Prosecutor Brian Barnes said Rose's confession would not stop the case from going forward. He said he planned to present testimony and evidence to a grand jury to seek an aggravated murder indictment against Rose and Jones. An aggravated murder conviction, said Barnes, could result in the death penalty.

On Monday, June 27th, a Lane County grand jury indictment charging Rose with aggravated murder and first-degree robbery was handed down. The indictment charged that Rose tortured and murdered Melissa Meyer "while deliberately effecting a human sacrifice."

Rose, despite his earlier admission of guilt in open court, pleaded innocent before Lane County Circuit Judge Douglas Spencer. The judge appointed Terrence Gough as Rose's attorney.

John Ray Jones, who turned 18 while being held at the Skipworth Juvenile Detention Center, was subsequently remanded to stand trial as an adult, was transferred to the Lane County Jail, and was indicted on identical charges. The indictment alleged that Jones strangled Meyer at a transient's campsite after first hitting her in the head with a machete. Jones, unlike Rose, would be protected under Oregon law and would not be eligible for the death penalty if convicted, since he was 17 when the murder was committed. He also pleaded innocent to the charges, and Eugene attorney Dan Koenig was appointed to represent him.

While awaiting trial, Rose continued to draw satanic symbols in his cell at the Lane County Jail. The drawings consisted mostly of inverted pentagrams with a goat's head in the center. Investigators photographed the symbols from time to time and would use them against him at his trial.

Rose's trial was finally got under way in April 1989 to a standing-room-only crowd of spectators in the courtroom of Judge Douglas Spencer.

Prosecutor Brian Barnes told jurors during the two-week trial that Rose and Jones took more than one hour to kill Melissa Meyer during the course of a ritualistic human sacrifice. At one point, Barnes presented the spell book and the set of "rune stones." He said that Rose told police he used them to predict the future. Barnes told the stunned jury that it was after a "roll" of the rune stones that Rose decided to kill Meyer, simply because the stones had told him to do so.

Defense Attorney Terry Gough called the prosecutor's version of the killing "nothing but smoke and malarkey." He admitted that Rose caused Meyer's death, but most likely by applying a choke hold after Meyer informed him that she was working for a rival of his. The type of work she purportedly performed was not specified. Gough insisted, however, that his client should not be convicted of aggravated murder because no aggravating circumstances were present in the slaying.

Prosecutor Barnes, on the other hand, argued that Rose committed aggravated murder because he and Jones kidnapped Meyer, stole her jacket, jewelry, and purse, and then tortured her, slowly choking her to death by standing on a thin wooden spear laid across her throat.

At one point in the trial, Barnes brought in a VCR. He played part of a videotape that depicted what authorities believed was an actual human sacrifice. Barnes alleged that Rose had watched the tape less than a month before Meyer was murdered.

At another point, Barnes placed a nationally recognized expert on satanic practices, Patricia Pulling, on the witness stand. He asked her several questions about items confiscated from the defendant.

The drawings and writings seized from Rose's jail cell, said Pulling, indicated a strong adherence to occult beliefs. She testified that the writings were consistent with someone who could have been controlled by a desire to explore deeper into the occult, perhaps to the point of even committing a human sacrifice. Books like those found in Rose's possession after his arrest, said Pulling, were commonly used by occultists to cast magical spells.

Pulling added that there comes a time when adolescents go beyond mere dabbling in satanic worship. They often pass through several stages, she told the jury, stages that include drinking human blood, use of dolls to cast spells, the desecration and robbing of graves, ritualistic mutilation of animals and, ultimately, the commission of a human sacrifice.

"Occultists believe that a human sacrifice frees the life force contained in every living body," said Pulling. "They think they can trap and use that force."

On Thursday, April 20th, 1989, after six hours of deliberations, the nine-woman, three-man jury returned with its verdict. They had found Jason Wayne Rose guilty of aggravated murder and first-degree robbery. Rose showed no emotion as the verdict was read.

"I'm sure he is very disappointed and he's sad because he did not believe he was guilty of aggravated murder," said Gough after the unanimous verdict. "He also feels some anger at things said in court he felt were untrue."

Under Oregon law, in order for a judge to sentence a defendant to death, a jury must unanimously decide that the attack on the victim was unprovoked, that it was premeditated, and that the defendant poses a future threat to society.

During the trial's penalty phase, Rose's attorney did not deny that Rose's attack against Meyer was unprovoked. He did argue, however, that Meyer's killing was not planned and that a mandatory 30-year prison term would effectively remove Rose as a threat to society.

"What is the value of human life?" Gough asked jurors. "You have the power to kill him. But if just one of you says 'no' to any one of these questions, Jason Rose lives. It's as simple as that."

On Tuesday, May 16, 1989, after nearly 13 hours of deliberations over three days, the jury decided that Jason Rose should die for his crime. Judge Spencer then sentenced him to death by lethal injection, making Rose the 20th person sentenced to Oregon's Death Row since reinstatement of the death penalty by voters five years ago. Rose's death sentence, which now goes to mandatory appeals, was the first time anyone had been sentenced to death in Lane County since 1927.

"Melissa would be happy," said a tearful relative of the victim's as she left the courtroom.

Less than a month later, John Ray Jones, dressed in a pale gray suit, appeared before Lane County Circuit Judge Gregory G. Foote for the beginning of his non-jury trial. In a case that doesn't involve the possibility of a death penalty, a defendant has the right to choose a jury trial or a non-jury trial.

During his opening statement, Prosecutor Barnes described how Meyer's killing also met the criteria for aggravated murder, the aggravated factors being kidnapping, robbery, and torture.

"There was intent to prolong the suffering of the victim," said Barnes. "The defendant told the authorities in Arizona that in his opinion she was tortured."

Barnes also pointed out how Jones had waived his right to remain silent, after which he admitted that he had participated in Meyer's killing. Jones, said Barnes, told authorities that he had been trained in first-aid and had checked the victim's pulse, finding that she was still alive before he stood on one end of the wooden spear that he and Rose laid across her neck.

Barnes also told the judge that a deputy sheriff would testify that Jones smiled and laughed when Rose made some "particularly callous statements about the victim's demise." Barnes maintained that Jones and Rose took an hour to kill Melissa Meyer as "they worshipped a god that demanded human sacrifice from them."

Dan Koenig, Jones' defense attorney, argued that his client only participated in Meyer's killing because he feared Rose and was dominated by him. During most of that fateful evening, said Koenig, Jones did not believe that Rose really intended to kill Meyer. Jones, he said, was so concerned that he wanted to try and get her away from the campsite.

After the first time Rose choked Meyer, said the attorney, Rose twice ordered Jones to kill her. The second time Rose ordered Jones to kill her, Jones picked up a machete and brought it down near the back of Meyer's neck, just as Rose had instructed, but he never actually hit her with it, said Koenig. Jones, said the attorney, was fearful that Rose would try and kill him after he finished off Meyer.

"It was a master-servant relationship that Johnny Jones had with Mr. Rose," said Koenig. "John Jones did only what Jason Rose told him to, directed him to, commanded him to . . . he did it under threat of his own life."

At one point in the proceeding, Koenig called a medical examiner to the stand who testified that Meyer, "in all likelihood," was dead before Rose and Jones stood on the spear they had placed across her neck.

On Thursday, June 8, 1989, Judge Foote ruled that John Jones clearly intended to kill Melissa Meyer. He had committed acts "to that end," but the most probable cause of the victim's death was a choke hold inflicted by Jason Rose. Foote then said he had found Jones guilty of intentional murder and third-degree robbery.

On Monday, July 10, 1989, Judge Foote sentenced Jones to life in prison, setting a minimum prison term of 25 years. He also fined Jones $5,000. Jones is now serving his sentence at the Oregon State Penitentiary in Salem, but it should be noted that the State Parole Board has the authority to reduce the minimum sentence if it so desires.

As of this writing, the slaying of Candice M. Roy remains unsolved. Although there were similarities between her death and Melissa Meyer's, there is insufficient evidence to positively link the two cases. Oregon State Police are continuing that investigation.

"SKINHEADS' 'BOOT PARTY' BLOODBATH!"

by Gary C. King

The tragedy occurred about 1:30 a.m. on Sunday, November 13, 1988. It could have been a scene from *Mississippi Burning,* a semi-factual movie about racial prejudice. But it wasn't. Instead it happened in Portland, Oregon, a city that has long prided itself on its racial and ethnic equality. The incident brought an aura of ugliness and shame to the City of Roses that had not been felt before and will not be soon forgotten.

The senseless violence began shortly after 27-year-old Mulugeta Seraw and two of his friends, all Ethiopian nationals, pulled up outside Seraw's southeast Portland apartment. They had just returned from a mutual friend's birthday party, which began early Saturday evening and continued into the next morning.

According to police reports based on witnesses' statements, Seraw had just climbed out of the backseat of his friend's car and was standing in the street saying goodbye to his buddies. Smiling broadly, Seraw waved at them as he walked across the street to his small apartment. It wasn't until he turned to cast a final glance at his pals that he saw the headlights of another car fast approaching.

The car, containing five people, stopped, its headlights shining directly into Seraw's friends' car. Some people would later say it was possible nothing would have happened had the car from which Seraw exited not impeded traffic. But it momentarily blocked the street, and that apparently was enough to anger the occupants of the other car.

Out of politeness and driver courtesy, Seraw's friends pulled forward to let the other car pass. However, passengers from the other car began yelling obscenities and making unfriendly gestures at the Ethiopians. Angry about being insulted, the Ethiopians stopped their car, not knowing who they would be facing when they got out.

Without hesitation, three white men from the other car jumped out, one by one, and began shouting more obscenities that escalated into racial slurs, apparently directed, at least at first, at Mulugeta Seraw.

One of the men, the third one to climb out and subsequently identified as the driver, wildly swung a baseball bat. Shouting racial epithets, he

159

focused first on one of Seraw's friends and struck him across a shoulder blade. When the attacker saw he had injured the man, he then turned his attention to Seraw.

By the time Seraw's friends realized what was happening and tried to intervene, it was too late. Mulugeta Seraw was already engaged in a fist-fight with one of the white men; he never even saw the bat-wielder come up behind him.

The sound of the baseball bat that struck Seraw in the head was earsplitting and could be heard all over the neighborhood. Mulugeta Seraw screamed in agony as he fell to the ground, his head suffused with pain. Together, in practiced unison, the three attackers feverishly put the boots to him.

It all happened quickly. When it was clear to the attackers that Seraw would remain down, two of them went after his friend. The bat-swinger, however, remained with Seraw.

Although his friends knew that Seraw was in serious trouble, they could do nothing to help him. Both had been injured and one was in con-siderable pain. It was all they could do to defend their own lives.

Seraw could see the bat coming again. He fee-bly reached out to try and fend off another blow from the attacker who remained with him, but he was just too weak to stop or deflect it.

The swinger struck his victim's skull again, this

time rendering Seraw completely helpless. Seraw attempted to say something, to plead for his life, but his words barely rose above a whisper and were unintelligible. The attacker, his blood lust nearing fever pitch couldn't care less. His only concern was to maim, then kill, his victim.

Seconds later, as Seraw's consciousness began slipping away, the assailant merely became a white blur against a midnight sky. Seraw probably was no longer aware of the viciousness under way.

The man with the bat bludgeoned Seraw one final time, so hard that the bat split down the middle. Seraw just lay there on the pavement, making guttural sounds, twitching helplessly as a gout of blood gushed from his head and formed a large puddle.

While the bat-wielder had been finishing off Seraw, the two other men had continued their attack on Seraw's friends. One of them could no longer fight back, and the other, apparently realizing he was no match for the three assailants, rolled underneath a car and feigned unconsciousness. Although it seemed an eternity for the victims, the attack was over in less than two minutes. The two Ethiopians watched helplessly as their attackers fled in the car in which they had arrived.

Witnessing the altercation from a safe distance, a concerned neighbor promptly notified the Portland Police Bureau. Several squad cars arrived minutes later from Central and East Precincts, as did teams of paramedics.

The neighbor provided the investigating officers with sketchy details of the attack and said that at first he thought he'd heard a gunshot. He soon realized, however, that what he'd believed was a gunshot was actually the sound of the baseball bat striking Mulugeta Seraw's head! Several other neighbors also told police they thought they'd heard gunshots.

Unfortunately, none of the witnesses had been able to obtain the car's license number. It had been too dark to see it as the car roared away. Nonetheless, after obtaining a description of the assailants' car, a team of officers vainly searched the neighborhood.

After sealing off the area, the officers reported their findings to headquarters, calling for a team of detectives to come to the scene, as well as a forensics wagon. Although it wasn't much of a prize, Detectives Tom Nelson and Mike Hefley won the assignment.

The victims were treated at the scene, but the paramedics, as well as the cops, knew that Mulugeta Seraw had little chance of surviving. All three were transported to a Portland-area hospital, where Seraw was pronounced brain-dead by attending physicians. Listed in critical condition, he died eight hours later.

Following additional treatment and observation, Seraw's friends were released from the hospital. Trying to make some sense out of what happened, they explained the incident to detectives Nelson and Hefley.

"My friends and me, we were down in the car and talking," said one of the surviving victims. "He [Seraw] had to be at work at seven o'clock in the morning, so he decided to get out of the car and go in." Seraw's friend told the detectives that the car with the attackers pulled up right after Seraw crossed the street.

"The driver of the car just showed up and jumped out carrying some kind of a stick," he said, and together the three men began beating and kicking Seraw. "They just opened the door and immediately they came."

He described the three attackers as young men, all with shaved heads. Each was in his late teens or early 20s and wore olive-colored military jackets with American flags on the sleeve and black workboots. Detectives Nelson and Hefley acknowledged that the assault had overtones of an attack by the East Side White Pride skinheads, a group of Hitler-worshipping, racist neo-Nazis.

The friend explained that he had tried to help Seraw, but was struck across the right shoulder blade by one of the attackers. He said there were two women inside the car, one of whom moved the car to a nearby parking lot while the street fight continued.

"The women inside the car were shouting," he said. "They were saying, 'Let's kill him. Kick him.' The men never said anything. They just jumped us."

As the violence continued, he explained, his other friend "went underneath the car."

"That's why he survived," he said. "They left him. Maybe they thought he was dead."

Seraw's friend told the detectives that he and the other surviving victim did not know the attackers and had no clues to their identity. He added that they did not believe Seraw knew them, either.

Although Detective Nelson readily admitted to the possibility that skinheads were involved in the attack, he stressed that he couldn't be 100 percent certain based on the sketchy details available. More investigation was needed, he said.

"All we have right now is three short-haired guys wearing boots," said Nelson. "We have no meaningful leads to suspects."

A definitive autopsy was conducted the following day at the Multnomah County Morgue by Dr. Karen Gunson, the deputy state medical examiner.

With Mulugeta Seraw's body lying on the stainless-steel autopsy table, a pathology technician shaved a large oval spot from his head. His skull, noted Dr. Gunson, had been fractured from above the right eyebrow to the midline point at the back of his head. Whoever hit him, she reported, had done so with tremendous force. Following removal of a portion of the skull to examine the brain, which revealed hemorrhaging, Seraw's skull was sutured back in place. Gunson reported that Seraw had died of head injuries due to "multiple blunt-force blows."

Although it was decided early in the investigation that beefed-up surveillance of the Portland skinhead community was needed, Detectives Nelson and Hefley also knew they had to look elsewhere for leads if they were going to clear the case quickly. They promptly requested assistance from the Intelligence Unit and from several other homicide investigators. They also did a routine background probe of Mulugeta Seraw.

Seraw, they learned, had come to Portland from Debretabor, a town in western Ethiopia, to leave behind the hardships of famine and civil war for a better life in the United States. Although he wasn't enrolled as a student, he hoped to someday earn a degree in business administration at Portland State University and eventually return to Ethiopia.

To accomplish his goals, he worked as a shuttle bus driver for a car rental service operating from Portland International Airport. Police learned that he was well liked by his co-workers and supervisors and was once named Employee of the Month.

Seraw regularly sent money home to his parents and five brothers and sisters in Ethiopia and was attempting to arrange for one or more of his sisters to come to Oregon to study.

"He had a goal to finish school, go home and help his family," said one relative. "Now their dream is shattered. The question is, what do we tell the family?"

Seraw was remembered as a gentle young man who had only nice things to say about people.

"He treated everyone very well and he was always happy," said a close friend and member of the Ethiopian Community Cultural Organization, in which Seraw was active. "He was one of those people who always could cheer you up. He didn't have time to be upset or mad. It's hard to have someone like that missing.

"Most of the recent emigres have seen hardship," continued the friend. "But this is worse than any kind of revolution. You try to make a home here where freedom rings and this happens. It doesn't leave a good taste in your mouth."

A good-looking young man, 5 feet 7 inches tall and 150 pounds, Seraw was slightly built, making it even more unlikely that he would have done anything to have provoked the attack that killed him. Furthermore, relatives assured police, it just wasn't in his character to start fights.

"He was a hardworking, friendly, very gentle

person," said a relative. "He would never provoke anyone. . . . My feeling is disbelief. If [Mulugeta] could be killed in front of his own house, what of the rest of us? This leaves everybody in fear."

The relative said that although he had no conclusive evidence of who killed Seraw, he said he believed the attackers might be linked to such racist groups as the Aryan Nations.

"All the indications are that [Mulugeta] was killed because he was a black man, that a white group of people attacked a black man without any provocation," he added.

"It's not only an outrage for the Ethiopian community," said a spokesperson for the Ethiopian Community Cultural Organization. "[It's an outrage] that any person in the community could be a victim of a senseless murder [and this] concerns the community as a whole—black or white or any color. . . . We think it is very possible that Mulugeta's [killers] are connected with other white supremacist groups in America."

The law enforcement community couldn't have agreed more. On Tuesday, November 16th, U.S. Attorney Charles Turner announced the FBI had joined the investigation. He said that the apparent racial motivation for the attack "strongly suggested" that Seraw's civil rights had been violated.

"We are going to examine the racial motivation behind the murder and whether those responsible have ties to people or organizations outside the state," said Turner.

Local law enforcement, assisted by the FBI, began doing their homework on the East Side White Pride group of skinheads. They soon learned that the group had ties with a former Grand Dragon of the California Knights of the Ku Klux Klan and, more recently, the leader of the neo-Nazi group White American Resistance (WAR).

East Side White Pride, according to the Anti-Defamation League of B'nai B'rith (a group that monitors the activities of right-wing extremist groups), also has direct ties to the Aryan Nations and the Aryan Youth Movement.

"Right now, [the skinheads] are the fastest-growing hate movement in this country," said the director of fact-finding for the Anti-Defamation League of B'nai B'rith in New York City. "In general, such hate groups are declining. But this wing is growing. One of the most troubling aspects is that it consists almost entirely of young people, ages thirteen to twenty-five."

In their attempts to connect the Portland skinheads to Seraw's death, surveillance efforts by the Portland Police Bureau's Intelligence Unit indicated that the skinheads in Portland are "not well organized."

"They surface infrequently, usually when they're trying to make a statement by attacking a nonwhite person or group," said one policeman, who requested that he not be identified because of the sensitivity of his work.

"Their numbers are small," he continued, "but based on activities over the past couple of months, it's obvious they are capable of loud action. They have no funding base that we know of. Many are employed."

Another policeman from the Intelligence Unit, who also requested anonymity, said skinheads began passing out recruiting literature at Portland high schools and in the downtown area about a month before Seraw's death.

"They tell the kids that as a white they're a minority," said the officer. "They're told to stand up for their rights and to write to a post office box to get the hate material. . . . They're very violent. To stay in the group you have to act out, hate all minorities, homosexuals, and Jews. You have to participate. If someone is knocked down, for example, everyone has to put the boots to him to make an example of the victim."

According to Officer Loren Christensen, in charge of monitoring white supremacist activity for the Police Bureau, the skinheads' actions often appear spontaneous.

"These people don't know five minutes before they're going to do something that they're going to do it," said Christensen. Another lawman, close to the Seraw case, agreed.

"For a good time, these guys go out as a group, drink, get all screwed up and go looking for people to put the boots to," the officer said. "Maybe it's a look that sets them off, maybe a person's name, maybe a gesture. The victims in the Seraw case didn't know who they were dealing with. They looked up and saw a bunch of kids sitting in a car. They didn't know they were looking at a keg of gunpowder."

According to Christensen there are about 50 hard-core skinheads and about 250 other white supremacists in Portland, and the numbers are increasing. While that number doesn't seem large, it's big enough to cause serious problems for the police and the city's residents.

For example, the skinheads regularly throw parties in April to commemorate the April 20th birthday of Adolf Hitler. On one such occasion, relates Christensen, a group of skinheads killed a dog and brought it to the party. They subsequently dismembered it, placed its head on the porch of a gay man and scrawled racist remarks with its blood on several houses.

Although the lawmen said they were learning a lot about skinheads and were making significant progress in the Seraw case as a result of their intelligence-gathering and surveillance efforts, they still weren't close to making any arrests.

In the meantime, a Multnomah County grand jury was convened to begin gathering information about Seraw's death. According to several sources, the grand jury had called in many people, several of whom were skinheads. Norm Frink, deputy district attorney for Multnomah County, stressed that the grand jury's efforts were only part of an information-gathering process and had not yet focused on indicting a specific suspect.

Sergeant Larry Neville of the Portland Police Bureau's Homicide Unit, however, said that detectives had received calls from several persons in the Portland area who offered information about possible suspects in Seraw's death. He said investigators had also received calls from as far away as Alaska, Ohio, New York and the Virgin Islands from people offering information. Although Neville would not reveal specifics about the tips, other informed sources said some of the information concerned skinhead activity.

Skinhead activity in 1988 was certainly no secret to Portland police, and their acts of violence were not necessarily limited to nonwhites. In February of that year, according to police reports, two skinheads approached a white man on the northwest side of town and asked his opinion about their group.

"What do you think about white supremacists?" they reportedly asked him.

"Not much, if you're an example," he responded. The skinheads knocked the man to the ground and attacked him.

In March, several skinheads armed with baseball bats threatened a family with children. In a separate incident, three skinheads attacked an Asian man as he and his family left a downtown restaurant.

In August, a skinhead stabbed a white man during a fight in northwest Portland, and the following month 20 skinheads attacked two white people in Washington Park. In that attack, one man was beaten unconscious and another kicked and thrown over the side of a hill. Some five minutes later, 20 skinheads caused an altercation at a downtown store and stabbed a black security guard. The guard, unlike Mulugeta Seraw, fortunately survived the attack.

By the time of Seraw's death, skinhead-related incidents had escalated dramatically and were being reported at the rate of one every 10 days. With the frequency and intensity of their attacks, police knew it would only be a matter of time before they committed a murder. Unfortunately, with Seraw's death, they were proved correct.

On Thursday, November 17th, Mulugeta Seraw was laid to rest at Portland's River View Cemetery, his grave shaded by a flowering plum tree.

"This afternoon there is a rage within all of us," said the pastor of a Seventh-Day Adventist Church where Seraw's funeral was held. "There is a war going on, a war between the forces of good and the forces of evil. Oftentimes the good and the innocent are caught in the cross fire. I believe this is what happened to our brother. Mulugeta was caught in the evil cross fire of the plottings of deranged men and women who are instruments of the devil. . . .

"We are ashamed and embarrassed that one who was a visitor to our city was slain like a common dog in the streets," he continued. "We must be determined that the blood of Mulugeta Seraw that was spilled in the streets of Portland was not wasted. We must labor to create an environment where our children, black and white and red and yellow, can live together harmoniously as children of God."

Later that evening, Portland Police Chief Richard Walker and other police and city officials met with some 350 residents at the King Neighborhood Facility in northeast Portland to lead a forum about what could be done concerning the increase in white supremacist violence. Walker stressed that police could intervene only when a crime was committed and could not arrest people because of their appearance or what they believed in.

"God teaches us not to hate, but to love," said Chief Walker. "While we may abhor hatred, especially on the basis of race or religion, hating someone is not a violation of the law. . . . We cannot protect you from people's thoughts and beliefs, but we will do everything we can to protect you from them if their actions turn to criminal activity."

Walker said significant headway had been made in the case. Detectives Nelson and Hefley, assisted by 15 other homicide investigators, were focusing on skinheads as their prime suspects. He declined, however, to name the suspects.

Oregon Governor Neil Goldschmidt, who made it publicly known that he was outraged by Seraw's death, sent a written statement to be read at the meeting.

"These are criminals with no other goal in life than the destruction of other human beings," the governor's statement said. "This is a time when we must join together and not let these criminals sick with hatred and bigotry kill our neighbors and friends."

The governor, through his spokesperson, said he would work closely with Chief Walker and Portland Mayor Bud Clark to fight the problem of racial hatred and violence.

Skinheads and other white supremacist groups "aren't welcome in Oregon and we want them to know," said Governor Goldschmidt. "We need to send a message to these groups that they won't find a home here. You won't find a home in this state."

As one day followed another, Detectives Nelson and Hefley, assisted by members of the Police

Bureau's Surveillance Unit and 15 other homicide investigators, questioned "anybody with a crew cut" about the case.

With the help of the grand jury's probe, which questioned many skinheads, the sleuths soon began to focus on three individuals: Kenneth Murray Mieske, 23, also known as "Ken Death" and "Bat Man," Kyle Hayden Brewster, 19, and Steven Rodney Strasser, 20. All were members of East Side White Pride, the largest skinhead group in the state.

One witness, Joan Warren, who at first was uncooperative, soon proved instrumental in placing the suspects at the death scene. Warren, described as Brewster's girlfriend, struck a deal with authorities early in the investigation. The state agreed to seek a one-year sentence for hindering prosecution in return for her guilty plea and testimony against the three suspects.

Warren told Detectives Hefley and Nelson that she was the one who drove the car carrying the three suspects on the night Seraw was killed. She had remained behind the wheel while the attack occurred. Her version, sleuths noted, conflicted somewhat with other versions, some of which identified the bat-swinger as the driver. They didn't know what significance, if any, to place on Joan Warren's version. Someone, however, was either lying or mistaken.

They had just left a party a few blocks away,

explained Warren, and were on their way to another apartment nearby. The incident began, she said, when the car carrying Seraw and his two friends blocked the street near Southwest 31st Avenue and Pine Street.

Warren said that as the Ethiopians passed, Strasser and Brewster began shouting obscenities and racial slurs at them, "seven or eight times." The Ethiopians responded, she said, by shouting obscenities back and making obscene gestures. The Ethiopians drove around the skinheads' car, stopped, and then got out.

Her story, noted Detective Hefley, certainly incriminated the suspects, but it often seemed opposite to what they had been told earlier by other witnesses. It seemed, at times, that Joan Warren was attempting to justify, or at least lighten responsibility for, the violence that occurred that night.

Warren told the detectives that she started to drive away, but Brewster yelled, "Stop the car, stop the car," while reaching for a .25-caliber handgun she kept in the vehicle. Then Strasser, Mieske, Brewster and Lisa Smith, Strasser's girlfriend, all got out of the car. Brewster began a fistfight with Seraw, she said, and Strasser began fighting with Seraw's friends.

Brewster had punched Seraw "two or three times" when Mieske walked up behind Seraw and hit him in the head with a wooden baseball bat.

Mieske struck Seraw two or three more times in the upper body and Brewster kicked Seraw about the head with his steel-toed workboots, standard footwear for skinheads.

As the fight continued, Warren related, she pulled the car into a parking lot across the street from Seraw's apartment, backing it toward the street corner. Once the fight was over, her friends jumped in, and they drove to her apartment and began drinking beer.

While at her apartment, they took out the wooden baseball bat used in the attack and found that it had been broken lengthwise. The next day, Warren cut the bat into small pieces using a power saw, after which she and Mieske drove to a park on the Columbia River where they soaked the pieces in gasoline and ignited them.

Warren led Detectives Nelson and Hefley to the park, where they recovered the baseball bat's charred remains. They subsequently turned the pieces over to the state crime lab.

Early Saturday morning, November 19th, utilizing information gathered by intelligence officers, Nelson and Hefley set up a stakeout at a southeast Portland location where they believed Kenneth Mieske to be hiding out. A short time later, they surprised Mieske and arrested him without incident. Although members of Seraw's family were told of the arrest, details were kept secret from the public because Kyle Brewster's and Steven Strasser's whereabouts were not yet known.

Later that day, investigators set up surveillance teams at several locations Brewster and Strasser were known to frequent. The surveillance continued the rest of that day, all that night and into the next morning. The sleuths watched several skinheads come and go from several locations, but none were the suspects they sought.

It wasn't until Sunday afternoon that police spotted the two remaining suspects at separate locations. Brewster was located first, at Northeast 31st Avenue and Flanders Street, eight blocks north of where Mulugeta Seraw was attacked. He was arrested without incident and brought in.

A short time later, acting on information from a number of sources, police converged on an area near Southwest Bonita Road and Hall Boulevard in Tigard here they arrested Steven Strasser. All three suspects were lodged in the Justice Center Jail. Kyle Brewster and Kenneth Mieske were held without bail on charges of murder. Strasser was accused of second-degree assault and held in lieu of $100,000 bail.

Mieske and Brewster were also charged with first-degree assault and racial intimidation. These charges stemmed from the September incident at a downtown store in which the black security guard was beaten and stabbed while attempting to remove the skinheads from the premises.

In a prepared statement, Police Chief Walker expressed relief at the arrest of the three suspects and credited Detectives Tom Nelson and Mike Hefley with solving the case. He also had this to say:

"This particular homicide has had a tremendous impact on the entire community, as the motive involves something that is so distasteful to the way almost all of us think. Even though an arrest has been made in this case, we must not forget that bigotry and racism do exist. We need to build on this tragedy to encourage better understanding and work to eliminate this type of intolerable behavior."

In the meantime, Multnomah County District Attorney Michael Schrunk announced that his office would not be seeking the death penalty in this case. It was a decision that angered many Portland residents.

"This is a terrible murder," said Schrunk in defense of his decision. "But the death penalty law doesn't seem to apply in this case."

He explained that under Oregon law, the death penalty is possible only in aggravated murder cases, where another crime, such as rape, robbery, torture, or kidnapping, was committed during the course of a murder.

On Tuesday, November 20th, a Multnomah County grand jury indicted Kenneth Mieske, Kyle

Brewster and Steven Strasser on charges of murder, assault and racial intimidation. The trio pleaded innocent and were held without bail. Separate trials were ordered for each defendant.

Strasser, police learned, had been a member of the Guardian Angels before joining the skinheads. He had also worked with handicapped people. What, then, they wondered, had compelled him to join a racist group that thrived on violence and intimidation?

A relative told the detectives that Strasser was afraid of not being accepted by his peers. He joined the skinheads, said the relative, at a time when it was faddish, when the gang was considered "cool," rather than racist.

"Even at the prom," said a relative, "he took a black girl. He still doesn't walk into this house and talk about white supremacy. He never has."

Kyle Brewster, the detectives learned, was born in Eugene, Oregon, but his family later moved to Portland. While attending Grant High School in Portland, he was chosen homecoming king of 1987. As the detectives probed deeper into his background, it became clear that Brewster took his skinhead membership more seriously than Strasser.

Detectives Nelson and Hefley observed the word "skins" tattooed on the back of his neck and "The South Will Rise Again" and "Right Wing" tattooed on his arms.

"To me [being a skinhead] is not a fad," said Brewster. "It's a serious political thing because I stand for my race and my nation. That's all I've got right now. And they're trying to take my nation away, 'they' being minorities and the left-wing liberals. . . . [Blacks] don't listen. The only things they understand is a fist through the face."

The detectives learned that Kenneth Mieske was born in Washington State and had lived in the Portland area for the past eight years. A high school dropout, he eventually earned a General Educational Development certificate. His employment record was sporadic and consisted mostly of seasonal construction jobs. He also played in a rock band at local clubs frequented by skinheads.

When the detectives searched Mieske's apartment, they found letters written by a relative of the head of the Aryan Youth Movement (AYM) and the skinhead leader who had roughed up Geraldo Rivera on the television show *Geraldo* on November 3, 1988.

During the search of Mieske's apartment, the detectives also found letters written by the head of the Aryan Nations, Church of Jesus Christ Christian.

As the post-arrest investigation continued, Detectives Nelson and Hefley uncovered another witness, Dee Dee Jones, 16, Mieske's former girlfriend. Jones told them that the defendants thought Seraw and his Ethiopian friends might be members of the Bloods or Crips, black youth gangs whose primary interest is in selling illicit drugs, particularly crack cocaine. She also provided information about the attack.

Mieske, Jones related, struck Seraw with the baseball bat. After the victim fell to the ground, Mieske, Brewster and Strasser kicked him in the head several times with their steel-toed boots. Jones described the attack as a "boot party" and said she had seen the three defendants attack other people in the same manner.

While waiting in jail for their trials, the three skinheads grew their hair long, partly out of fear of retribution from nonwhite inmates who might recognize them as the racists they were, and partly to bolster their images before the judge and jury.

However, none of the cases went to trial.

On Monday, May 1, 1989, Ken "Bat Man" Mieske, fearing federal prosecution for civil rights violations that could result in a life sentence with no chance of parole, struck a plea agreement with the Multnomah County District Attorney's Office.

Appearing before Judge Philip Abraham, Mieske pleaded guilty to murder and first-degree racial intimidation in connection with Seraw's death. He also pleaded no contest to first-degree racial intimidation in the stabbing of the black security guard at the store in downtown Portland prior to Seraw's killing.

"The pleas are being entered as a result of complex and very tough negotiations with the federal government," said Randall Vogt, Mieske's lawyer. The U.S. Attorney's Office agreed not to prosecute Mieske if he pleaded guilty to the Oregon charges and agreed not to challenge the sentencing recommendation of life with a minimum of 20 years. "The threat of federal prosecution was an important element" in Mieske's decision, Vogt added.

"This sends a very strong message to anyone who wants to commit racist crimes in Portland, Oregon, and we hope that never happens again," said Deputy District Attorney Norman W. Frink Jr. "I don't think we could have gotten anything better if we'd gone to trial. . . . This guy got hammered. This was no bargain for Mr. Mieske."

The following month, Judge Abraham sentenced Mieske to life in prison with a minimum term of 20 years without the possibility of parole or work release.

"This racially motivated murder directly challenges the Constitution of this country," said Abraham at sentencing. "A man lost his life because of his race."

On Friday, September 1, 1989, Kyle Brewster pleaded guilty to first-degree manslaughter after cutting a deal with the prosecutor's office, admitting that he aided and abetted in killing Seraw.

He also pleaded guilty to first-degree assault for attacking Seraw's friends and pleaded no contest to three counts of first-degree intimidation. He was sentenced to 20 years in prison.

On Friday, October 27, 1989, following lengthy plea negotiations, Steven Strasser pleaded guilty to first-degree manslaughter and second degree assault for his part in the attack that killed Mulugeta Seraw.

Appearing before Judge Abraham, Strasser apologized to Seraw's relatives. He also said, "I'll never again be a part of a group that advocates violence." Abraham sentenced him to spend nine to 20 years in prison.

On Friday, February 2, 1990, Lisa Smith, Strasser's girlfriend, appeared before Multnomah County District Court Judge Frank L. Bearden and pleaded guilty to a charge of first-degree racial intimidation. Smith admitted that she aided and abetted the assault on Seraw and his friends.

As a result of plea negotiations, Judge Bearden sentenced Lisa Smith to one year in jail and five years of probation, setting a condition that she not associate with any racist groups.

From his cell at the Oregon State Correctional Institution, in an area reserved for inmates who are disciplinary problems, "Ken Death" Mieske expressed some regrets, all selfish, about Mulugeta Seraw's death.

"If this had never happened," he said, "I'd be

out with my band, cutting an album. I'd probably be touring now."

Is he sorry for what happened?

"Now that I'm serving a twenty-year minimum, yeah, I'm sorry," said Mieske.

Following a private hearing by the Oregon State Parole Board, Kenneth Mieske became even sorrier. His parole date was extended to November 17, 2018, 10 years longer than the 20-year minimum imposed by Judge Abraham.

EDITOR'S NOTE:

Lisa Smith, Joan Warren and Dee Dee Jones are not the real names of the persons so named in the foregoing story. Fictitious names have been used because there is no reason for public interest in the identities of these persons.

"SIX LOVELY GIRLS FOR SATAN'S FLESH EATERS!"

by E. E. Gilpatrick

The working girls saw the items scattered on the sidewalk outside the door of the real estate office in the shopping center at the corner of Illinois #83 and St. Charles Road in Elmhurst, Illinois. They knew instantly something was terribly wrong. Strewn on the sidewalk were Lorraine Borowski's shoes, scattered keys, a broken key chain, and some cosmetics. The door to the real estate office was still locked, and there was no trace of Lorraine.

It was a few minutes before 8:00 o'clock on Saturday morning, May 15, 1982. Lorraine A. Borowski, age 21, was the senior member of the Saturday office staff and had left her home in the Elmhurst Terrace Apartments in Elmhurst, one of Chicago's western suburbs, about 7:30 to have the office open at 8:00 when the rest of the Saturday office staff was due to arrive.

Elmhurst police were called immediately. It was

apparent there was more involved than a mere disappearance. Generally, in the case of a missing person, police wait 24 hours before beginning an investigation, but because of the ominous circumstances, a squad was dispatched immediately to take a look, with investigators to follow. The patrol officer questioned the real estate office workers who had waited by the door of the real estate office for him. They were able to add no more than the evidence there on the sidewalk.

The investigators arrived only moments after the patrol officer. They began an immediate canvass of other stores and offices which were beginning to open in the shopping center. In the building supply store, the manager looked at the investigators incredulously. He found it hard to believe that Lorry, whom he knew, was not in her office. He'd seen her getting out of her car in the parking lot as he was unlocking the front door of his own store.

As an experienced manager, he always looked around behind him before putting the key in the lock of the front door of his store. When he approached the door that morning he'd looked back; he'd seen her, and at that hour she was parked right in front of her office. It would only take her a matter of seconds to get to her office.

No one else in the shopping center had seen her. Owners, clerks, and managers had seen cars and trucks coming and going. That's what a suburban shopping center is all about. None were memorable. The lawmen closely examined Lorry Borowski's car. There was nothing in it or about it that was incriminating.

The investigators went back to the Elmhurst Terrace Apartments on the possibility that Lorry had returned home because of sudden illness, or for some other reason. Maybe a friend had driven up to her car seeking help in a personal emergency, and Lorry left her car in the parking lot to go with the friend. Her family might know something. Her mother knew only that something was very wrong. It was not at all like Lorry. She was a conscientious girl. She would never have walked away from responsibility for the office without a word to anyone. Her family had no idea where she was, but were apprehensive.

Lawmen felt no need to into details, but the Elmhurst police and the investigators from the sheriff's office in Du Page County, in which Elmhurst is located, were also concerned.

On May 23, 1981, Linda Sutton, age 28, who lived in the 5000 block of West End Avenue, was abducted. Her mutilated body was found 10 days later in a field near the Rip Van Winkle Motel in Villa Park, Illinois. Villa Park is on the other side of Illinois Route #83 west of Elmhurst. The Sutton Case was an active case, but, as yet, no arrests had been made. The body of Rose Davis, age 30, from Broadview, about three miles southeast of Elmhurst, was found in an alley in Chicago. She'd been strangled, stabbed, and mutilated. In both cases, the left breasts of the victims had been cut off.

Now, Lorraine Borowski of Elmhurst was missing. Two weeks later on Saturday, May 29, 1982, a young woman by the name of Shui Mak, who lived in Lombard, the next town west of Villa Park, was abducted while she was walking along a road in Hanover Park in northwest Cook County, in which the city of Chicago is located. Hanover Park is about 10 miles northwest of Elmhurst.

On Saturday, September 11, 1982 Carole Pappas, age 42, wife of Chicago Cubs pitcher Milt Pappas, drove her burgundy and white 1980 Buick out to a quality department store in a Du Page County shopping center in Wheaton, Illinois. No trace of her has ever been found.

All the while, friends and relatives of Lorraine Borowski were spending every night and weekend trying to find Lorry. They searched vacant lots, forest preserves, parks, country roads, and anywhere else they thought a body might be. Her mother, hoping against hope, wanted to believe someone was, perhaps, holding her in bondage, but at least she were alive. A psychic had been called in who said Lorry would be found "within 18 miles in a shack in a cemetery." All the cemeteries in the western suburbs were searched. Nothing.

On Sunday evening, October 10, 1982, an investigator called Lorry's mother to inform her a body had been found. Police believed it to be the body of her daughter. The decomposed remains would have to be examined by pathologists, but clothes described as having been worn by Lorry at the time of her disappearance were found nearby. Some adolescents had gone into the Clarendon Hills Cemetery a few miles due south of Villa Park to play. Under a thicket near a tall, lone evergreen at about 3:30 Sunday afternoon they discovered some remains which piqued their curiosity enough so that they went to find a caretaker to report their find.

Bursting into tears, the mother exclaimed, "What bothers me is that we were there . . . If we had stayed longer, we might have found her. We were always hoping that she was all right, that someone was just holding her somewhere. I'm glad we found her, not this way, but I'm glad."

Chicago radio personality Wally Phillips had launched an air waves effort in an attempt to find Lorry Borowski. Through his efforts, toward finding out who was responsible for her disappearance and death. Investigators were looking under every stone, but there was little to be had in the way of leads. The body had apparently been exposed to the abrasions of nature for most of the five months Lorry had been missing. A dental check confirmed that the body was that of Lorraine Borowski, age 21. Beyond that, most was speculation.

The coroner's office of DuPage County called in a university anthropologist to work with them in an effort to generate some information as to the cause of death and, hopefully, some of the circumstances surrounding that death. The DuPage County pathology team was able to find out little. The remains were carefully packaged to be sent to some of the world's most noted anthropologists in Ohio. Their luck was little better. As close as they could come was that there was some evidence to suggest that the victim may have been stabbed to death either with a sharp knife or an ice pick.

Now, the investigators had at least some data on which to work. The first phase of the investigation had been to find the body and in so doing get an idea of what had happened. It appeared what had happened was abduction and homicide. On the plus side, the initial emotional shock had long since worn off for Lorry's kin. The victim's mother had been working with the investigators for months. The relationship became very close. She said some officers, "became almost like family," even to the extent that occasional problems and disagreements arose, but, like good family, they worked them out. "We were always bugging them, driving them nuts, sometimes getting in the way of their investigation, but they always put up with us. They did everything they could. You couldn't want a better department working on the case."

Most homicides are committed by someone who has some relationship to the victim. In this homicide there appeared to be no connection. Investigators were even confident that not only was there no connection between the perpetrator or perpetrators and the victim, but there was no discernible connection among the various victims. Certainly there was nothing in Lorry Borowski's background which suggested a solution. She was what, in these irrational times, most parents would want their daughters to become. She was described as a "hard-working kid who was constantly busy. She seemed happy with her life and with her job. She was a good kid and we really miss her."

Chicago investigators had tapped into the investigation. Sandra Delaware, age 18, of Chicago, who had a prostitution record, was found stabbed and strangled on August 27, 1982. Her left breast had been cut off. It seemed the murders were no longer confined to the western suburbs. Media picked up on the sensational crimes in what they were calling the Jack The Ripper Murders. It would be later that the crimes would more accurately be called the murders of the

Cannibal Gang.

Possibly it's the intrepid sleuth of a former age who captures the imagination of the romantic who lies lurking in the soul of us all, but in a modern, fast-moving city, it's often impersonal, highly instrumented, mechanically augmented scientific crime detection which will crack a case. Computers immediately spring to mind, but equally important are maps, county engineer's plats, distance logs, tables, charts, personal records, public records, and as always and most important of all, the sharp, trained, experienced eyes and ears of dedicated investigators.

Some of the victims were from impeccable backgrounds; others were known hookers. The combined list of friends, relatives, and associates of the known victims comprised a list pages long. All had to be checked out. Months and months of investigation were involved. Maps and charts were major tools in this probe. One can be easily deluded into thinking that simply because the best in modern, scientific equipment is on the job, the paraphernalia will immediately spit out the solution. It won't; it can't. Science can evaluate, record, and reproduce, but the logic, discernment, and decisions still must come from the human mind of the lawman.

Generally, the bodies and disappearances were centered in the Du Page county area, but not always. One victim had been a resident of Chicago's elegant Gold Coast. Another had been a streetwalker whose body had been found under a bridge in a lower-class Chicago area. There was no mistaking, however, the mutilations and missing left breasts, or sometimes both breasts, in those cases where the body was still in adequate condition to make that determination.

Calendar and time charts were part of the investigation. By correlating the days and the dates of the crimes with the geography of the crimes, the investigators hoped to establish a time-place context of the killer or killers which might tend to point to the place where they lived, where they might be located, or might tend to indicate who or what they were. Again, the information was not simple and pat. Investigators had come to believe they were looking for a person or persons who kidnapped, sexually abused, mutilated, and killed women of procreative age. This indicated young men at the peak of their sexual vigor.

One victim had been Beverly Washington, age 20, of Chicago whose body had been discovered on October 6, 1982. Her left breast had been amputated, and as with most of the other victims, the amputation seemed to have been accomplished with a single smooth cut. In none of the cases was there any indication of hacking or even multiple cuts. Strangely, on the same day, October 6th, Raphael Torado and a friend, both of Chicago, were standing by a phone booth on the corner of North and Damen Avenues in Chicago. A car drove by and shots rang out. Torado was killed and the friend was permanently condemned to a wheelchair as a result of their gunshot wounds.

These victims were not women, nor were they abducted. The murder and attempted murder, however, did appear to be random. Neither victim had any apparent troublesome connections in dope, street gangs, personal or business relationships.

As closely as the investigators could catalog the crimes, 15 women had been killed, plus the two men hit, a total of 17 victims. After the discovery of Borowski's body the killings ended. The investigative effort was intense. Lieutenant Kenneth Lepic of the Du Page County Sheriff's Department was heading up the investigation. The maximum pressure was coming from Du Page County area, and they knew the heat was on. Lepic was pleased. The lawmen seemed to be headed in the right direction.

The abductions happened so fast no one saw anything. All lists of known sexual deviates in the area proved fruitless. All had to be checked out. Areas near the locations where the victims were abducted were canvassed for information. Nothing. Next, early in November, the areas where the bodies were found began to undergo minute scrutiny.

The remains of the body of Linda Sutton, the first victim, had been found in a field near the Rip van Winkle Motel on North Avenue in Villa Park. Investigators went to talk to the management. The Rip van Winkle was an inexpensive motel which catered to truck drivers and less affluent travelers. Part of their clientele consisted of transients who rented inexpensive rooms by the week or the month. There were those, also, who might have called the Rip van Winkle Motel a hot mattress factory.

With the dispassion that characterizes the dedicated lawman, probers came into the motel manager's office to begin a hand search of registration records. The search would disclose overnight transients who lived less than 10 miles from the motel.

Generally, only those who are knowledgeable in the field of crime, as a lawman or a habitual criminal, are aware of the importance of an auto registration number. It would never occur to one dallying for an evening to enter a false registration on the motel card. To others who have much to conceal, giving a phony plate number is as important as, "Never give 'em your right name." Thus, each registration card was a challenge.

The investigators rolled up their sleeves and dug in. The management helped all it could. Most names could be dismissed out of hand, some almost cried out to be investigated, and others imply looked curious. In the transients' list there were a number of possibilities, but nothing on the face of it that looked promising. It seemed unlikely that the weekly, or semi-permanent, residents' list would produce much. It seemed unlikely anyone would bring a body home with them. But, knowing the imponderable twists and turns of the criminal mind, the investigators grabbed a stack of registration cards of the semi-permanent residents.

One investigator found an interesting group. They were four young men in their twenties. For a time they'd rented two adjoining double rooms. They had moved out of the motel some months before the body of Linda Sutton had been discovered in a field near the motel, but the quartet of young men had been there long enough to learn the locale intimately — when the manager was there, when the lights went on, and the parts of the grounds where people seldom went. Two of the men were brothers who, according to the motel records, were having their mail forwarded to an address only a short way down North Avenue.

The detectives asked the manager if he recalled the group. The manager thought for a minute; vaguely, he did. They were cultists or satanists. He'd heard that they had secret rites in their rooms. They'd had girls in, prostitutes he was pretty sure, for some of the goings-on. The investigators asked how long the sessions lasted. The manager had to admit he didn't recall ever seeing any of the girls walk out with any of the four men.

Spurred by a vain hope, probers had a lab crew check the rooms, but as logic would dictate months after the foursome had lived there, no usable evidence was found despite a thorough search.

Investigators now proceeded to an address in the 900 block of West North Avenue to have a talk with Andrew Kokoraleis, age 20, and his brother, Thomas C. Kokoraleis, age 23. The detectives had in mind to informally ask the Kokoraleis brothers a few questions to determine if there was a possibility they might know something of the disappearance of Lorrane Borowski or of the other victims. As murder is not generally a social affair, the investigators at the time had predicted there was an outside possibility the highly-charged goings-on at the motel may have somehow been indirectly connected with the disappearances. If they were lucky, they might pick up a lead.

Only Tom Kokoraleis was home. The detectives introduced themselves and asked if they could come in to chat. They said they'd hoped to see both Tom and his brother, but Tom said his brother was out, although he was expected home before long. As they waited for Andy to return, the investigators began to make friendly observations which led to small questions. It must be more comfortable living on North Avenue than at a motel. In spite of labs, scientific advances, or electronic instrumentation the key to effective criminal investigation is the knowledge contained in the investigator's mind. Two things any successful investigator knows is that he or she can never tell what might be discovered on any given call.

Secondly, a good investigator without scientific proof, logical reason, or legal validation knows when the subject is ducking, dodging, or even lying outright in response to questions. As the questions become more intense, this is precisely what Tom Kokoraleis began to do, it seemed to the questioner. Their recollection was that as they asked questions about Linda Sutton, he was answering in relation to facts involved in the disappearance of Lorraine Borowski. Such answers may have been deliberate deceptions or simply an outpouring from an overly stressed mind. Why?

The investigators ran up their colors. They advised Tom Kokoraleis of his rights and told him there were inconsistencies in what he was telling them. They suggested it might be easier to talk and get a more precise delineation of the facts at headquarters. As Andrew Kokoraleis hadn't shown up, the investigators made arrangements for someone to meet him when he arrived home.

In the interrogation room, the detectives told Tom Kokoraleis that they thought he was lying to them. He maintained he was telling them the truth. The investigators responded by saying, if that were the case, he'd have no objection to taking a lie detector test. They hastened to advise him that even if the test showed he were lying, that information couldn't be used in an Illinois court of law as evidence against him. Kokoraleis said the machine would show he was telling the truth. The polygraph, or lie detector, test, which Kokoraleis voluntarily consented to, led the polygraph operator to believe Kokoraleis was not being entirely candid with the police.

For the next two days, Tom Kokoraleis took investigators to the motel, to fields in Du Page County, to Chicago, to streets, and to alleys to point out elements in his story. At first, the evasions persisted, but when it became apparent that the investigators were not going to let up, the story became more exact, the locations more precise, and the guilt more specific in the minds of the lawmen.

In the interrogation room with a tape recorder going, for the last time investigators asked Thomas Kokoraleis to tell them how it happened. Kokoraleis admitted he knew about the death of a girl in Chicago. He knew because he'd been there and he'd watched as his good friend Robin Gecht, age 27, killed her. The ceremony was held in a chapel up on the second floor of Gecht's Chicago home. Gecht was an unemployed carpenter. Services had been held there for nine or ten women Kokoraleis knew about. He thought there had been more, but he wasn't certain. Gecht was the one who conducted the "services."

The services began by all of them joining in raping the victim. "All of them" meant the Kokoraleis brothers, Robin Gecht, and Edward Spreitzer, age 23, a self-employed electrician. They didn't always kill together. From victim to victim, it could be various twos or three of them, but Gecht was their spiritual leader and had shown them how to kill their victims.

The service began by cutting the victim with knives or stabbing her with an ice pick. When she was screaming steadily, they would then join in raping her over and over. They would continue until the victim's mind could no longer stand the assault, and she lay helpless. Gecht, acting as high priest, would then step behind the altar, which was draped in a scarlet scarf in the manner of the Black Mass. Satan's minister Gecht then read verses from the Bible to mock and deride Satan's arch-enemy, Christ. To desecrate God's most beloved creation, Man, Gecht impressed on his students that the most important thing was to "leave their mark" on the victim. He then took a thin, strong wire and looped it around the victim's left breast. With a firm, strong stroke, he pulled the wire straight, very neatly cutting off the breast in one smooth move. Sometimes the procedure was repeated on a victim's right breast.

Kokoraleis said at that time Gecht had nine or ten breasts in a box, but later he had about 15. Continuing with the ceremony, Gecht then cut the breast into pieces and each communicant was given a piece. Finally, in Satanic communion, together each ate his piece of breast. As inured as they thought they were to the depravities of some men, the detectives had to stop to compose themselves. As they did, Kokoraleis explained that was why he knew what to do with Lorraine Borowski. He said he, his brother, and Edward Spreitzer had been the ones who'd abducted her from in front of the real estate office in the shopping center in Elmhurst and had taken her to the Rip van Winkle Motel for the sacred rites. Because at this point the investigators were beginning to question their own sanity, they laid out a selection of photos of some of the apparent victims of the Cannibal Gang. With no hesitation or uncertainty, Kokoraleis immediately picked out the picture of Lorraine Borowski.

The information was transmitted to Chicago investigators who were working on cases believed to be the work of the cannibal gang. Gecht and Spreitzer were picked up. Armed with a search warrant, the Chicago sleuths found evidence in the second floor chapel of Satan in Gecht's home to corroborate some of Thomas Kokoraleis's statement. In Du Page County, sheriff's police picked up Andrew Kokoraleis. The chief of the Du Page Sheriff's Police, Robert Soucek, stated publicly after the three arrests in Du Page County were made that all the suspects were now in custody. He added, however, that the investigation was continuing on the Sutton case, and that the group was suspected in that case also.

Soucek was asked about the satanic worship aspect of the case. Soucek conceded the group may have been involved in some type of cult. "The ones we talked to never called it a cult, but there's a strong connection among all these guys," the chief said. "I don't think anybody knows at this point what they were up to, but there were strong sexual, perverted as they are, common bonds," among the group.

The case was immediately forwarded to the state's attorney's office. First Assistant State's Attorney Michael Higgins said, "A number of other murders could be tied to the group." He said the state's attorney's office was carefully going over all the evidence, because "a lot of work has to be done to make cases. There is no rush now, because everyone is in jail."

The wheels of justice may turn slowly, but they turn inexorably. Largely because the evidence found on the second floor of his home was incontrovertible, Robin Gecht was the first of the cannibal gang to be convicted. At the end of September, 1983, in Cook County Court in Chicago, he was found guilty of the attempted murder, rape and aggravated battery in the mutilation-murder of Sandra Delaware, whose body was left under the bridge in the 1800 block of West Fullerton Avenue in Chicago. Gecht was sentenced to 120 years.

On April 2, 1984, Edward Spreitzer was described by prosecutors as "a sadist — someone who gains pleasure from seeing other persons suffer." That day, Spreitzer pleaded guilty to murdering four people, to wit: Rose Davis, 30, whose body had been found in an alley in the Gold Coast district; Sandra Delaware, who he'd killed in the company of Robin Gecht; Shui Mak, whom he held down while she was raped and mutilated; and lastly, the killing of Raphael Torado, who had been slain as he stood by a telephone booth talking to a pair of his friends. Spreitzer was sentenced to natural life on each of the four counts of murder plus additional sentences on charges of rape, deviant sexual assault, kidnapping, and attempted murder.

At 11:00 a.m. on Tuesday, May 15, 1984, exactly two years to the hour after the body of Lorraine Borowski was left there, a bus pulled up to the thicket where the body had been dumped, and the jury hearing the evidence against Thomas C. Kokoraleis got out to look at the scene.

The jury of 10 women and two men listened to the tape in which Thomas Kokoraleis described the method of killing. One courtroom spectator fainted; another dashed out of the courtroom gagging and holding her hand over her mouth. Order in the court was re-estalished. The prosecution said Kokoraleis "held the key to the door where Lorraine Borowski would spend her last few minutes in hell." He later said, "Surely she knew she was about to be raped. But, what she experienced was an evil so overwhelming that her mind and body couldn't deal with it, and she lost consciousness, thank God!"

The defense contended Kokoraleis was "a borderline retarded boy who was harassed by police and talked into making a confession." Actually, he was only there at the commission of the crimes because he was a voyeur of sadism, sexual perversion, and murder. As the defense saw it, he wasn't actually a perpetrator.

The jury failed to grasp the defense's fine distinction and on May 18th found Thomas C. Kokoraleis, now age 24, guilty of the abduction, rape, and murder of Lorraine Borowski. While awaiting sentencing, Kokoraleis said he'd take police to the field where Carole Pappas was buried. With Kokoraleis leading, the detectives went to the field Kokoraleis designated. No body or evidence of a body was found. On September 8th Kokoraleis was sentenced to life imprisonment.

On September 25th, Kokoraleis was indicted along with his brother Andrew and Edward Spreitzer for the murder of Linda Sutton. At the same convening of the grand jury, Andrew Kokoraleis and Edward Spreitzer were indicted for the murder of Lorraine Borowski.

Under Illinois law, Andrew Kokoraleis and Edward Spreitzer are presumed to be innocent of the murder of Lorraine Borowski unless and until convicted of such crime in a court of law. Likewise, all three are presumed to be innocent of the killing of Linda Sutton unless and until similarly convicted.

" 'DISCIPLES' STRANGLED THE TEENAGE SEX KITTEN!"

by Jaye Fletcher

For the poor, no matter where they live, life can be a tough proposition. But in Chicago's highrise housing projects, life can be mean as well, and remarkably cheap. The Robert Taylor Homes on the city's near south side is not only Chicago's but the U.S.'s largest low income housing project. Its long blocks of stark, multi-storied buildings house over 42,000 people—most of them black—all of them poor.

There are no lawns at Robert Taylor, no driveways or backyards or porches; no swingsets or lawnchairs. Only row upon row of faceless, graceless buildings, each one sectioned off into hundreds of small, cement-walled apartments. It is an urban jungle, where the strong prey upon the weak and the weak hide. Or die.

Reggie Brown was luckier than most residents of the Robert Taylor Homes. He had a job. A janitor in the complex itself, he knew it wasn't much of a job, but it was better than none at all. Now, at 6:15 a.m., on the morning of December 22, 1981, Reggie Brown was on his way to report to work. As he eyed the littered landscape, he shook his head. It was always the same. He would go home in the late afternoon after working all day to keep the grounds as clean as possible. But every morning when he returned, the same litter would be strewn across walkways, in the entrances and hallways of the giant stone buildings. Stairways sparkled dangerously with broken bottle glass, walls were defaced with sprayed-on gang slogans, empty beer cans and wine bottles dotted the gangways.

As he was passing the 4352 South State building, Reggie Brown noted another dangerous, but certainly not uncommon, condition. There was a fire burning in a trash can just alongside the outside elevator door. Reggie crossed the parkway and threw several armfuls of snow onto the burning trash before continuing on his way to check in at the maintenance office. He made a mental note to stop back later, empty the car and drag it back around the side of the building where it belonged.

At 7:15 a.m., the janitor returned. The fire in the trash can had been doused by the snow, but the can's contents still smoldered with thick, damp smoke. Reggie put on his heavy canvas work gloves and grasped at the can, intending to drag it around the corner to the dumpster—then, he stopped and stared unbelievingly into the can.

It took a moment to fully comprehend what he was seeing. They were charred and twisted by fire and they'd apparently been wrapped in some sort of blanket or cloth, but they were undoubtedly legs. Human legs. Reggie Brown turned and ran wildly for the telephone.

The police arrived within minutes. As a crowd began to gather around the grisly contents of the trash can, the officers made the decision to move the can, along with its contents, into a small maintenance room nearby and to wait there for the homicide experts.

The plainclothes detective team from Area One Violent Crimes arrived on the scene almost simultaneously with Dr. Robert Stein, the Cook County Medical Examiner. Together, they carefully tipped the trash can and slid the gruesome remains, still partially wrapped, out onto the cement floor. Dr. Stein knelt and began his preliminary examination.

Glancing at his watch, the medical examiner noted the time and pronounced the still-unknown victim officially dead. Absurd as such a pronouncement might seem in a case such as this one, the medical examiner was merely complying with Illinois law, which states that only a licensed physician can actually pronounce a human being dead. Horrifying mistakes have occurred in the past when nonmedical personnel had been permitted to make this most final of all decisions, and the current law had been in effect for many years.

Continuing with his examination of the charred, ruined remains, Dr. Stein stated that the body was that of a black female, probably a young woman or a teenaged girl. He also felt, although an autopsy would be needed to be certain, that the woman had been strangled or choked as well as having been set afire. Her eyes seemed to bulge nearly out of their sockets, consistent with strangulation, and deep ligature marks were virtually cut into her throat.

After 10 or 15 minutes, the medical examiner had completed his preliminary examination and gave permission for the police forensic experts to photograph the remains and to take samples of the various materials on and around the body. Lawmen, meanwhile, made note of the victim's clothing which, although badly burned, was still recognizable. The dead girl was wearing designer jeans, a blue shirt under a white sweater, red leather gloves and gold boots.

Tangled in the body's cloth wrapping, which was now identifiable as a bedsheet, the detectives found a gold clutch-type purse. There was very little inside the purse, only a few scraps of paper and a birth certificate for a Stella Fernandez, with a birth date which would now make her 16 years of age. A squadrol was called from the nearest district to transport the body to the morgue for autopsy, and the detective teams began their canvass of the building and the neighborhood.

One of their first stops was at the home of the Fernandez family, several blocks from where the body had been discovered. Family members verified that their 16-year old Stella, when she last left the house, had been wearing designer jeans, a blue shirt, white sweater and gold boots. Dental records would have to be compared, but the detectives had no doubt that the young woman's body they'd found that morning was in fact that of Stella Fernandez. A routine check through the police department's juvenile records showed that the 16-year old had twice been arrested; once for disorderly conduct and another time for prostitution. Her short life had been sadly typical of so many youngsters raised in the urban high-rise ghettos.

The detectives' interviews with building residents turned up some interesting leads. One man told them that a family had recently moved out of a fifteenth-floor apartment, but that the family's three sons, all in their 20's, returned to the apartment on and off with friends. One of the sons, according to this man, had been at the apartment the night before with a young woman and the two of them had had a rousing argument inside the vacant apartment. The man who told all this to the detectives said he had been able to hear much of the argument through the thin walls of his adjacent apartment. The detectives went downtown for a photo of the murdered Stella Fernandez to show to the neighbor, but he said that the girl in the photo was not the same girl who'd been involved in the argument the night before.

On the twelfth floor of the building where Stella Fernandez' body had been found, detectives discovered another vacant apartment—this one showing signs of a recent fire against one of the bedroom walls. They ordered the crime lab to take samples of the burned debris inside the apartment, to be compared microscopically with samples taken from the trash can in which the body had been found.

By mid-afternoon, the detectives had found and interviewed several people in the 4352 South State Street building who knew Stella Fernandez or who said that they'd seen the girl in and around the building on numerous occasions. In the midst of these interviews, the primary detective team assigned to the case was suddenly contacted via their portable radio and told to head downtown immediately and to report to the watch commander at the communications room of police headquarters. They were puzzled at the unexpected summons, but responded at once.

Upon their arrival at police headquarters, the communications watch commander explained that a call had come in through the 911 emergency switchboard which he thought would interest them. It did.

At precisely 13:59:46 hours, the zone dispatcher answered a telephone call to 911. A woman's voice stated in a loud whisper: "I know who killed the sixteen-year old girl who was burned up at 4352 South State. He lives at 4410 South State." The woman then gave an apartment number at that address and hung up. The detectives listened several times to the tape, then thanked the watch commander and left police headquarters to head back toward the Robert Taylor Homes projects.

The Chicago Police Department's emergency communications network is extremely sophisticated and the detectives had been able to see, on a screen above the dispatcher's console, the address and apartment number from which the woman's call had been placed. They now drove to this building and knocked at the apartment door. Several people were inside the apartment including two women. But everyone inside claimed no knowledge of the mysterious telephone call to police headquarters. One of the occupants of this apartment, a 25-year-old man, suddenly became extremely evasive and hostile when the detectives asked whether anyone knew or had been acquainted with Stella Fernandez. He became so abusive and defensive that the sleuths decided to take him in for questioning.

Once at the detective area, the young man seemed to calm down somewhat, and he admitted that he "thought" he knew the girl in the photo which the detectives had shown him. But he claimed not to have seen Stella around for some time, and denied knowing anything about her death. Detectives asked whether he would voluntarily submit to a polygraph exam, and the young man agreed. Once the lie detector test was completed, the polygraph operator told the sleuths that he believed the young man was perhaps withholding some kind of information, but that he did not appear to have actually participated in the crime itself. Detectives then released the man without charges, but cautioned him to keep in touch in case they needed him for further questioning.

The investigating detectives had been hoping to uncover a witness or informant in the apartment from where the anonymous call had been made. In that way, they would have had some facts at their disposal before confronting the occupant of the apartment where the killer was supposed to live. But since this particular lead had fallen through with the denial of the women that they had even made the call, and the inconclusive results of the polygraph exam, they now had no choice but to go to the apartment of the supposed killer and see what they were able to dig up.

In checking with the Chicago Housing Authority registration, detectives determined that the apartment was registered to one Albert Fields, although several other occupants were listed as well. When detectives arrived, Albert Fields was not at home, but several other people were, including Field's girlfriend, Shalanda Merrill, or "Candy" as she was known on the street, and Ronald Jackson, a friend of Fields. Candy was only a few years older than the murdered Stella Fernandez had been and she, too, was a hardened product of the projects. She readily admitted to the detectives that she'd known Stella, and said that, in fact, she'd been with the girl just the night before when they'd met at a restaurant down the street for coffee. Candy seemed unusually chatty, and seemed to give the detectives whatever information they asked.

Candy said that Stella Fernandez had for a time "belonged" to a man named Roy Horton, but that Horton had been killed in a robbery attempt the previous year. She added that Stella had lately been "hanging with" a guy known to her only as "Little Dave." She didn't know Little Dave's real name or where he might be found.

The other occupant of the apartment, a hugely obese black man named Ronald Jackson, listened as the detectives talked with Candy, but had very little to say on his own behalf. He admitted that he had known Stella Fernandez, but denied knowing anything about her murder. Finally, the detectives left without having learned anything substantive from the interviews. They left word with Candy and Ronald Jackson that as soon as Albert Fields returned home, they wanted him to contact them for an interview.

Later that evening, Albert Fields contacted the detectives, saying he'd heard they were looking to talk to him. Fields told the probers that he'd known Stella Fernandez and that he, along with Candy, had seen the girl just the night before. When they asked Fields his whereabouts for the remainder of the night, he told them he'd been arrested for disorderly conduct about 9:30 p.m., and hadn't been released until after midnight. He said he'd gone right home after that and, along with his girlfriend Candy, had spent the rest of the night in his apartment. The interview was concluded then, with the detectives issuing the same directive to Albert Fields as they had to the others—stay around in case we need to talk further with you.

Now that they had apparently gotten all they were going to get from the various people interviewed, the detectives did some checking on their own. And what they discovered looked interesting, indeed. In checking through the district arrest reports from the previous evening, they learned that Fields had been telling the truth about his arrest for disorderly conduct. What Fields had failed to mention, however, was that another man had been arrested with him—one Dennis Wilson, known on the street as Little Dave. Little Dave had been bonded out at the same time as Albert Fields, 12:35 a.m., but strangely, he hadn't been seen at home or around the neighborhood since.

Even more incriminating, the detectives learned that all of the men, Ronald Jackson, Albert Fields and Dennis Wilson, alias Little Dave, were members of the Disciples, a vicious and powerful south side gang. The Disciples were an offshoot of the old Black P Stone Nation street gang which had risen to prominence in Chicago during the 1960s, when such gangs were frequently subsidized by Federal funds, under the guise of community development youth groups. Those gangs, including the notorious El Rukns and the Disciples, were no longer composed of wayward teenagers, but had matured and organized until now they represented a black underground version of Organized Crime. They dealt in extortion, blackmail, prostitution, gambling and drugs.

The Disciples are a highly organized gang, with a hierarchal structure similar to that of the early mobs of the 1920's and 1930's. So it was not all that difficult for the detectives investigating Stella

217

Fernandez' death to learn exactly where in the Disciple organization each of the three men stood.

By talking to confidential informants on the street and to gang specialists within the police department, the detectives learned that Dennis Wilson, alias Little Dave, was a lower echelon member. As such, his position would be to follow and carry out orders of his superiors, whether those orders meant committing a robbery, stealing a car, or whatever.

In contrast, Albert Fields was a pharoah of the Disciples, or one of the ruling members. He, and his counterparts, were the ones who actually held meetings to decide which criminal activities their troops were to become involved in, and to what extent. The pharaohs, or ruling members, were also the ones to determine the guidelines for disciplinary action against one of their gang members who might have transgressed the discipline code of the organization.

It was Ronald Jackson, the obese black who'd been in Fields' apartment with Candy, who held what the detectives considered to be the most interesting position with the Disciples. For Ronald Jackson was an enforcer. It was Ronald Jackson, and others like him, who allowed the Disciples to hold their reign of terror over neighborhood business owners, prostitutes, gamblers, drug users and other victims of the Disciples' chokehold.

Whenever someone refused to pay, or refused to follow orders, or otherwise displeased the pharaohs of the Disciples, it would be Ronald Jackson or another enforcer like him who would be sent to deal with the wrongdoer.

While they were asking questions about Ronald Jackson, the detectives learned that on the afternoon of December 21st, the day before Stella Fernandez' body was discovered in a burning trash can, Ronald Jackson had been seen brandishing a gun and talking darkly about a "job" he had to carry out. In the parlance of the street, the sleuths took this to mean that he had been assigned as enforcer to carry out an execution.

While the detectives felt that Ronald Jackson's "job" might be connected to the murder of Stella Fernandez, all they had thus far was speculation. So, on December 26th, four days after the murder, they picked Ronald Jackson up and brought him into the detective area headquarters for questioning.

At first, Jackson refused to cooperate at all, maintaining repeatedly that he didn't know what the detectives were talking about. But, when they convinced him that they in fact had people who would come in if necessary and testify about seeing Jackson with the gun and hearing him talk about the "job" he had to do, Jackson finally opened up—somewhat. Jackson now told detectives that he had in fact been carrying a gun on

December 21st, but he said that he was only bringing it to Albert Fields who, according to Jackson, had asked to borrow a gun.

Why would Albert Fields need to borrow Ronald Jackson's gun? Jackson said that he didn't know the details, that Fields had simply told him someone had "ripped him off" and he needed the gun. Jackson now said he assumed Albert Fields needed the gun to frighten someone into paying back some disputed money.

The detectives weren't satisfied with this version of Jackson's story, but without any solid evidence against the man, they had no choice but to conclude the questioning and let Jackson go. Next, investigators brought Albert Fields in for questioning. Like Jackson before him, Fields was at first extremely evasive and hostile. Fields also denied Ronald Jackson's story about the gun, claiming instead that Jackson always carried a gun and that he, Fields, had never asked Jackson for the loan of his weapon.

While the detectives had to release Albert Fields too, they knew that there would now be trouble between Fields and Jackson because of the differing versions each man had given the sleuths. They hoped eventually to capitalize on that trouble, but meanwhile, they sought to bring in the other two people who seemed to be part of this group—Candy Merrill and Dennis Wilson, alias Little Dave. Little Dave seemed to have disappeared from his usual hangouts, but Candy was easy enough to find and she was brought into the area headquarters for questioning.

When they had last spoken to Candy Merrill, shortly after the discovery of Stella Fernandez' body, the young woman had been open and talkative. Her attitude now was exactly the opposite, and she glared sullenly at the questioning detectives. But the sleuths, through years of experience with people under these circumstances, felt that Candy Merrill was more than quiet and uncooperative—she was frightened. While Candy had very little to say, and repeatedly denied knowing anything about Stella Fernandez' death, she did tell the detectives about an incident which they felt might have great significance to their case.

According to Candy, Albert Fields had been very angry at Stella because the girl had, indeed, "ripped him off." Candy said that several nights before the murder, she, Albert and Candy had all spent the night at Albert's apartment. When he awakened the next morning, Albert Fields said that twenty dollars was missing from his wallet and he accused Stella of having taken it. Stella denied this, and offered to undress so Fields could see for himself that she didn't have his money. Stella had pulled off one of her boots and shook it upside down so Fields could see there was nothing in it. She asked him then if she should undress, or would he take her word for it that she did not have his money. Fields had said the girl didn't need to undress, but he ordered her to pull her other boot off. She did and a twenty-dollar bill fell out on the floor. Fields was enraged, but Stella continued to insist that he had given her the money the night before and had just forgotten about it.

Shortly after telling the detectives about this incident, Candy was released. The detectives now held a conference to see exactly what they had and to decide how to proceed from here. Was it actually possible that Fields, or perhaps Ronald Jackson or even Little Dave, had killed the 16-year-old Stella Fernandez because she'd supposedly stolen $20 from Fields! Could a human life be worth so little? The questions were merely rhetorical, because the detectives knew well that people were killed every day for less.

Ronald Jackson was picked up again and this time the detectives had something to work with. They told the obese enforcer that they knew about the incident with Stella having supposedly stolen Al Fields' $20. They made it clear that they knew exactly what Jackson's position with the Disciples was and they knew that Albert Fields was a pharaoh and as such, Jackson's boss. As they continued the pressure, Jackson began to crack, making mistakes in his varying versions of events. Finally, he told them what they had known already but which they had thus far been unable to prove. He said that Albert Fields had decided Stella Fernandez was to die because she'd stolen his $20.

Jackson insisted that while he had been present in Fields' apartment during Stella Fernandez' murder, he had not actually taken part. He said that Fields beat the girl to the floor and then wrapped a telephone cord around her neck. Fields and Little Dave had then taken the ends of the telephone cord and pulled in opposite directions until Stella was dead.

It was a cold-blooded story, but not entirely true. Albert Fields was found and arrested for murder several days after Ronald Jackson. Little Dave and Andy had both disappeared, but were finally located in a San Francisco motel and taken into custody. According to these three, it was Ronald Jackson who directed and supervised Stella's murder. He'd held a shotgun on the girl while the others strangled her to death. At one point, while Albert Fields and Little Dave were strangling Stella, Candy had picked up a plastic milk crate and beat the girl about the head with it.

All four defendants went on trial in October, 1983, and all four were convicted and sentenced. Ronald Jackson, the enforcer, received 80 years in the penitentiary. Albert Fields was sentenced to 30 years. Little Dave was convicted of conspiracy to commit murder and received a seven-year sentence while Shalanda Merrill, known as Candy, received three years and nine months for conspiracy.

EDITOR'S NOTE:
Reggie Brown is not the real name of the person so named in the foregoing story. A fictitious name has been used because there is no reason for public interest in the true identity of this person.

A Skinhead rally.

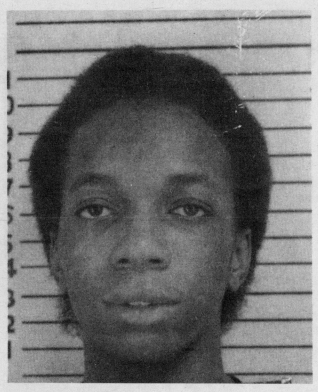

Larry Donnell Williams.

Jason Wayne Rose arrives for arraignment.

Drawing of an inverted pentagram with a goat's head —
a common symbol of devil worship.

Federal marshals transport Maurice Jerome Barnes III into custody.

Barnes' victim, Osage Indian Victor Louis Red Eagle.

Felipe Beltran.

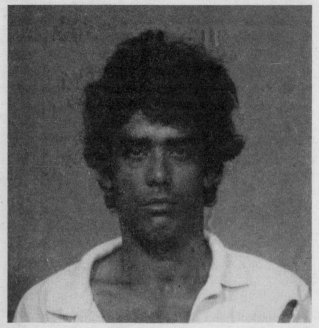
Rolando Ocana.

Jesus Fernandez.

Scene of cult worship.

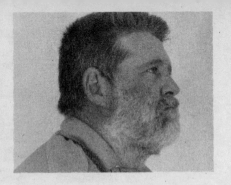

Michael Ryan.

Sarah Maria Aldrete.

Mark Kilroy.

Adolfo Constanzo (left) and Martin Quintana Rodri-
quez (right).

A cult cauldron full of bones, a turtle shell and possible human blood.

"SATANIC MUTILATIONS IN THE GRAVEYARD!"

by Jack G. Heise

They were called "The Devil Kids" by the investigators and prosecutor who alleged they were members of a Satanic cult. One member of the group was quoted as saying they "killed just for the hell of it."

Another member said they wanted to see someone die, but they wanted to see the person die slowly and painfully so they could enjoy the experience.

The case began for the Harris County homicide investigators in Houston, Texas, on the morning of August 14, 1985, when a Rest Haven Cemetery employee was dumping grass clippings and spotted the corpse.

When the homicide detectives arrived, one of the veteran investigators looked at the body and said, "I've seen a lot of man's inhumanity to man, but this has to be the worst ever."

A fellow detective agreed. "The guy must have

died one hell of death."

The evidence was visible.

The victim, a white male, in his late teens or early 20s, was sprawled on the ground with his feet and hands tied with ropes. There was a bandanna with a piece of pipe in it to form a garotte around the neck. Strangulation had caused the victim's eyes to pop out, and one of the eyeballs had been gouged out of the socket.

Part of the victim's hair had been burned, but apparently the fire had been extinguished by the blood from the battered skull. All of the youth's teeth had been knocked out by blows that bashed the facial features beyond recognition.

Stab wounds and slashes covered almost the entire body. It appeared someone had attempted to carve initials or some kind of sign on the flesh.

Lying in the hot sun, the corpse had started to decompose, indicating it had been there for at least several days.

"What in hell do you make of that?" the detective asked as the investigators waited for the lab technicians to arrive and record the scene.

"Somebody sure must have hated his guts to do a thing like that," a detective responded.

Trampled grass around where the corpse lay indicated that more than one person had taken part in the grisly mutilation and slaying.

"Drugs?" a detective questioned. "Those guys

play pretty rough."

An investigator scowled at the suggestion. "I don't know," he said. "Murder in a graveyard is strange, and the way he was mutilated, I'm just wondering . . ."

"Yes?" he was urged.

The veteran detective said he had heard about some Satanic cults around Houston and suggested the victim might have been killed as a sacrifice in one of their rites.

"Like that Charles Manson family out in California a few years back?" a detective questioned. "They were into some freak religious stuff and killed a mess of people, including the movie actress Sharon Tate."

"And more recently that case they have out there on a guy called The Night Stalker," a detective said. "We got a report on it from the NCIC."

In the Night Stalker case, the suspect had killed a number of persons and had left mystic symbols, scrawled with the blood of the victims, on the walls at the scene of the slayings.

When taken to court for a preliminary hearing and ordered to stand trial on charges of first-degree murder, the "Night Stalker suspect raised his manacled arms as he was being led out of the courtroom and shouted, "Hail Satan!"

The crime scene experts completed their work and the corpse was removed by deputies with the Harris County medical examiner for a postmortem examination.

One of the detectives suggested, "There isn't a chance that we'll find any eyeball witnesses out here. Let's get back to town and see if we can get the guy identified and find out what in hell this is all about."

Checking with the Missing Persons Bureau, the investigators came up with the name of Dennis Keith Medler. A dental chart comparison confirmed the identity of the 19-year-old youth. He had no criminal record, and narcotics squad officers hadn't heard the name.

Sleuths contacted persons who had known the slain youth. Several said they heard that Medler had been with a group who was into Satanism, but he dropped out because he thought it was weird. However, they were unable to come up with any names.

"I've got a hunch on how we might come up with a lead," one homicide detective said. "There are a number of book stores around town that are into that stuff. One of them might recognize the name."

At the first book store they visited, the operator told them that he did not recognize the name of Dennis Medler, but he gave them a crash course in Satanic culture and devil worshipping.

"A long time back, it was the flower children," he said. "Then it was the hippies. Now in the 80s it's Satanists. We can't stock enough of the literature, icons and heavy metal rock records and tapes."

He said most customers were young persons. He suspected many were into drugs and he thought there might be a dozen or more covens, as the Satanic worshipers called their groups.

The fastest moving items in his shop, he said, was the "Satanic bible, black candles and icons."

"What's a baphomet?" a detective asked.

The book store operator explained it was a goat-headed medallion usually worn on a necklace to replace the traditional cross. He said another icon worn by Satanists as a necklace or bracelet was the pentacle. It was a medallion formed as the upside down "Star of David."

He said the Satanic bible, and a number of other books written on devil worship, had been authored by the founder of the Church of Satan in San Francisco, who had portrayed the part of the devil in the film "Rosemary's Baby."

"You guys ever read any of his stuff?" the book store operator asked.

"Hell, I never even heard about it," a detective responded. "What's it all about?"

"You guys are investigating a murder," the shop owner said. "How does this strike you?"

He picked up a copy of a book and read the introduction that outlined the basics for devil worship. These were the seven signs of sin: greed, pride, envy, anger, gluttony, lust and sloth.

He turned to a chapter on sacrifices on which the author had written, "The only time a Satanist would perform a human sacrifice would be if it were to serve a twofold purpose; to release the magician's wrath in throwing a curse, and, more important, to dispose of a totally obnoxious and deserving individual."

"I'll be damned!" a detective snorted. "You guys can sell crap like that?"

The operator laughed. "I don't suppose you guys even listen to any of the words in heavy metal rock?"

"Words?" a detective questioned. "I thought all it was was screaming and making a hell of a racket that's supposed to resemble music."

The book shop operator quoted a line from the lyrics of a rock group in which they sing, "Well, now I'm killing you, watch your face turn blue," and a line from another group in which they sing, "Howl like a wolf and crush the cross."

"Can you give us any name of the people who buy this stuff?" a detective asked.

The operator shook his head. "We deal in cash, and we don't ask for names."

"How can we locate some of these people, other than just standing around and waiting for them to come in?" a prober asked.

The operator shrugged. He said that most often, Satanists wore black clothes, particularly black rock T-shirts and black boots. Their jewelry was the pentacle and baphomet.

"If you locate any of them, you'll know them," the operator said. He advised the detectives to look for tattoos. Coven members are into tattoos heavily with the number "666" or the pentacle on their shoulders, arms and palms of their hands. He explained that the number "666" is referred to in Satanic literature as the mark of Anti-Christ.

At the end of a week and after more visits to book stores carrying Satanic literature, the detectives learned a lot about devil worshipping, but nothing about who had committed the grisly graveyard murder or for what reason.

Meanwhile, the report from forensic pathologists stated that the cause of Medler's death was strangulation. He had choked to death by swallowing his own teeth. The pathologists stated that Medler had been alive and most likely conscious during most of the mutilations to his body.

"Do you suppose the murder is connected to that Satanism crap we've been hearing?" a detective asked. "Or have we just been taking lessons on how rotten some people can be?"

"Devil worshipping, weirdos, or whatever you want to call them," another detective said. "Somebody had to be mighty weird to put that kid Medler through the torture he suffered before he died."

The sleuths agreed that the evidence indicated more than one person had been involved in the gruesome murder, and if they belonged to a cult, or a coven as they called it, it was unlikely any of them would voluntarily talk about what had happened.

"We've got to get some kind of a break," a detective said. "But I've got no idea where it can come from."

What appeared to be a break came with a telephone call from the police in Pearland, a suburb of Houston.

An officer reported that a short time earlier they had received a call advising them to check out a pickup truck parked in a field and to look into a toolbox in the bed of the truck.

"We checked it out," an officer said. "There's a body in the toolbox. He looks to be a kid in his teens. We've left everything just as it is because the truck is outside the city limits and in your jurisdiction."

The Harris County homicide investigators hurried out to Pearland and were taken to where the truck was parked. A visual examination showed that the youth had been shot through the head and appeared to have been dead for several days.

"Do you know who called you?" a detective asked a Pearland officer.

He said the call had been placed by a girl who gave them her name and address. She lived only a short distance from where the truck had been abandoned.

"We haven't talked to her," the Pearland officer said. "We figured the case was in your jurisdiction and you'd want to talk to her first."

After the crime scene experts and deputies with the medical examiner's office arrived, the sleuths left with the Pearland officers for the address that had been given.

A teenage girl and her parents were waiting for them. They invited the detectives into the house.

Obviously distraught and near tears, the girl was urged by her parents to tell the detectives what had happened.

Nervously and in jerky sentences, the girl related that on Monday evening her 16-year-old boyfriend had stopped by the house to visit. Shortly after he arrived, he had told her that he had something in the truck that he wanted to show her.

She said he had lifted the lid of a toolbox in the truck and there was a body inside it.

"Did you recognize the person in the toolbox?" a detective asked.

The girl shook her head negatively. She said she had asked her boyfriend who it was and he told her it was one of his friends, 16-year-old Wayne James Schubert, and that he had shot him.

"Why?" a detective asked. "I mean did he tell you why he had killed him?"

"Not exactly," the girl answered. "All he told

233

me was that he had gone to visit his friend and something came up and he shot him."

The girl related that her boyfriend had urged her and then threatened her to go with him in the truck (which belonged to Schubert). They drove to an isolated field and abandoned the truck, then walked back to the house and spent the night there.

The parents explained that the youth was a frequent visitor to their home. He was the son of a single parent and had sort of become family to them. They had no objection to his spending the night after he had called his mother to tell her where he would be.

"That was Monday night," a detective said. "You didn't call the police right away. Why?"

The girl couldn't answer the question. She said she had been upset about seeing the dead person in the toolbox, but didn't know what she should do about it.

"You must have talked about it after you came back home," a detective suggested.

The girl said that was true. "He was acting and talking kind of crazy-like," she said. "He talked about being with some people who worshipped the devil, and they believed that it was all right to kill somebody if they deserved it."

At the mention of the devil worshipping, the detectives became more interested in what the boyfriend had talked about.

The girl was asked if she knew someone by the name of Dennis Medler, or if her boyfriend had mentioned that name.

The girl said she didn't recall his mentioning that name. In fact, he never mentioned the names of any of the persons in the Satanic group.

She related that her boyfriend had called his mother in the morning and she came to the house to pick him up. After he left, she began to cry and her parents forced her to tell them the reason. When she told them what had happened, they advised her to call the police immediately.

Receiving her boyfriend's address from the girl, the detectives hurried there. The youth's mother answered the door and informed them he was not there.

Asked where he was, she told them that she was aware her son had been using drugs. When she picked him up in the morning, he appeared to be irrational. She called a drug counselor who had been treating the boy and he suggested that he be placed in a rehabilitation center in San Antonio. The woman said she bought plane tickets and the counselor had taken her son there.

Informed that her son was being sought as a prime suspect for a murder, the mother was shocked and unwilling to believe that he could have done such a thing. When told the victim had been Wayne Schubert, she was even more confused. She said she had thought that Wayne was one of her son's best friends.

The detectives asked if she knew that her son had been involved with a Satanic group. The woman said she knew he had some material on witchcraft, but thought it was only a passing fantasy.

She could not recall ever hearing her son mention the name Dennis Medler.

The detectives obtained an arrest warrant for the youth and a search warrant for his home.

The suspect was taken into custody at the drug rehabilitation center in San Antonio and returned to Houston where, because of his age, he was turned over to the juvenile authorities.

When questioned in the presence of an attorney, the boy was confused as to why he had shot his best friend. All he could say was that an urge had come over him and he went to his friend's home and shot him.

The boy said he did not know Dennis Medler or anything about the grisly graveyard murder. He gave the investigators the names of his friends. They were checked out, and none could be found who had known or associated with Medler.

The investigation into the murder of Medler appeared to have reached a dead-end. The detectives had checked out all the persons they could locate who had known the victim, without finding anyone who would admit knowing why he had been killed.

Then, a teenage youth accompanied by an attorney came to the sheriff's headquarters. The lawyer said he wanted to talk to the detectives who were investigating the Medler murder.

When he and the youth were taken to the room with the detectives, the attorney said, "My client has something to tell you that I think you will be very much interested in."

"We're all ears," one detective said.

"Not yet," the attorney said. "I think someone from the district attorney's office should be present. I want it on record that my client has come in voluntarily to make this statement, and that his participation in certain things that took place were against his will."

The detectives called the district attorney's office, and Assistant D.A. John Petruzzi came down to hear the statement.

After the meeting was set, the attorney told the youth, "Now, you tell them what you told me this morning."

"Where do I start?" the obviously nervous youth asked.

"Start right in at the beginning," the attorney urged.

"Tell them about how you became involved with this group who are into Satanism."

At the mention of Satanism, the detectives

came to full attention.

The boy explained that he and a number of other young people had been reading and practicing various things, primarily witchcraft and black magic, in what they called a coven.

He said he hadn't been very impressed with the meeting until he had been hitchhiking with one of the members and they had been offered a ride by a man.

The youth said that, without warning, his companion slashed the driver's throat, threw the body out of the car and drove away in the vehicle.

The detectives were well aware of the case. The 25-year-old victim had survived the vicious slashing. He had been able to give a description of the teenage boys he had picked up. The case had been investigated as an attempted murder and car theft, but no suspects had been located.

"You say that you did not know in advance that your companion intended to cut the driver's throat or steal the car?" Petruzzi asked.

"I wouldn't have gone with him if I'd known he was going to do that," the youth answered. "Afterward, I asked him why he did it and he said, 'Just for the hell of it.'"

Asked to give the name of his companion, the boy named a 17-year-old youth.

"That's it?" a detective asked.

"Not quite," the attorney responded. "There's a lot more." He nodded for his client to continue.

The youth related that on Saturday morning following the slashing throat incident, he and his companion attended a coven meeting at the apartment of a 19-year-old youth who was also a member of the Satanic cult.

The informant said that during a discussion of black magic, the older youth had drawn a knife from a sheath he was carrying and asked, "You want to see what a blade like this will do if you know how to use it?"

After more discussion about killing people, the informant said, the other two youths had taken him to an apartment where there was the bloody body of a man on the floor. The victim had been stabbed and his throat slashed.

The informant said he'd been shocked and fearful at the sight of the victim and asked the youth with the knife why he had killed the man.

He quoted the youth as saying, "Just for the hell of it. It gives you a real high to see someone die."

The detectives were also aware of the murder. The victim had been 25-year-old Ronald Monahan. The case had been investigated as a homicide committed during a burglary. They hadn't come up with any suspects.

"You'd be willing to testify in court that you saw the murder victim and heard the person admit that he had killed the man?" D.A. Petruzzi asked.

The attorney answered for him, saying his client would testify only if he was guaranteed immunity from prosecution.

Petruzzi said he was certain that could be arranged.

One of the detectives whispered to another, "Man, this is going to take a couple of tough ones off the book for us."

"Does your client know anything about the murder of Dennis Medler?" a detective asked.

"We're coming to that," the attorney replied. He nodded to his client to continue.

The informant said that after being shown the bloodied corpse of Monahan, the two he was with had told him how they had murdered a member of the coven, named Dennis Medler. They said they had some kind of a falling out with him and that, according to the Satanic bible, anyone who deserved to be killed should be killed in ritual, so they had taken Medler to the graveyard to kill him.

"They were all hopped up about it," the informant recalled. "They told me that it took a long time to kill him and how each of them had beaten and cut him during a ceremony."

One of the detectives let out a soft whistle and said, "I'll be damned. We've hit the jackpot."

D.A. Petruzzi asked, "You have names of the others?"

The informant looked to his attorney. He nodded to continue. The informant named two boys, 16 and 17 years old and a 16-year-old girl who had been present at the time Medler was killed.

"Anything else?" Petruzzi asked.

"That's about it," the attorney answered. Turning to his client he said, "Now tell them why you came to see me and why you are here."

The informant explained that after they left the apartment where Monahan had been slain, they told him they wanted him to get a good sharp knife because he had been selected to kill the next victim in order to become a solid member of the coven. He said they hadn't selected a victim as yet, but thought it might be a girl.

As the informant hesitated, the attorney said, "They mentioned a name, didn't they, as a possible victim?"

The informant nodded. He said the name of Pam had been mentioned. She had been a member of the coven, but had not been with them at the time they killed Medler. Pam had disappeared shortly after the murder and could not be found. They were looking for her, fearful that she might tell someone what she knew about Medler's murder.

The informant said that after he parted company from his two companions, he was frightened. He said he did not want to kill anyone and was fearful that if he refused, he would be selected as the next victim, just as Medler had been

241

when he had a falling out with the members of the coven.

"That's when he informed his parents and came to me," the attorney said. "I want it clearly stated on the record that my client was not involved or present at the time Monahan or Medler were killed and that he had no prior knowledge that the person he was with intended to attempt to kill the car driver and that we've agreed that he should receive immunity for his testimony in that case."

Petruzzi said the record would show that. His client could remain free without bond, but would guarantee to be available and testify after charges had been placed against the other coven members.

After the attorney and his client left, the detectives went into a huddle with Petruzzi. They asked how soon warrants could be issued to have the suspects taken into custody.

Petruzzi warned the investigators not to rush the cases. He pointed out that the informant could testify as an eyewitness to the assault upon the motorist. His testimony, however, for the murders of Monahan and Medler would be primarily hearsay.

"You want to wrap up the Monahan and Medler murders solid?" Petruzzi asked.

"We sure do," one detective replied. "What more do we have to have?"

Petruzzi explained that the witness had mentioned the girl Pam who knew about the Medler murder, but had not been present or taken part in it. If she could be located and would be willing to testify, there would be two witnesses and a much stronger case.

"I'll draw the warrant for the others," Petruzzi said. "We'll just hold off having them issued until you can see what you can come up with. It ought to be a lot easier now that you have names to work with."

He added that all of the suspects were teenagers and, as soon as they were taken into custody, they would have to be turned over to juvenile authorities.

"I'm sure I can have them certified as adults in the murder of Medler," Petruzzi said. "But that is going to take time. If we can nail down the Medler case solid, it will be the easiest to prosecute."

With the names the witness had given them, the detectives began a quiet search for Pam. They learned that she and the 16-year-old girl had been living at the apartment of the 19-year-old suspect. Pam was no longer there and no one seemed to know where she had gone.

On Sunday morning, the detectives were alerted to a murder in northwest Harris County. The victim was a young woman who had been shot eight times.

When the investigators arrived at the scene, it was noted that the victim had the numbers "666" and a pentacle tattooed on her left shoulder and forearm. She also had a tattoo of a flying horse and a top hat perched on a skull on her right forearm and shoulder.

"My God, maybe we waited too long," a detective said.

"I don't know," another prober said. "She looks to be older than the girl Pam we've been looking for."

The tattoos, however, definitely suggested that she must have been at one time a member of a Satanic cult.

The corpse was taken to the Harris County medical examiner. Pathologists were able to definitely state that the victim was not Pam.

Unable to identify the victim as anyone reported missing in the Houston area, the detectives filed a description of her with the National Crime Information Center to be sent to all police agencies.

She was a white female, in her early 20s, with dark shoulder-length hair and brown eyes, five-feet two-inches and 120 pounds.

The investigators thought she might have been a nightclub dancer, but no one answering that description had been reported missing in Harris County. She had not been killed at the spot where her body had been found and had likely been dumped there following the slaying. Detectives did not think this new murder was part of the cases they had been investigating.

Following a tip, the sleuths located Pam in Louisiana. When informed that the detectives knew about the Medler murder, Pam agreed to tell them about it and return to Houston to testify in exchange for a promise of immunity from prosecution.

She related that she and the 16-year-old girl had been staying in an apartment with two of the male members of the coven. She said the Medler murder had been planned two weeks before he was killed.

Pam said they were all into devil worship, reading the Satanic bible and practicing black magic. She said they often talked about killing someone just to see the person die, but that it was only talk.

It came to a head when one member suggested that Medler would be the perfect victim. The Satanic bible said that it was all right to kill someone if the person deserved it.

Medler had been selected because he had fallen out with the group. They discussed the method of killing Medler, and when someone suggested shooting him, the others objected that it would be too quick and easy; they wanted to see the victim die as slowly and painfully as possible.

Pam related that on the night of the murder,

she and the 16-year-old girl and four male members of the cult had been in the apartment when the final plans were made to kill Medler.

One of them suggested that, to make it a real sacrifice, the murder should take place in a graveyard. The problem was how to get Medler to the cemetery.

She said one member called Medler and invited him to go mushroom hunting with them. Medler had not accepted the invitation readily, but the person who called said he knew a good place near a cemetery where they could possibly find the kind of mushrooms that produce hallucinations.

Pam said she did not want to participate in the murder, so she pretended to be ill and went to bed.

She said the group left the apartment around midnight and returned in the early morning hours. Medler was not with them and the others were covered with blood.

"They were excited, real high," Pam recalled. "They were all talking and bragging about the part they had taken in the murder."

In the affidavit, Pam stated that the 16-year-old girl had related to her in detail the murder of Medler. According to the girl, as soon as the group arrived at the graveyard, they jumped Medler and tied his ankles and wrists with rope. When Medler asked what they were doing, one of them told him, "Hey, Dennis, this isn't anything personal. We just want to see somebody die."

"Why me?" Medler had asked.

"I told you, just for the hell of it," he was told. "We had a meeting and decided to kill somebody. You're the odd man out."

She said a bandanna with a piece of pipe in it was placed around Medler's neck. The garotte was slowly tightened until Medler's eyes bulged out.

Medler had pleaded with them if they were going to kill him to do it quickly or knock him out first.

"Hell, no!" one member of the group shouted. "That wouldn't be any fun. We want to watch you die real slow!"

According to Pam, the 16-year-old girl told her that she used a butane lighter to attempt to set Medler's hair on fire, but someone hit him in the head with a piece of pipe and the blood put the fire out.

"He just wouldn't die," Pam quoted the 16-year-old. She claimed that they had all taken turns beating and stabbing Medler.

One member suggested knocking out Medler's teeth so that when his body was found the police couldn't identify him.

Repeated blows with the pipe to Medler's mouth had knocked out his teeth, but Medler swallowed them. One person tried to get the teeth out of Medler's throat, but failed.

Pam quoted the 16-year-old as having told her that after Medler died, she had been given a knife and asked if she wanted to carve her initials on Medler's belly. She refused the offer and then was asked if she wanted Medler's penis as a souvenir. She also refused it.

The 16-year-old told Pam that it was the most exciting experience she'd ever had in her life and began to talk about who the next person might be to sacrifice.

Pam claimed the group continued to talk about the murder of Medler and excitedly recounted how Medler's eyes had "bugged out" during the time he was being strangled.

An interrogator asked if the group had been high on drugs at the time.

Pam said she thought they had used some drugs, but that the high was from the murder.

She claimed there was talk about the next sacrifice and how the killing should take place. One person suggested that the next time they should not strangle the person, but instead just slash him and let him bleed to death.

"You knew all about this but you didn't come to the police?" Pam was asked.

She explained that the group who belonged to the Satanic coven were all friends, but that after the murder, she became afraid of them. She said she wanted to leave, but was fearful that they would find her and she would be selected as the next sacrifice.

"If they thought I told on them, according to the Satanic bible it would be all right to kill me because I deserved to die," she said.

Asked why and when she had left Houston and went to Louisiana, Pam said that a relative of a group member learned about the murder and knew she had not taken part in it. She said he offered her $400 to leave Houston and forget about anything she knew about Medler's murder.

She accepted the offer readily and went to visit a distant relative in Louisiana, hoping that the others would not know where she had gone.

With the affidavit from Pam and the previous statement from the youth who had voluntarily come to the sheriff's office with his attorney, murder warrants were issued for the four male members of the group and the 16-year-old girl.

The suspects were taken into custody. Two of the male defendants were 19 years old and held as adults to stand trial. A 17-year-old youth and the 16-year-old girl were turned over to the juvenile authorities.

A petition was immediately issued requesting that the 17-year-old and 16-year-old be certified to stand trial as adults.

The district attorney's office realized that the most difficult case would be to have the girl certified. They chose that case to be heard first. The hearing was held before Juvenile Court Judge Robert Lowery on February 21, 1986.

Special Prosecutor Roger Haseman presented the state's case. He informed the court that the defendant had been 16 years old when the crime took place in August, but was now 17.

The defense attorney did not deny that his client had been present at the time Medler was murdered, but he claimed she had gone with the group to hunt mushrooms and did not know the murder had been planned.

Pros. Haseman refuted the statement by presenting evidence that the defendant had purchased rope that had been used to tie up Medler. He also cited the statement from Pam who said the girl had come into her room and told her, "We're going to kill Dennis Medler tonight. Do you want to come along?"

There was also Pam's statement about how the defendant had attempted to burn Medler's hair with a cigarette lighter.

Haseman also presented a statement by one of the other defendants who said that when one of the group had begun strangling Medler, the girl had screamed, "Wait! Don't kill him so quick! This is fun."

Haseman concluded his argument by stating that, although the defendant was young, it had been a very violent crime and she should stand trial as an adult.

Judge Lowery agreed and ordered the defendant certified as an adult.

Following the hearing, she was taken before State District Judge George Walker on a charge of first-degree murder. After hearing the evidence against the defendant, Judge Walker ordered her held for trial and set bond at $25,000.

The juvenile court hearing for the 17-year-old boy was nearly a replay of the earlier hearing for the girl. Prosecutor Haseman introduced evidence which showed that the defendant had been in on the murder plot and had participated in the slaying.

Haseman informed the court that the defendant had been on parole for an offense he committed at the time of the murder and that, while on parole, the defendant got angry at a relative and fired a gun at him.

At the conclusion of the hearing, Judge Lowery ruled that the 17-year-old youth should also stand trial as an adult

Following the hearing, a relative told news reporters that the defendant had told her two years earlier he had "sold his soul to the devil."

"The boy who did what was done in that field at the cemetery" was not the boy she knew, the woman was quoted as saying. "When you get into devil worshipping, you get into drugs. In the end, what happens is exactly like what happened."

With the five defendants certified to stand trial

as adults, the prosecutors had to decide how they should proceed. They could either try the five jointly or each one separately.

They decided to try each one separately and selected Harold Glenn "Jack" Smith to be the first because he was the acknowledged leader of the group and had picked Medler as a victim because of a dispute he had with him.

Assistant D.A Jim Peacock presented the state's case. The trial began on August 14, 1986.

The defendant, when he appeared in court, had a changed appearance from when he was first taken into custody. His long hair had been trimmed and styled, and he wore a three-piece suit with white shirt and necktie. He sat silently, staring through large horn-rimmed glasses as a jury was selected.

As soon as the panel was sworn in, the prosecution and defense attorneys clashed over the admission into evidence of a statement Smith had given shortly after his arrest. The defense claimed it had been gained illegally because Smith had not been adequately advised of his legal rights and had been threatened by his interrogators with the death penalty unless he talked.

The court examined the statement and ruled that it could be introduced as evidence. It was a blow to the defense and definitely a first-round victory for the prosecution.

The prosecution spent days introducing a constant barrage of witnesses and evidence to support the murder charges.

When the case was finally completed, it was the defense's turn. They called Smith to testify on his own behalf.

Smith began by denying he was a member of a Satanic coven or that he had been involved in plotting Medler's murder. He said the group had discussed killing somebody, but he had considered it a joke.

He related that he had gone with the others and Medler to the graveyard to hunt for mushrooms, but did not know they planned to kill him until he was ordered by the others to tie Medler's feet.

Smith testified he was surprised when the assault on Medler began and denied taking part in the victim's torture and mutilation.

On cross-examination, Peacock challenged the testimony, asking Smith why he hadn't fled when he learned about the group's intentions.

Smith replied that he feared for his own life. He said if he deserted the group, they would have likely done the same thing to him.

As a rebuttal witness, Peacock recalled Pam. She repeated how she had heard Smith bragging about how he had applied the bandanna garotte to Medler's throat and had laughed when Medler's eyes "bugged out," and then he used a piece of pipe to gouge one of the eyeballs out of its socket.

Peacock gave an emotinal closing argument. He recounted the torture Medler had suffered and, at one point, fell to the floor to demonstrate how Medler had been knocked to the ground and bound.

The defense contended in its closing argument that Smith had told the truth when he said he had not known about the plan to kill Medler and had not taken part in the torture.

The defense counsel attempted to discount the testimony of Pam by branding her a "conniver and survivor" who would say anything to save herself.

On Wednesday, August 13, 1986, the panel received instructions from the judge. Surprisingly, they were out only 45 minutes before a buzzer sounded form the jury room to announce that they had reached a unanimous finding.

The court was called back into session as the panel returned to the jury box. A foreman handed the court clerk their verdict.

To a hushed courtroom, the clerk read that they had found Harold Glenn "Jack" Smith guilty of first-degree murder.

Smith appeared to be stunned by the verdict, but after a few moments to compose himself, he turned to where Pam was seated in the courtroom and smiled at her.

The court ordered the panel to remain sequestered until they could determine a penalty.

The penalty phase began the following morning.

Pros. Peacock asked the panel to recommend the maximum penalty of life in prison, since the state had not asked for the death penalty.

He downplayed the Satanic aspects of the case that had been brought up during the trial, saying that it was done for thrills more than any part of a ritual.

The defense introduced witnesses who described Smith as being shy and non-violent and kind to small animals.

Peacock challenged this testimony with witnesses who testified they had seen Smith kill and sacrifice animals.

As the final witness for the defense, Smith took the stand. He said he was sorry that the jurors had not believed his story and said he was sorry about Medler's death and would do anything to bring him back to life.

Tearfully, Smith pleaded with the jurors to give him probation, saying he would repay them and society by making a useful life.

The panel was sent out to deliberate a verdict. They remained out longer this time than they had when they had found Smith guilty.

After 3 1/2 hours, the buzzer sounded and they informed a bailiff that they had reached a unanimous decision.

They recommended that Smith be sentenced to life in prison plus a $10,000 fine.

Following the sentencing, Smith's attorney said his client was stunned by the maximum penalty.

Reporters questioned Pam following the trial. She said she felt a little sorry for Smith, but felt he got what he deserved. She said she expected to testify in the trials of the four other defendants who had been charged with Medler's murder.

Peacock was asked when he expected the other defendants to be brought to trial. He said it would depend upon what developed following Smith's conviction. He said he felt it was likely some of the others might enter guilty pleas as a result of Smith's trial and the severe penalty he had received.

Peacock said he was not ordinarily in favor of plea bargainings, but if sufficient penalties were imposed as the result of a guilty plea, it would save the court a lot of time and money.

No charges have been filed for the murder of Ronald Monahan or the deadly assault upon the motorist whose throat had been slashed.

Peacock stated that they had ample evidence to proceed in either case, but would wait until all the defendants had gone to trial for the Medler's murder.

"There's plenty of time to consider those cases later," Peacock said. "And much will depend upon the severity of the penalty if the defendants are found guilty."

At the time of this writing, trials for the other four defendants are still pending. They must be presumed innocent until it can be proved otherwise in a court of law.

"MURDER WASN'T ENOUGH FOR THE KILLER-CULTISTS!"

by Walt Hecox

July 13th was on Tuesday in 1982, a bright, warm summer evening on the San Francisco Bay. The tugboat operator passed close to the little islands known as the Two Sister off San Rafael's McNear's Beach as he pulled the little craft away from the aggregate company's docks on the Marin shore.

The body was bobbing like a cork on a fishing line in the shallows not far from the islands. Obviously it was anchored to the bottom. The tugboat operator noticed that immediately. It was not drifting with the tide, but rising and falling atop the wavelets. There was no question about it being a corpse. The dead man's head showed clearly through the clear, plastic wrapping.

As he slowed his engines and pulled the tugboat closer to the floating cadaver, the first thing the skipper thought about was calling the police. But officers of the law are rare on the surface of the

San Francisco Bay and those who are there are usually taking the day off to go fishing. The sailor did the next best thing and radioed the United States Coast Guard.

When the Coast Guard patrol craft—it was far too small to enjoy the status of a cutter—seamen investigated the incident they discovered the body was attached to an outboard motor which was lying in the muddy bottom of the bay about six feet below the surface.

Obviously the person inside the plastic and bamboo wrapping which covered most of the corpse had been in the water for some time. Even while it was in the water a putrescent odor rose from the macabre bundle. The sailors in the little patrol boat decided that since the corpse had been in the water that long, a little extra soaking would do no further damage. They towed the body to the Mare Island Naval Shipyard at Vallejo not far from Carquinez Straits where the Sacramento river empties into the bay. There it was turned over to Solano County deputy coroner and sheriff's deputies, roughly 10 miles from the point where it had been found in Marin County waters.

Deputy Coroner William Breaker and Detectives Lynn Fowler and Richard Halsey of the Solano County Sheriff-Coroner's Department, knew they had a jurisdiction problem on their hands soon as they contacted the officer in command of the patrol boat. The floating corpse in the plastic and bamboo wrapping was definitely not their body. They promptly contacted the Marin County Sheriff's Department and informed the dispatcher that the dead man—and they were positive he must have been murdered—had apparently been found in Marin waters.

Twilight had faded into darkness and evening became late night by the time the body had been found by the tugboat operator, towed to Mare Island and Solano County officials had been summoned and examined the corpse. When the Marin County Sheriff's Department was notified the body had been found in their waters, Deputy Ray Maynard was sent to Mare Island to investigate the matter.

Deputy Maynard discovered that the body was wrapped in a beige, corduroy type slip cover and a bamboo window shade, all of which was covered by a clear, plastic sheet. All of the items around the body were bound by a silver covered tape, the kind used by plumbers to secure duct pipe joints, a hemp rope and a black, plastic, coaxial television antenna cable. A brown, terrycloth hand towel was stuffed in the dead man's mouth.

Because of the advanced state of decay and degeneration of the corpse, and a lack of facilities for properly storing it inside the mortuary normally used as a morgue in Solano County, the body was kept outside overnight and Dr. Harold Brazil, a Vallejo pathologist, performed the autopsy outside the building, in an area beside the crematorium, the next morning.

Witnessing the operation were Detectives Fowler and Halsey of the Solano County Sheriff's Department and Deputy Maynard from Marin. During his examination, Dr. Brazil discovered duct tape had been used extensively to secure the plastic wrapping around the body. The same tape was wrapped around the dead man's neck and ankles. A heavy rope, about two inches in diameter, was wound around the neck twice and extended to the ankles, which were also wrapped twice.

The body was, in Dr. Brazil's words, extensively putrefied. The skin was beginning to separate and slough off in layers. It had become reddish-black and green in some areas and was bloated. The entire body was swollen, which had provided the buoyancy to bring it to the surface. During the operation, Dr. Brazil, and the sheriff's representatives present, took about three dozen photographs.

The pathologist found two narrow stab wounds which passed through the dead man's heart and probably killed him. He also discovered a star shaped cut on the left side of the head. Beneath the wound the skull had been fractured and the muscle tissue reduced to pulp.

Although the murder victim was wearing a white T-shirt, blue polyester trousers and brown socks, no wallet or identification of any kind was discovered. Still attached to the body by about a six foot length of "bungi" cord, was a nine horsepower Wards Sea King outboard motor.

Dr. Brazil told the attending officers that the heart wounds had killed the man and that his skull had been fractured by a blunt, heavy instrument at about the same time he was murdered. He added that the man had been dead for from five to 15 days, probably a week.

Back in San Rafael, the county seat of Marin County, Sergeant Rich Keaton, a veteran detective with the sheriff's department, was keeping in touch with what was happening in Vallejo. He remembered that a San Rafael man had been reported missing by a relative on July 5th and wondered if the body found floating in the waters off the Two Sisters might not be his. The man's name was Richard Baldwin.

Early the next morning he contacted one of Baldwin's relatives who told him she had tried to contact his close friends and had been able to reach all except two of them. She also told him Baldwin had contracted to have a remodeling job begin on his house and that the work had started July 6th. Since the seventh, she said nothing had been done, although the work was scheduled to continue. She said that Baldwin, who specialized in repairing and renewing antique automobiles in a shop on Front Street in San Rafael, frequently carried large sums of cash and that because of this he had told her he was going to purchase a safe in which he planned to store the money and other valuables overnight. She added that she did not know whether he had bought the safe.

Sergeant Keaton then telephoned Sergeant Ted Lindquist of the San Rafael Police Department, a homicide detective, and asked him to search Baldwin's home in an area outside of town known as Venetia Meadows and the repair shop, which was within city limits.

Later that day, investigators learned that Solano County authorities had called for help from the California Department of Justice Laboratory in Santa Rosa. Richard Waller, a criminalist employed by the DOJ, had responded and concentrated his early efforts on identifying the body found in the bay.

Because of the advanced state of decomposition of the corpse, it was necessary for Waller to pull the skin from the fingers, insert material to brace it from the inside, ink them and secure fingerprints. Using this method he managed to get a complete set of prints from each hand. They were matched with prints Baldwin had made while applying for a business license and proved beyond any doubt he was the murder victim. Later, a forensic odentologist verified Criminalist Waller's findings.

Early on the morning of the 15th, Sergeant Lindquist, Sergeant Walt Kosta, his partner, Sergeant Keaton and several other deputies met in the sheriff's office and discussed the case. They were not sure at the time whether the murder had occurred in San Rafael, thus making it a city police case, or in Venetia Meadows, thus putting responsibility for the investigation in the hands of the sheriff's department investigators.

With a relative's permission, the detectives entered the repair shop on Front Street and examined the inside. Almost immediately they were convinced that if Baldwin was a murder victim, he had been killed in the shop. The investigation would be the responsibility of the San Rafael Police Department, and specifically Sergeant Lindquist's.

As they entered the shop they saw, in an open area beyond an ancient Rolls Royce, what appeared to be a large amount of blood on the floor. Sawdust and wood chips had been spread across the top of the fluid, but it had soaked into them. There was ample other evidence of violence in the room. There was also blood on the fender of the Rolls and a large amount of blood was discovered on the other side of the shop.

A baseball bat was leaning against the wall near the door. Its handle was cracked and what appeared to be blood stained its fat end. There was also what looked like dried blood in the bathroom sink and some on one of the ancient automobiles awaiting repair. Remembering Sergeant Keaton's description of the body found in the bay, Sergeant Lindquist noticed a bungi cord on a bench in the shop and a heavy piece of hemp type rope on the ground just outside the front door. He also found a large roll of silver colored duct tape, the same type and color used to bind the dead man and to secure his wrappings, on a bench in the shop.

When the body and the material with which it had been weighted and wrapped were returned to Marin County, Sergeant Keaton discovered a repair tag on the outboard motor which had been used as a weight. It named a shop in Sausalito, a small city in Marin County located just below the north end of the Golden Gate Bridge.

Deputies Don Hulett and Ray Maynard were called to examine and photograph the blood-stained items, plus the cord, rope and other items the detective believed might possibly be involved in the murder. These included a bloodstained wrench and screwdriver.

Moving onto Baldwin's residence in Venetia Meadows, the detectives could find no sign that anyone had forced his way into the house. Yet each interior closed door had been opened and left ajar and on one bedroom door a deadbolt had been broken and the door removed from its hinges. Inside the bedroom closet there were several two inch by four inch wooden blocks on the floor and a vacant space between them about two by three feet wide which might have contained a safe.

The detectives immediately began canvassing both the neighborhoods around the repair shop on Front Street and the home in Venetia Meadows. From a neighbor of Baldwin's in Venetia Meadows, Sergeant Lindquist learned that at about four p.m. on the afternoon of July 6th a ratty looking, early 1970's model Ford or Chevrolet pickup driven by a young white man in his late teens or early twenties had backed into his fence and damaged it. The driver had apologized and said he was working for Mr. Baldwin, adding that "I have to fix this fence."

At the time, the young man appeared to be in a hurry and told the neighbor with the damaged fence he would return to repair it later and drove away. The neighbor said he had not seen Baldwin since that day. He noticed at the time that Baldwin's blinds on the front windows of his house were open, a circumstance he considered unusual. Sometime between noon and one o'clock on July 8th he noticed his fence had been repaired.

After questioning all of the friends on the list provided by Baldwin's relative who had reported him to be missing, Sergeant Lindquist began to search for the two friends the relative had not been able to contact.

One of these friends, a man named Mark Richards, had been the man who was scheduled to build the improvements on Baldwin's house July 6th and who had worked there that day but had not returned on the seventh.

Was it possible, the investigators wondered, that there was another body in the bay off Marin County? Or was Richards implicated in Baldwin's murder? Possibly his failure to continue to work on Baldwin's house on the 7th was pure coincidence. Sergeant Lindquist looked into Mark Richards' background and discovered he was, although unlicensed, a private contractor who employed several young men and specialized in home improvements. He was also, the detective learned, one of the dead man's closest friends.

Turning his attention to the outboard motor which had been used as a weight with which to anchor Baldwin's body, the sergeant contacted Sergeant Keaton of the sheriff's department and asked if the outboard repair shop listed on the tag which had been attached to the motor had been contacted.

Sergeant Keaton told him that Detective Don McQuarrie of the Sausalito Police Department had visited the repair shop and been told by the proprietor that he had repaired the motor for a man living in Sausalito August 9, 1980. He said the manufacturer of the motor was Chrysler Corporation and added that Ward's normally used Chrysler products in its outboard motors.

Sergeant Kosta, meanwhile, returned to

Baldwin's repair shop in search of further clues which might help solve the crime. While he was there the telephone rang at 2:10 in the afternoon. When the detective answered the telephone he spoke to a man who first identified himself as "Mark" and later said his full name was Mark Richards. He explained that he was trying to complete an improvement project on Baldwin's house and had been trying to contact him for several days without success.

"What he said made sense, but he sounded nervous and apprehensive," Sergeant Kosta informed Sergeant Lindquist when telling him about the conversation later in the day.

Through the relative who had reported Baldwin missing, the detectives learned that the dead man had carried many credit cards which were missing when his home and shop were searched. Checking back through the companies who had issued the cards, Sergeant Dave Miller of the Marin County Sheriff's Department learned from a Montgomery Ward representative that Baldwin's account there had been inactive for about two years but that $868 had been charged to it a couple of days before July 13th. The account had a $1,000 limit.

This information was relayed to Sergeants Lindquist and Keaton. Lindquist also learned that Sergeant Keaton had received an anonymous telephone call earlier from a person who said he worked for Mark Richards and that something

268

strange was happening. The young man said one of his co-workers, whom he knew only as Crossy, had told him he had been involved in a "ripoff" and murder and that it had netted him a large amount of money and credit cards.

The informant had arranged to call Sergeant Keaton later that day. While the detectives waited apprehensively that afternoon, the informant kept his promise. Urged by the officers to identify himself and let them conduct an extensive interview, he agreed. That evening, the young man, who identified himself as Art Conway, met with the detectives and Marin County Deputy District Attorney Terry Bourne.

He said he was a third-year pre-dental student at the University of California and his record was spotless. He'd never even been convicted of overtime parking. He lived, with his parents, in San Anselmo, another of Marin County's many suburban cities.

Conway had started working for Richards, a lifelong acquaintance of his family, on a summer vacation job on June 30, 1982. There were several other young men employed by the contractor including one whose nickname was "Crossy."

The young man said he had been told by Crossy that he had been involved in a ripoff. More than $1,400 in cash had been stolen, a safe, jewelry which had been found in the safe and the registration certificates for about six automobiles. Many credit cards had also been stolen, Conway was told.

From another of Richard's employees, Conway learned that the ripoff had taken place in the victim's shop. While the thieves were there, Conway was told, Baldwin had entered the shop and Crossy had hit him in the head with a baseball bat. After murdering the man, the thieves had gone several times to Baldwin's house and taken away truckloads of Baldwin's property.

Conway was also told that Crossy intended to get rid of the body by tossing it over the side of a boat their employer, Mark Richards, who had engineered the robbery and murder, had purchased for that purpose. The boat, Crossy told him, was currently parked in his driveway.

Crossy said the boat was acquired from a man who owed him $1,600 for work he had done. Richards had said he had paid 3,000 for the little cruiser. The man had been trying to sell it for $3,600, Conway was told.

Conway told the investigators he knew that Richards had money problems. On July 3rd, he said, he had received a check for $50 for the work he had done for Richards, plus a $110 check. When Conway had endorsed the check and used it to pay for repairs on his automobile he was told shortly thereafter it had been returned "stamped, refer to maker." He said he returned the check to Richards, who promised to replace it but had thus far not done so.

The second employee of Richards who had spoken to Conway about the murder told him that during the past few days Crossy and another young man had been on a credit card spree.

Conway went on to say that he had been in Richards' home on July 14th and seen what he believed to be a new video cassette or disk player with a Ward's brand on it. Richards had explained he had received the item from someone who owed him money. Shortly thereafter, a relative of Richards had entered the room wearing an expensive necklace and said, "See what Mark got me."

On July 6th, Conway said, he had seen Crossy leaving the job in an ancient, blue Ford pickup and been told "he had business to attend to." The pickup, he said, belonged to Richards, but Crossy drove it back and forth to work. Later, Conway said, on about July 13th, he had seen a green safe in Richard's garage.

There was only one major problem with Conway's statement. He did not have any complete names of any of the people with whom he had talked. He knew them all by their first names of nicknames.

On the off chance he might be able to locate one of the people he had talked with, Conway was shown a Novato High School year book. To his knowledge both Crossy and the other young man lived in Novato. The detectives' hunch paid off. After a short time, Conway was able to identify a photograph of the second young man who had mentioned the murder. His name was Matthew Quisling. Like Conway, Quisling had a crime free record, lived with his parents in Novato, northernmost of Marin County cities, and worked as a laborer for Richards.

He said that on July 12 he had been told by Crossy that a man had been beaten, robbed and murdered in San Rafael. Crossy told Quisling it was he who had hit the person over the head with a baseball bat and that he did so more than once.

Once the man was dead, Crossy had said, the people committing the robbery had taken the pink slips to several automobiles which were parked in the garage. Crossy had mentioned both a "shop" and a "house" and Quisling was not sure which place was the crime scene. Crossy had told him that he, Richards, and another young man, Harry Templar, had been involved in the incident.

Within the past week the young man said he had dropped both Crossy and Templar off at homes in Novato and indicated he was willing to point them out to the detectives.

He also said that on July 14th, Mark Richards had given him a .44-caliber Ruger Blackhawk revolver, serial number 83-27182. Richards had explained he was turning the gun over to Quisling in lieu of cash for his work. He was advised by Richards not to try to register the weapon. Quisling turned the gun over to Sergeants Kosta and Lindquist. The detectives made a quick check on the registration of the weapon and discovered it had belonged to Richard Baldwin.

Next, Sergeants Lindquist and Kosta worked through the night preparing a search warrant for the home of Richards, on Butterfield Drive in San Rafael, and the two homes in Novato Quisling had pointed out as the places where Crossy and Templar lived. That morning they took both Quisling and Art Conway to the home of Judge Robert Smallman who issued search warrants for all three places.

The detectives called in everyone who had participated in the investigation and made plans with them to visit the homes occupied by Crossy, Harry Templar and Richards. They still did not know Crossy's full name, but Quisling had pointed out both their homes to the detectives early that morning and they had seen the ancient blue Ford pickup parked in front of Crossy's home.

Plans were made to search first Richards' home on Butterfield Drive in San Rafael, then continue on to the homes of Templar and Crossy in Novato. Because they had been working 36 hours without sleep, neither Sergeants Kosta nor Lindquist planned to participate in the arrest. The loss of sleep, they feared, might impair their judgment.

More than a dozen officers were involved in serving the search warrant. Sergeants Lindquist and Kosta parked an unmarked car in front of Richards' house and they immediately spotted the blue Ford pickup they had seen in front of the house identified as Crossy's earlier.

Other police units moved into place, sealing off the street to incoming traffic. While they did, two young men and an older person emerged from Richards' house and began loading the pickup with debris. They filled the truck's bed, then attached the boat to it and began to drive away. After being allowed to progress about two blocks, a marked police car moved in and stopped them. The two young men, later identified as Crossan Hoover, Harry Templar and Mark Richards, were arrested.

When they entered Richards' house the investigators discovered a great amount of strange literature and items. The literature concerned a cult known as "Pendragon" and some of the items were medieval.

The detectives did not think much about the literature at the time. They were looking for hard, physical evidence connecting Richards to the murder and they discovered a lot. A roll of duct tape the same color as that used to bind Richard Baldwin's body was discovered in Richards' house.

Two guns, both registered to Baldwin, were found there. Black television cable of the same type used to help tie the wrappings around Baldwin's body were found in the bed of the pickup truck. A bloodstained boat seat was also found in the back of the pickup.

Baldwin's house, car and shop keys were found in the door jamb of the pickup.

At Hoover's home, Detectives Mike Keller, Jim Cook and Steve LaBounty discovered a gun registered to Richard Baldwin and a quantity of "Pendragon" material. Nothing which would serve as material evidence was found in Templar's residence. However, they did find a young man there who told them a weird story about plans for an "Imperial Marin." They learned eventually that Richards had been organizing a group of from eight to 10 young men into a cult with which he planned to take over all of Marin County.

The plan involved cutting Marin off from the rest of California by blocking off Highways 1 and 101 to the north and blowing up the Golden Gate and Richmond Bridges. A laser beam would be mounted atop Mt. Tamalpias for defense against aerial attack and the possibility of using the beam to blow up the oil refineries in Richmond were discussed.

Each member would become a noble. Richards

had given them such titles as Lord of Nature, Lord of the Land, Lord of Angel Island, other geographical locations in Marin.

Richard Baldwin, strangely enough, was listed as Lord of Transportation, although there was never any evidence he was a member of the group.

Richards would be Pendragon, highest lord of them all, and he used his organization to convince at least two teenagers they should help him, for $5,000 and a car to murder Baldwin.

After their detention, Richards, Hoover and Templar were interrogated extensively at San Rafael Police Headquarters. Sergeant Keaton from the sheriff's department assisted in the questioning.

Richards at first refused to admit he knew anything about the murders. Later he said he believed he had been framed by his teenaged employees.

Hoover was another story. He waived his rights and immediately began telling how he and Templar and Richards had lured Richard Baldwin to his shop with the intention of murdering and robbing him. He told how he had clubbed Baldwin in the head with the baseball bat while Richards distracted the victim with conversation. The young man described in detail how he had pounded the screwdriver into Baldwin's chest with a hammer twice. He had also stabbed Baldwin in the temple with the same weapon and once it had penetrated the skull, spun it around so it would scramble the brain.

Microscopic examination revealed that the coaxial cable found in the blue pickup at the time the search warrant had been served on Richards' home had once been a part of the cable used to bind Baldwin's body. Fingerprints found on checks which had been cashed on Baldwin's account after his death belonged to Richards.

Harry Templar, who played a minor part in the murder plot and was very young, was granted immunity for his testimony.

Mark Richards 28, was sentenced to serve life in prison without possibility of parole. Judgment was passed June 4, 1984.

Crossan Hoover, 19, was convicted of first-degree murder and sentenced to from 25 years to life in prison.

EDITOR'S NOTE:

Harry Templar, Matthew Quisling and Art Conway are not the real names of the persons so named in the foregoing story. Fictitious names have been used because there is no reason for public interest in the identities of these persons.

"THREE SLAIN BECAUSE THEY WERE WITCHES!"

by Bruce Gibney

The woman was a beauty. Long blonde hair streamed past her shoulders, bordering a delicate, pretty face. She had clear blue eyes and a winning smile. Only a few crow's feet wrinkles indicated her age was closer to 40 than 20.

Her companion stood well over six feet tall, had shoulder length hair and a thick beard that dominated the face. Naturally, his nickname was "Bear."

The two stood beside Highway 101 north of San Francisco on January 11, 1983, hitchhiking a ride to nowhere. They had no destination, no set itinerary.

An El Camino stopped for the couple at 10 a.m. The driver was a 30-year-old San Diego man named Jon Hillyar. Hillyar was staying with friends in Santa Rosa and made it a habit to pick up hitchhikers.

"Where to?" he asked.

"Don't matter," Bear replied.

"Canada," the pretty blonde said. Seated between the two men, she fixed her gaze upon the driver. As they neared Santa Rosa, she nudged her companion.

Bear turned and looked at Hillyar. Suzan was more susceptible to energy levels than he was, but he started feeling it too. Little jumpy sensations — electricity.

Hillyar would never have picked them up if he had known about the electrical impulses the two called "bad vibes." He would have certainly kept on going or perhaps called police if he had known anything about their nomadic, murderous past.

But he had only their appearances to go by. And they looked harmless enough. A guy with a beard and a sleeping bag. A woman with long blonde hair and an Indian blouse. At 30, Jon was old enough to remember when people like them had invaded the Haight-Ashbury section of San Francisco, smoking dope, passing out flowers, and making headlines in the process.

Displaced hippies, flower children. Drifting around, living like innocents, Hillyar was only doing them a favor.

It turned out to be a tragic mistake.

Frank J. Falzon and Carl C. Klotz are homicide inspectors with the San Francisco Police Department. On March 7, 1981 they went to a triplex on Shrader Street in the core of Haight-Ashbury to investigate a missing person report.

The woman missing was 23-year-old Keryn Barnes, a sometime artist who had been living in the Haight area and taking classes at the nearby San Francisco Academy of Art. Friends became concerned when Keryn failed to show up at a party they had thrown in the neighborhood. A girlfriend had gone to her apartment and was surprised when no one came to the door. She went back later in the afternoon but the door was still locked.

"I had a funny feeling that something had happened to her," she told police. "I felt funny when I touched the door knob."

She had reason to be concerned. The Haight is famous as a spawning ground for the hippie movement in the 1960s. But police know it as a violent, high crime area where drug murders and assaults are routine. Inspectors Fazon and Klotz went to the Victorian-style building on Shrader Street to check out the complaint. The superintendent opened the door and they went inside.

The apartment was cluttered with stretched canvasses and art supplies but showed no sign of a break-in or ransacking. They searched the bedroom, found the bed was made and the clothing hung neatly on hangers in the closet. It didn't appear that the room had been used for several days.

Inspector Klotz stepped outside and asked the superintendent if the tenants had access to the garage or other rooms in the building. Pulling a cigar from between his lips, the super said there was a basement that some tenants used for storage. It was locked, but residents had their own keys.

The detectives found Keryn downstairs in the basement. Her fully clothed corpse was wrapped in a blanket and tied with cording. It had been stashed behind some boxes that had been piled up apparently to conceal the body. Her skull had been fractured and she had been stabbed twice in the neck.

The detectives were hard pressed to find a motive. The coroner found no evidence of sexual assault, and the apartment showed no signs of ransacking. Drugs were dismissed as a motive when friends said Keryn didn't use any.

The lawmen learned that until a week ago, Keryn had shared the tiny apartment with a transient couple she had met at a coffee shop. The man was in his mid-30's, wore shoulder length hair and a beard, and went by the name "Bear." The woman was named Suzan, had long blonde hair and wore colorful Indian blouses and blue jeans. The threesome had been together for about a month and had returned recently from a hitchhiking trip to Arizona. Keryn's friends didn't know much about her roommates. One described them as "late blooming hippies" who practiced vegetarianism and kept to themselves. No one had seen them since Keryn dropped out of sight.

The couple apparently had no intention on returning to the apartment. The knapsacks and camping gear they took on the trip to Arizona were gone and there was nothing in the apartment that could be linked to them.

The investigators had composite drawings of the two made and distributed copies to officers who patrolled the Haight-Ashbury-Western Edition area.

A few people were brought in for questioning but nothing came of the interviews. Klotz and Falzon didn't know if the couple was mixed up in the murder of the 23-year-old artist, or if it was a coincidence that they left the apartment shortly after she dropped out of sight.

The two worked leads in the case for almost two weeks. Then the clues dried up and they went on to solve other cases. There was no shortage in the city—gay murders in the Castro Street District, drug slayings in the Filmore—and it would be two years before they heard her name again.

Alderpoint is a speck of a town in Humboldt County, 200 miles north of San Francisco. On May 3, 1982 a farmer was inspecting his land when he found a decapitated, badly decomposed corpse under a layer of chicken manure.

The autopsy revealed the victim was a male Caucasian in his late 20s or early 30s with tattoos on his left forearm. He had been shot in the side and then burned before being buried under the manure.

The victim wasn't from Alderpoint and police suspected he was probably a hitchhiker who caught the wrong ride. They were only partly correct.

Two weeks earlier Clark Stephens, a 28-year-old resident of Garberville, left a local restaurant after breakfast and headed back to his small farm on the Mattole River.

A friend went to visit Stephens but found he wasn't home. When the friend returned a few days later and Stephens still wasn't back, he called police.

Humboldt County investigators took down the report but didn't act upon it until they learned of the body found in Alderpoint.

Stephens matched the height and weight of the victim and had tattoos on his left forearm. Fingerprints confirmed their suspicions.

Though authorities knew the identity of the victim, they still didn't know the motive for his murder. Stephens was suspected of raising marijuana on his farm. But it seemed unlikely he had been slain for his weed crop, since it was May and the crop was too green for harvesting.

Robbery was not likely. Stephens' house had

not been broken into, and he rarely carried large sums of money when he made his trips into town.

Humboldt County investigators learned Stephens went into Garberviille twice a week to buy supplies and eat at the restaurants.

On one of his last trips, he was accompanied by a couple wearing backpacks and hiking gear. A clerk at a local dry good store remembered the couple and assumed they were living with Stephens because of the amount of groceries he bought. The man was in his 30s, about 6 feet tall, and had long dark hair and a bushy beard. The girl was about the same age with blonde hair.

Authorities didn't know if the couple lived in Humboldt County or were passing through. This isolated, sparsely populated county with its soaring redwoods and torrential rains is home to hundreds of long-haired entrepreneurs who grow high grade marijuana on illegal farms. Transients are not uncommon, particularly during the planting season in summer and early fall.

Stephen's killer might have been anyone. Time passed and investigators went on to other cases. No one made the connection between the slaying of the suspected pot grower and the murder of the art student in San Francisco. There was no reason to. The cases were separated by time and geography, and it would take a third murder before lawmen made the connection.

A produce worker named Jack Irons was in front of his fruit stand pyramiding a bushel of apples on the counter when an El Camino with three people inside pulled off Highway 101 and drove into a field.

Irons heard someone yell for help and turned to see two men grappling on the ground in front of the El Camino.

There was a woman, too, a pretty woman with long blonde hair and wearing blue jeans and sharp pointed boots.

She used her boots to kick the man on the ground. "He was yelling, 'Help, help, someone help me.' " Irons went past the counter for the phone. He didn't know what the fight was about and he didn't want to know. As he punched the number for the police the man who was on the ground got up and ran for the car.

A deliveryman pulled off the highway in time to see the scuffle. He pulled up behind the El Camino and blew the horn, figuring that the disruption of the horn blast would cool them off.

Instead he saw the man with the shaggy beard take a gun from the car and push the other man to the ground. The gun fired twice. The deliveryman watched in disbelief as the man with the beard stood up and walked back to the El Camino with the girl.

A Somona County Sheriff's deputy arrived at

the fruit stand expecting to break up a fight. Instead, he found Jon Hillyar lying dead in the dirt and two very excited witnesses standing around him.

The two witnesses described the gunman and his girlfriend and said they headed south toward Healdsburg. The deliveryman had been close enough to see the license plate number, which he gave to the officer.

An all points bulletin was put out on the gold, late model El Camino, along with descriptions of the occupants and the advisement that both were wanted on suspicion of murder.

Healdsburg Police Officer Steve Bouchard received the radio alert at 11 o'clock as he was headed onto Highway 101. Suddenly the yellow El Camino shot by and took the second exit onto Dry Creek Road.

Bouchard chased the car down the road to Lyton Road and onto Highway 128 to the resort town of Calistoga.

Bouchard soon received the backup of the California Highway Patrol, Napa County Sheriff's Office and the Calistoga Police Department.

The El Camino got as far as the Calistoga city limits before it slid out of control at the intersection of Maple Road, crossed a gravel road to a private ranch and came to a halt in a vineyard. The bearded driver and his blonde-haired companion ran from the car for a waist-deep stream that ran parallel to the private road. They were half way across when a Napa County deputy pulled his revolver and ordered them to halt.

The couple was taken to Somona County Jail in Santa Rosa and charged with suspicion of murder. The bearded suspect told deputies he was 32 years old and his name was "Bear." The woman refused to give her age or her name.

Their fingerprints were sent to the Criminal Intelligence and Identification bureau in Sacramento. "Bear" was Michael Carson, 32, of San Francisco. The woman was his wife, Suzan Thornell Hamilton Carson, 40.

In a search of the El Camino, detectives found a recently fired .38-caliber revolver and two unpublished books listing former California Governor Jerry Brown, present Governor George Deukmejian, President Ronald Reagan, and other political figures as marked for death.

Lawmen asked the Carsons why they wanted the politicians dead. Michael shrugged and said they would have to ask his wife. Suzan said the politicians mentioned in the book were witches and she and her husband had a moral obligation to kill witches.

Detectives asked if her moral obligation had resulted in any deaths. Suzan nodded. "We have committed several murders," she said. "It is our moral obligation to kill witches even if such slaying must be committed in the full view of eyewitnesses."

The Carsons were arraigned in Santa Rosa Municipal Court, January 1983. An arraignment is normally a simple process lasting a few minutes. The Carson arraignment, however, was stalled for almost an hour, as Suzan refused to accept her court-appointed attorney, declaring that her religion mandated she have the same attorney her husband did.

"I won't let that man near me," she said, pointing to the attorney appointed by the court. "I will not speak to him. He is not my lawyer. He will never be my lawyer. My husband's attorney is my attorney."

Judge John Gallagher explained that having separate attorneys was desirable because the couple might wish to pursue separate defenses.

Michael Carson turned to a reporter and shook his head. "We are political prisoners. I want everyone to know that I have written a book that explains everything, but the authorities have confiscated the book. The book is the key to our defense. We are prisoners of our consciences, but we are not criminals."

The judge decided the Carsons could be tried together and have the same attorney represent them. He also agreed to amend the murder complaint to "Michael and Suzan Carson, also known as Michael and Suzan Bear" after Michael argued he had taken his surname because the bear had special religious significance.

Humboldt County detectives, meanwhile, had built a case against the Carsons in the murder of alleged pot grower Clark Stephens. The Carsons matched the description of the couple seen in the grocery store with Stephens, and the gun taken from the El Camino was the same one used in the shooting.

The Carsons were also wanted for questioning in the murder of Keryn Barnes. Detective Falzon had linked them to the slaying after reading of their arrest on the police telex.

The couple resembled the two hippies who stayed with Keryn at her apartment. They also matched the couple who had attended a party with Keryn.

The San Francisco detectives went to Santa Rosa and attempted to question the Carsons about the murder. But neither appeared interested in talking to police.

The same could not be said for the press. The Carsons eagerly sought out reporters, wanting their story to be heard by as many people as possible. That meant getting outside Santa Rosa.

In April the Carsons wrote a letter to *San Francisco Chronicle* columnist Herb Caen, claiming they had not received publicity in the "more important press."

Caen, the most widely read columnist in the Bay area, decided they deserved their shot and wrote a small story in his weekly column. The media picked up on it and besieged the small county jail with requests for interviews.

On April 28th, they got what they wanted, as did Detectives Frank Falzon and Carl Klotz, who were "advisers" at the press conference. Their job was to make the couple aware of their constitutional rights and to keep them on a narrative track.

That morning the Carsons appeared before a dozen reporters and television technicians. Dressed in red prison jumpsuits, the two gave a rambling, sometimes stream of consciousness account of their nomadic travels and the murders of Keryn Barnes, Clark Stephens and John Hillyar.

Michael did most of the talking. "We insist on pre-trial publicity," he said.

"We want to get our story out to the people."

He said he and his wife had drifted to Haight-Ashbury in the 1967 Summer of Love, adopting a hippie lifestyle that practiced free love and use of psychodelic drugs.

That led to wanderings through Europe, the American Southwest and California. They professed strong feelings of pacifism, practiced yoga and vegetarianism and converted to a form of the Moslem religion.

In late 1981, they returned to San Francisco and befriended Keryn Barnes. They moved into her apartment and the three later hitchhiked to Arizona and stayed with friends. They decided to return to San Francisco in January, 1981, with Keryn going on ahead of the Carsons, who wished to spend another day in Arizona. On the way to San Francisco, they got caught in a blinding winter rainstorm and had to wait it out in a motel in Oxnard, California. That night Suzan began receiving "vibrations" while lying naked in the bed.

"Suzan is a yogi and a mystic with knowledge of the past, present and future events," Carson explained. "In the motel the vibrations told her that Keryn was an evil force and that Suzan should slay her."

Michael said each time his wife asked out loud if she should murder Keryn, the thunder would clap.

When they arrived in San Francisco, they went to the Shrader Street apartment and waited for Keryn. When she arrived, Michael took a pan off the kitchen stove and hit her on the head three times "as hard as I could." When she made a sound, he said he stabbed her twice in the neck with a small paring knife, then wrapped the body in a blanket and hid it in the basement.

The couple fled that night, hitchhiking rides up Highway 101. Near Garberville, they befriended Clark Stephens, whose car had broken down and who was hitchhiking back to town.

After the car was fixed, Carson said, they went back to Stephens farm and stayed as guests for two weeks. They then left but a year later they returned and again stayed with Stephens.

It was a good time, with beautiful scenery, good food and occasional trips into town. Then, one evening, Suzan tapped her husband on the shoulder and shot him a look. "She had another flash," Michael said. "I said him, too, and she said yes, he is a demon and must be killed."

Michael took a gun that was in the cabin and waited until Stephens had turned away before shooting him twice in the head and once in the side. He then dragged the body outside and burned it with gasoline to purge it of evil spirits. The Carsons said they later buried it on the farm in Alderpoint.

Jon Hillyar was killed for the same reason as the others. "The man was a witch," Michael said. "He used his powers to sexually abuse Suzan."

That would have been difficult, since the three of them had just met and were sitting in the front seat together. Suzan, however, was certain she had been sexually abused by Hillyar, that Hillyar was a witch, and that he should die.

Michael said he demanded that they stop, and then started a fight. Once they got Hillyar down on the ground, Michael took the .38 and pumped two slugs into the helpless man, then fled in the El Camino.

Michael said, he had no choice but to kill the "witches" that were posing as mortals. It was a part of his religion to cleanse the world of these unclean, evil spirits.

"We are Moslem vegetarian warriors trying to rid the world of witches. We had to kill them. It was part of the Koran."

Suzan kept her gaze on her husband's face most of the time, with her left hand placed on his right arm. She smiled and occasionally stared at the others in the bland, almost bare interrogation room. She showed no discomfort when Michael said she was the one that gave the orders to kill.

"We fear for the future of this country," Michael said at the end of the five hour interview. "Witchcraft, homosexuality and abortion are the ruin of everyone in this country. They are causes for death."

Michael ended the marathon press conference by saying he hoped he would first be tried in San Francisco where the courts were more tolerant and his story would be heard by a wider audience.

In May, 1983 he got his wish when the Carsons went on trial for the Keryn Barnes murder. During the two-week-long trial, the Carsons gave testimony that Keryn Barnes had been murdered because she was a "witch and a vampire" who was trying to drain the health of Suzan Carson.

The jurors did not believe in witchcraft and found the Carsons guilty of first-degree murder. On June 16th, Michael Carson was sentenced to 26 years to life in prison, while Suzan was given a 25-year to life sentence.

The two will now stand trial for the murders in Sonoma and Humboldt Counties, with the previous murder conviction making them eligible for the death sentence if convicted in either case. The trial begins in Sonoma County early in 1985. Until they have been able to defend themselves in court, Michael and Suzan Carson must be considered innocent of all charges against them.

"A HUMAN SACRIFICE TO SATAN!"

by Charles W. Sasser

It was four nights before Halloween — Tuesday, October 27, 1987 — when the fire alarm went off at the home of Victor Louis Red Eagle outside the small Osage County town of Hominy in north-central Oklahoma. It was a silent alarm. It went through a security firm located in Tulsa, 30 miles to the southeast, and was then relayed to the fire department in Hominy. It was 1:46 a.m.

Five minutes later, Hominy Fire Chief Philip Wilson and three of his firemen were riding their screaming truck east on Highway 20. They went out a mile, then hooked right for another mile to where the sprawling wood-and-rock residence of the richest man in the community perched on top of a hill surrounded by prairie.

"There were no lights on at the house and no cars there," Fire Chief Wilson said. "We didn't see any smoke or fire at first. We thought it was a false alarm. But then, fire heat from inside busted out a window and we saw smoke."

One of the firemen crawled through the broken window and unlocked that front door to let fire-fighters rush inside. Apparently, no one was home. Wilson said that 13 separate fires were beginning to kindle throughout the two-story mansion. The house was filled with silence and thick smoke.

Within a short time, the blazes were out, including one in an upstairs bedroom. Chief Wilson's flashlight beam darted as he hurried through the house checking for more fires. He noted that the furnishings were expensive wood and leather, the house well-kept. In the living room, into which the firemen had first entered the residence, Wilson's light beam looked eerie and diffused by the lingering smoke.

Suddenly, the beam froze like an icicle. It spotlighted a man lying on a short leather sofa. Firemen had missed him before. It was almost as if the corpse had appeared there out of the smoke.

"He was lying face down on the loveseat," Wilson said. He was wearing jeans and a tee-shirt. His legs were bent at the knees and sticking up because the sofa was too short for him. There was blood on his head. I thought he had been shot in the back of the head."

Osage County is the largest county in Oklahoma. It is also the most confusing in terms of law enforcement jurisdiction.

Before statehood, Osage County was known as the Osage Nation. When the reservation was split into individual allotments after 1907, white cattlemen ended up with much of the land. It is the finest tall-grass pasture in the world. That land, however, which remained under American Indian ownership, also remained under federal and tribal jurisdiction. That is why a crime occurring on one ranch falls under the authority of the county sheriff, while a crime occurring on a neighboring ranch might require the magistracy of federal authorities.

When the chief criminal investigator for the Osage County Sheriff's Department arrived at the scene of the apparent homicide shortly after 2:00 a.m. and determined that the crime had occurred on Indian land, he immediately notified the Tulsa regional FBI office. FBI Agent George Zeigler met the deputy at the Red Eagle mansion within the hour. He found the chief criminal deputy to be a rawboned man with the cowboy look of that part of the world. A 15-year veteran of the sheriff's department, Deputy Bill Williams had earned a widespread reputation for being thorough and quick. While Agent Zeigler officially took charge of the fledgling probe, in all practical terms he was to share investigative responsibility with Investigator Williams and with Osage County Sheriff George Wayman.

The body was quickly identified as that of Victor Louis "Louie" Red Eagle, 38, a full-blooded Osage Indian and the great-grandson of former Osage Chief Fred Lookout, the last hereditary leader of the Osage Nation. Virtually everyone in Osage County knew the wealthy bachelor resident of the VLRE mansion, as it was sometimes called. Those who did not know him personally at least knew him by reputation.

At first, authorities reported, Red Eagle appeared to have been slain not by gunshot but by a terrific blow to the back of the head. The unknown weapon had apparently not been left at the scene. A flammable fluid—lantern or lamp oil—had been sprinkled on the dead man's clothing and throughout the house and then set afire. Firemen had extinguished the blazes in the house; Red Eagle's clothing had only been scorched before those flames died out on their own.

Maybe, detectives said, the motive for murder was robbery. Maybe. Reportedly, crime-scene experts combing the house for evidence recovered nothing to point investigators toward either a motive or a suspect. Sheriff George Wayman could only tell newsmen, "Foul play is indicated in the death of Mr. Red Eagle. The preliminary investigation indicated the victim had been struck on the head and fires were set in every room in the house in an effort by the assailants to cover up this crime."

The next day, Wednesday, the office of the

State Medical Examiner released autopsy findings that Red Eagle had been neither shot nor beaten to death; he had died from manual strangulation.

"Somebody choked him to death," said Deputy Bill Williams.

"Do you have any suspects?" reporters asked. "It's not going to be another one of the 'Osage County Mystery Murders,' is it?"

For decades, murder in the wide-ranging Osage country has attracted national attention, especially during the 1920s Oklahoma boom days when the discovery of oil brought the tribe unprecedented wealth. Crime was so commonplace in the wild boom environment that the violent deaths of Osages attracted scant attention outside the county. Inside the county, however, terror mounted. When the Osage Tribal Council called on the U.S. Bureau of Investigation, as the FBI was then known, for help, it cited at least two dozen killings of Osages that were being ignored by local authorities.

The FBI's first big claim to fame came as a result of breaking these cases. Bureau agents posing as cowhands and cattle buyers soon obtained evidence against a displaced Texan named W. K. Hale, a wealthy white rancher who owned or leased thousands of acres in the Osage. His conviction for murder in 1926 led the *New York Evening World* to comment: "Even lurid fiction pales beside the story of these Osage murders."

Although the "Osage Reign of Terror" was over, the "Osage County Mystery Murders" has become part of the lore of the land, to be recalled whenever another prominent Osage is killed, whatever the motive. It was brought up 17 years ago when Osage rancher E. C. Mullendore III, the great-grandson of still another Osage, Chief Charles Brown, was slain. His murder, the subject of countless articles and at least one book, is still unsolved.

It was being brought up again now with this latest slaying of an Osage tribal member.

"We'll find out who did it," lawmen promised the press. "It will not be one of the 'Mystery Murders.' "

That was one promise, law officers speculated, that might come back to haunt them.

Lacking solid evidence or clues, Investigator Williams and Agent Zeigler delved into Red Eagle's background and lifestyle in expectation of uncovering some motive for murder. Find a motive, went an old homicide rule of thumb, and you find the killer.

"Naturally, his close friends and relatives are all stunned and can't believe that this would happen," exclaimed a Red Eagle kinsman. "He has no enemies that we know of. Everyone just thought the world of him."

"Victor Louis was what I would consider to be a prominent member of the Osage community," said a Bureau of Indian Affairs official in Osage County. "He was a very giving young man. He contributed generously to functions put on by the Osage. He was a wealthy young man."

Investigators reportedly learned that Victor Red Eagle was an only child who never married, held no formal job, liked travel and the theater, and was "very jealous of his privacy." He lived in Tulsa until two years earlier, when he moved back to the Osage and constructed his estate. The house had gold-plated bathroom fixtures.

"That house that he built was absolutely a mansion," said the BIA official. "I consider it kind of a monument to himself."

Red Eagle's wealth, according to news accounts, derived from a complicated system of mineral rights. When the tribe divided the land into individual allotments, a wily full-blooded chief stipulated that "only the top 18 inches" of land could ever be sold. Members of the Osage tribe continue to own all mineral rights underneath the county. Individual Indians receive payment from oil and gas exploitation based upon "headrights," which cannot be sold, only inherited. One headright is equal to one of 2,229 parcels of interest in all oil and natural gas income.

Red Eagle owned "in excess" of four headrights. In 1981, the quarterly payment for one headright was $10,000. That meant Red Eagle would have received more than $160,000 cash for that year.

"How about money?" detectives asked, still searching for a motive for the Indian's slaying. "Did he keep large amounts of cash around the house?"

No one who knew Red Eagle reportedly believed he would have kept more than $100 cash around the house at any one time. That was hardly enough to motivate a robbery—unless the perpetrators thought he kept more.

As puzzled lawmen pursued their investigation into the victim's background, they soon uncovered a darker side to the dead man's life. According to subsequent testimony and reports, Louie Red Eagle was a homosexual who had fought bouts against alcohol and drugs.

"He, like a lot of Indians and other people, had a problem with alcohol," a relative allegedly told investigators. "But he kept pretty well abreast of it."

It was through his drinking and drugs that the wealthy Osage allegedly became acquainted with some people who attended wild, days-long parties at Red Eagle's rural residence. The parties were also attended by local juveniles who went there for alcohol and marijuana because area law officers had no jurisdiction on Indian land.

Red Eagle's housekeeper explained away the wild parties in her later testimony by calling her former boss a "generous, abused man" of whom other people were always taking advantage.

"He liked to have a good time," she said. "He fed everybody who came out there to his house."

Chief Criminal Deputy Williams conceded as much: "When you're as rich as he was and as willing to part with your money as he was, then people are going to swarm to you."

Calling Red Eagle a "professional victim," Williams recalled several police incidents during which Louie Red Eagle had been a victim of a criminal action. Red Eagle's homosexuality, Williams said, led to one such incident that occurred three or four years earlier.

Police reports record how Red Eagle had hired another presumed homosexual to be his chauffeur; Red Eagle did not have a driver's license. One night, the chauffeur robbed Red Eagle, beat him without mercy, and then ran over the fallen Indian with his own car. Fortunately, Red Eagle survived.

He had not been so fortunate this time.

A number of motives presumedly presented themselves through the investigation into the dead man's background. The possible motives, said Deputy Williams, were a homosexual love triangle; robbery or extortion, a sour drug deal; an alcoholic altercation.

Sleuths could reasonably be certain of only one thing—Red Eagle's assailant was likely someone he knew. The house showed no signs of forced entry. The house was also equipped with elaborate burglar and fire alarm systems. Although the fire alarm had sounded, the burglar alarm had remained mute.

"That means Red Eagle probably let his killer into the house with him," Williams concluded.

Lacking a better place to begin, the Osage deputy and the Tulsa FBI agent focused their energies upon questioning the guests of a party Red Eagle gave at his house just two nights before his death. About 15 to 20 people attended. Red Eagle's housekeeper reportedly stated that drugs and alcohol were plentiful and that Red Eagle hosted it dressed in woman's clothing.

"Did anything else unusual happen the night of the party?" lawmen asked partygoers. "Was there a fight or a quarrel? Anything?"

The general contention seemed to be that, within the limits of the term "wild," Red Eagle's party had been a peaceful affair. Only one minor episode marred it.

Red Eagle's housekeeper allegedly stated that recently her employer had begun responding to community complaints over juveniles attending his parties by barring them from the premises. That led to a brief confrontation between the Osage homeowner and a 17-year-old Hominy Indian youth named Maurice Jerome Barnes III, commonly called "Trey" because of the numerals following his name. Barnes demanded admittance to the festivities, but Red Eagle turned him away.

"Trey was drunk," a witness reportedly told officers. "He argued with Louie, but Louie made him leave. They didn't get violent about it or anything. They just argued and Trey left."

According to Deputy Williams, Trey Barnes had built up an unsavory reputation with local police. "He was really wild and capable of doing anything," Williams said. Just a few weeks earlier, local lawmen purportedly captured the Hominy youth on a stolen motorcycle following a hair-raising high-speed chase. Crime reports also listed him as a suspect in a number of area burglaries.

Still, being turned away from a party seemed a poor reason to plot murder.

Police routinely interrogated Trey Barnes along with Red Eagle's other friends and acquaintances. Deputies recalled that Barnes, like the others, readily supplied an alibi for the night of the slaying. Supposedly, he had been in the company of other friends that night. These friends would vouch for him.

Detectives moved on down their list. A second name floated to the top. That led the sleuths to an Osage man named Prentice Crawford, 21. Subsequent testimony exposed Crawford, a 300-pound effeminate-looking individual, as a homosexual who'd had a love affair with Red Eagle. Red Eagle had recently terminated the liaison, according to testimony, partly because he had caught Crawford stealing money from him.

Confronted with these allegations, Crawford allegedly denied them vehemently and also provided an alibi for the night of the crime.

That, for the time being, again left police stymied. They continued down their list, questioning everyone who might have had any contact with the deceased, however casual.

It was also during this early stage of the investigation that detectives scented out what might constitute yet another possible motive for murder. Only this one proved so bizarre that the astonished lawmen were at first reluctant to place any credence in it. Rumors — and, later, testimony and official statements — paired Trey Barnes and Prentice Crawford in an outlandish episode involving Satanism and a Satanic curse.

According to statements and court records, Prentice Crawford believed he was the son of the Devil and that his mother had sold him to Satan before he was born. Allegedly, he had once sacrificed a cat and spoke of his desire to sacrifice a human being. As the Devil's own son, he reportedly believed that he had the power to place curses on his enemies. Witnesses said he tried out this power by obtaining a lock of Trey Barnes' hair and placing a Satanic curse on his friend after the two young Indians had quarreled.

Even more significantly, a young woman friend

of the two Indians reportedly told authorities that, "Prentice believed Louie Red Eagle was an evil man because of the way he lived."

She paused when she took the witness stand. Then she concluded, "The Devil lives in Hominy . . ."

"Red Eagle was *not* sacrificed to Satan!" a deputy declared with fervor. Other skeptics throughout the county likewise dismissed the idea as absurd.

Officers continued to check out stories and alibis; they felt that the Osage's death somehow stemmed from his last party at the mansion. Deputy Williams said he soon learned that Trey Barnes had boldly lied in order to provide himself an alibi. That cast fresh suspicion upon the slender Indian teenager.

"We found witnesses who saw him at places other than where he said he was the night of the murder," Williams said. "He was seventeen and still a juvenile, so I set up an appointment for him and his (nearest relative) to meet me at the police station in Hominy."

The small police station sits next to the fire station and is built into a storefront structure. Williams recalled that Barnes arrived "acting like Charles Manson." Inside the small back room at the stationhouse, the Indian youth allegedly stared at the opposite wall and dispassionately answered questions by mumbling out of the corner of his mouth.

At first, Williams said, Barnes repeated his alibi. But then, confronted with discrepancies, he surprised the case-hardened deputy by suddenly and unexpectedly admitting that he had been present when Victor Red Eagle was strangled to death. But, he said, he was not the killer.

The killer was Prentice Crawford.

"Why?" the deputy asked. "Why was he killed?"

Much later, the veteran deputy shook his head and said, "I still don't understand why Red Eagle was killed. There just didn't seem to be a motive. Barnes talked about contributing factors of why he went along with Crawford—such as robbery, such as Barnes being mad at Red Eagle for not letting him into the party, such as Crawford threatening to snitch to the police on Barnes for a burglary they'd committed if Barnes didn't help him kill Red Eagle, such as Red Eagle threatening to break off homosexual relations with Crawford. But there just didn't seem to be any one sound reason for the homicide."

Unless that one sound reason was Satanism.

The plot to murder Red Eagle began, Trey Barnes would later swear in a court of law, because of the Satanic curse Crawford laid on his friend several weeks earlier. Barnes stated that Crawford insisted the only way to rid Barnes of the spell was to have a human sacrifice—"and the sacrifice was going to be Louie Red Eagle."

Barnes continued his statement to the court by saying that Crawford believed he had been visited by a shepherd who was Satan, his father. "(Prentice) told me I should pray to his father for power and strength."

Thus set on their course of destruction in the name of Satan, the two young Indians apparently met at a Hominy drive-in restaurant on the night of October 27th. Barnes testified he got into a blue Ford with Prentice Crawford. They motored to the nearby farm where Crawford lived with his family. It was just two miles away across the fields from Red Eagle's mansion. They left the Ford at Crawford's farm and walked across the fields to Red Eagle's. It was shortly after midnight when they arrived. Red Eagle was alone at home. His nocturnal visitors explained that they were having car trouble and needed to use a telephone. Knowing the pair and unaware of the plot being hatched against him, Louie Red Eagle let his tribesmen come inside.

"Was the plan to kill him?" Deputy Williams asked Trey Barnes.

"Yeah. We were going to throw him down the stairs to make it look like an accident."

Instead, Barnes was to testify, Crawford picked up a green wine bottle left from Red Eagle's previous party. While Trey Barnes and Red Eagle were talking in the kitchen, Crawford sneaked up behind their unsuspecting host. Suddenly, he swung the bottle in a vicious arc that caught the wealthy Osage on the back of his head and brought him to his knees. Crawford swung the bottle again. Red Eagle dropped to the kitchen floor with a muffled cry of pain and surprise.

Crawford snatched the half-conscious man around the throat and began choking him. Red Eagle begged his former friend not to kill him.

"He said he'd give each one of us fifty dollars if we'd leave him alone," Barnes said in this paraphrased excerpt from his confession.

It took the millionaire 15 minutes to die. Barnes testified that he dashed to the kitchen and returned with a plastic bag, which Crawford pulled down over Red Eagle's head to aid the strangulation. As Red Eagle gasped his final breaths, Prentice Crawford threw back his head and shouted, "This is my gift to you, Father!"

"Then," testified Barnes, "he (Crawford) told Louie that he loved him and that it was going to be okay. Then he said, 'Goodbye.' "

Victor Louis Red Eagle lay dead on the floor.

Barnes then described how, in an effort to cover up the crime, the killers dragged the fresh corpse from the kitchen into the living room where they dumped it on the loveseat. Afterward, they poured lamp oil on the body and at various locations about the house and set the mansion afire.

"I guess you know the rest of it," Barnes reportedly concluded.

Barnes' confession lent a certain urgency to the homicide probe. Hominy is a small community. It wouldn't be long before word about these developments got around. Delivering Barnes to the mental ward of nearby Central State Hospital for safekeeping, Investigator Williams moved quickly in an effort to obtain and preserve vital evidence. Procuring a search warrant, he led fellow deputies in a surprise raid on Prentice Crawford's farmhouse.

Apparently, however, the raid wasn't that much of a surprise. The bloody clothing which Barnes claimed he and Crawford hid inside hollow stone pillars framing the Crawford driveway was now gone. In fact, Williams said, the police raiders uncovered nothing that would even remotely link Crawford to the murder, other than some magazines and drawings indicating that the accused killer might have been associating with Satan worshippers.

Deputy Larry Sharp described one of the drawings by Crawford as "a human being, but it didn't have the face of a human being. It had wings."

Prentice Crawford purportedly denied any complicity in the Red Eagle slaying.

"He has obtained a lawyer," said Deputy Larry Sharp, "and isn't saying anything right now."

Trey Barnes' apprehension and the authorized raid on Prentice Crawford's residence ended Osage County lawmen's involvement in the Red Eagle investigation. Williams turned all evidence and control of the probe to FBI Agent Zeigler. During the weeks that followed, the feds canvassed across Osage County attempting to dig up further evidence to corroborate Barnes' accusations against Crawford. While the inquiry pulled in loose ends, Trey Barnes turned 18 still in police custody. He would be certified as an adult to stand trial. Prentice Crawford remained free; no formal charges had been lodged against him.

The stalemate finally ended on Wednesday, February 3, 1988, more than three months after the night of the Red Eagle murder, when a federal grand jury indicted Prentice Crawford and Maurice Jerome Barnes III for first-degree murder. Almost immediately, Barnes agreed to turn state's evidence against Crawford in exchange for his being permitted to plead guilty to a reduced charge of second-degree murder—and a reduced sentence. Conviction of first-degree murder carries the death penalty. Crawford, on the other hand, was not to break his silence about the matter until May, when he finally took the witness stand.

Prentice Crawford's trial for his life began on May 28, 1988 with Federal Prosecutor Ben Baker describing the defendant's life as having been side-tracked by the "barbaric reality" of teenage alcohol and drug abuse.

"For Prentice," he said, "the alcohol and drugs mixed with some strange mixture of Satanism or spiritualism (became) a one-way road to murder."

Hushed jurors clung to their seats in shock as Prosecutor Baker drew from his star witness, Trey Barnes, the startling story of Satanism in Indian country and how that led to the brutal slaying of Louis Red Eagle.

When the defense took over, Prentice Crawford mounted the stand in his own behalf and broke his silence.

"What Trey said was an outright lie . . ." he asserted. "I did not kill Louis Red Eagle. Trey Barnes killed Louis Red Eagle."

If Trey Barnes failed to draw a clear picture of why Red Eagle was killed, Prentice Crawford was even more vague about a motive. In his testimony he hinted only that Barnes wanted to avenge himself against the wealthy Osage because of his having been barred from the party. He also testified that Barnes feared Red Eagle's homosexual behavior. He said that Red Eagle showed Barnes newspaper clippings and photographs of high school athletes with whom Red Eagle claimed he'd had gay affairs.

"Louie was telling us he had been to bed with this one, that he had been to bed with that one. Then he told Trey he was going to bed with him next."

Barnes, Crawford said, became very angry and tore up the pictures.

Crawford claimed that Barnes and he went to Red Eagle's prairie mansion the night of Red Eagle's death merely to get drunk. "No one said anything about murdering Louie."

Crawford insisted he was not in the kitchen when Barnes struck Red Eagle with a wine bottle. He said he fled from the house while Barnes was strangling the hapless victim. He ran from the house and collapsed in the yard because his legs "felt like rubber and wouldn't work . . . The last I saw of Louie alive, Trey was standing on his throat . . . I heard a gurgling noise."

While running out of the house, Crawford said, he slipped in Red Eagle's blood and fell. That was why he had blood on his clothing.

Crawford testified that he was still huddled terrified in the yard when Barnes came swaggering out of the house carrying $70. "The cheap bastard didn't even have a hundred dollars!" Barnes purportedly sneered, in obvious reference to Red Eagle's cash offer to ransom his own life.

While Prentice Crawford denied involvement in the Osage's death, he did testify that he helped Barnes burn the house to cover up the crime, that he and his (relative) burned the bloody incriminating clothing the two accused killers first hid in the hollow driveway pillars at Crawford's house, and that they likewise concealed all details of the crime from investigating authorities. Those acts constituted separate serious crimes on their own. Crawford, in effect, confessed to them while attempting to avoid complicity in the murder itself.

In his closing argument to the jury, Prosecutor Ben Baker scoffed at the defendant's testimony.

"Can you imagine standing on someone's throat, balancing on one foot, to strangle someone?" he asked. "Red Eagle died with a 300-pound Indian (Crawford) on his back with his hands around his neck . . . It would be tragic to punish Barnes, then send Prentice free to go back to Hominy where he believes he is the son of Satan, and believes he has the power to call for a sacrifice and carry out the sacrifice himself."

Satanism as the motive for the Osage slaying must have been a hard one for the Tulsa federal jury to swallow. On Friday, June 3, 1988, Prentice Crawford was acquitted of the charge of first-degree murder. Shortly afterwards, however, a second federal grand jury indicted him for first-degree arson, accessory to a murder after the fact, and withholding knowledge of a felony. If convicted, Crawford could be facing up to 48 years in a federal prison.

In the meantime, Maurice Jerome "Trey" Barnes III pleaded guilty to second-degree murder and, on September 1, 1988 received a sentence of 12 years in a federal penitentiary. Prentice Crawford awaits trial, and until and unless he does stand trial before a jury of his peers, he must be considered innocent of all accusations against him.

Locally, although the murder of Victor Louis Red Eagle was solved, it still takes its place as one of the "Osage County Mystery Murders" because of the allegations of Satanism that surround it. Exactly why Red Eagle was killed remains a part of the enigma. Cowhands, Indians, and others in the largest county in the state of Oklahoma still look at each other sometimes in the night and wonder aloud if Red Eagle really was an offering to Satan.

"MURDERED AT THE FOOT OF
A VOODOO ALTAR!"

by Richard Shrout

It was no big secret in the Miami Beach neighborhood that Miguel Perez sold drugs. The Miami Beach Police SIU (Street Unit Investigations) group, which investigates organized crimes and narcotics, already knew about him.

Even when they know something illegal is going on, it isn't too often that honest citizens want to get involved. So when Felipe Beltran called and said he wanted to help the police make a drug bust, Detective Lauri Wonder, who spoke Spanish, went to see him.

"Felipe Beltran called about somebody dealing narcotics in an apartment building he managed," recalled Detective Wonder. "He said, 'Look, my apartment is right across the way, directly across. If you look through this peephole' — now he's telling me how to do a drug transaction — 'if your guy stands here in my apartment, we'll have cameras and everything, and he can make a buy from

317

Miguel Perez.

" 'I'll let you use my apartment, but I don't want to be involved, you know. But I want to be around when your undercover cops can go and bust him, once you get the signal,' Beltran said.

"I didn't need him," said Detective Lauri Wonder. "I didn't need him at all. Everybody knows Miguel Perez. I mean I'm out on the streets. You know who you can buy from. I bought cocaine from Miguel Perez a long time ago. He's been arrested before.

"In comparison to kilos, he's a small-time dealer in grams or ounces. But he could supply more if you wanted it. That was our intention. He had a separate apartment from the one he lived in, where he dealt drugs. A lady would come with a baby carriage there. That's supposedly how the drugs came in."

Conducting a drug sting on a small potato like Miguel Perez was pretty low on the priorities of the Miami Beach Police Department. Felipe Beltran got very angry with them when they didn't act immediately on his generous offer.

At 11:30 on the night of June 10, 1985, a lady in the apartment building heard shouting, followed by a series of gunshots and the sound of someone running. She called the police and then hid under her bed until they arrived.

Officer Hector Trujillo was patrolling the zone from 41st Street to Government Cut, a place on

South Beach where the luxury cruise liners headed out to the Atlantic Ocean. He arrived at the address on Pennsylvania Avenue at 11:34 p.m. Other units arrived simultaneously.

The door to Miguel Perez's apartment was ajar. The officers entered cautiously with guns in their hands. They saw a bullet-riddled body of a man on the floor. They checked the other rooms to make certain that no one else was there. Then they notified the department's Persons Unit, which among other crimes, handles homicide investigations on Miami Beach.

Several sergeants arrived with a team of investigators. Detective John Murphy was appointed the lead investigator, to be assisted by Detective Robert Hanlon. They sent several members of the team to begin canvassing the building's occupants while they examined the crime scene.

In the bedroom and kitchen area were tables with vases of flowers and arrangements of religious figurines, which the detectives recognized as Santeria altars. Santeria is a mixture of African deities and Catholic saints, a religion akin to Voodoo that is popular in Cuba and the Caribbean islands, as well as in the Miami area. It imposes no ethical or moral restrictions on its members, but teaches a system of rituals and offerings to bring good luck and ward off bad luck. It is not uncommon for criminals to practice Santeria, hoping to prosper in their illegal deals and keep police and enemies away.

It obviously hadn't done Miguel Perez any good that night. But the significant thing was that none of the figures of saints had been knocked over or disarranged. Underneath one was some folded money, placed as an offering to the deity it represented. No dresser or desk drawers had been pulled out. There was no evidence that the place had been searched. Nothing in the apartment seemed disturbed.

Except for the body, which lay in a pool of blood, with one arm thrown out, leaving a red swipe mark on the floor, it was a tranquil scene.

However, Detectives Murphy and Hanlon noted that on a table were a brown bag containing packets of marijuana and cellophane packets of a white substance suspected to be cocaine, neatly packaged and ready for sale. But the drugs were just there, still undisturbed.

A large wad of money — $491 to be exact — protruded from the victim's pocket, just to add to the mystery.

"At that point," recalled Detective Murphy, "we had a little problem. We couldn't immediately see why the victim had been killed. The narcotics were there, the man had a large amount of money in his left pocket which was totally visible, plus the jewelry he had still on his person. The apartment wasn't ransacked."

We thought it must be a revenge-type thing,"

agreed Hanlon, "due to the fact the money was there, the narcotics were there, and nothing was taken from the apartment."

It did not look like a drug "sting," but like a "hit," pure and simple. Crime-scene technicians from the Metro Dade County Police Department arrived and began a methodical search of the premises and the victim's accumulated papers, such as bills and receipts.

Technician Tommy Stoker summarized their findings: "There was a note in Spanish tacked to the front door. It read: 'I'll be right back.' There were six nine-millimeter casings and some spent projectiles on the floor. There were bullet holes in a window, bullet holes in the doors, bullet holes in the walls.

"From what I could determine, it appeared that whoever was doing the shooting probably stood just inside the front door.

"The next day we went back to examine the outside. In the alley, we noted blood on the electrical circuit box on the west wall of the building. There was also a cigarette pack with blood on the cellophane."

Dr. Valerie Rao, a Dade County assistant medical examiner, arrived at 2:30 a.m. to examine the corpse before removing it for autopsy. She announced that there was "scant rigor and minimum posterior livor." When asked what that meant, she smiled and answered, "It means that he's recently dead."

It was the only thing they didn't need a theory to explain. Miguel Perez had bullet holes in the center of his chest, on the right nipple, on the right forearm above the elbow, on the lower left back, on the back of the right shoulder, on the back of the right knee, and on the front of the leg on the shin.

But the cursory examination of the body revealed some additional mystery: the victim had a sutured area on the scalp from very recent medical treatment. There were also unexplained bruises and abrasions on his knees.

The body was removed. It was now the morning of June 11th. Detectives Murphy and Hanlon started investigating the background of Miguel Perez.

"We contacted our investigation units and also the Drug Enforcement Agency, Immigration, and more Federal authorities," recalled Murphy, "to see whether we had a big-time drug dealer or just a street-level guy."

They found that Perez had a previous arrest record. His probation had expired on March 7, 1984. His life had expired one year, three months, and three days later. From the Dade County Occupational License Division, they learned that Perez had a license as a "peddler." It didn't specify what it was that he peddled.

The interviews of the building's occupants

hadn't revealed anything. Many spoke only Spanish, and all were frightened. Later on the 11th, a detective saw a man nervously loitering in the alley behind the apartment. He said he'd just learned of the crime and thought a relative of his had been shot. He was asked to come to the police station later, where he could be interviewed by a Spanish-speaking officer.

The victim's relative, Phillip Ruiz, was questioned in Spanish by Detective Bob Davis. He related that Miguel Perez had been beaten and robbed on June 9th, the day before the murder. He said he believed that two men, who lived four or five blocks away, were responsible for the assault. His reason was that they were constantly in the area, and he had seen them around the apartment prior to the incident. Miguel Perez had even described the attackers to him.

Detective Charles Metscher showed Phillip Ruiz over 150 photographs of known and suspected criminals, on the slim chance that one might resemble the victim's description of those who assaulted him. Finally, Phillip Ruiz tentatively identified a picture. The name on the back said the man's name was Jesus Fernandez. It was a secondhand identification, based on the victim's verbal report, and although they would try to check it out, the lawmen didn't have too much confidence in it.

A check of nearby hospitals and clinics revealed that Miguel Perez had been treated at Mount Sinai Hospital on the 9th of June for a severe scalp laceration. That explained the fresh stitches on his head and the abrasions on his knees, at least. It also probably accounted for the blood found on the electrical box and cigarette wrapper in the alley.

It might not be too unusual that a drug dealer got mugged. The question was, did the beating and robbery relate to the murder? If not, there would be little to gain by finding Jesus Fernandez, the man whose mugshot was picked out of over a hundred others by someone who had previously seen the man, but hadn't witnessed the attack.

The victim's relationship with others who lived in his building had not yet been determined. At 6:30 p.m. on June 12th, Detectives Murphy and Hanlon located the manager of the building where the shooting had occurred. He explained he had just taken over the job and claimed he didn't know the occupants very well.

He advised the sleuths that the previous manager, who had lived in an upstairs apartment, had disappeared several days before the crime. There were rumors that he dealt in drugs, he said. He claimed he didn't know the man's name.

The neighborhood consisted of once-decent hotels, whose ancient rooms had long since been converted into small efficiency apartments, rented by the "season," month, or week. Some of the renters were old people on Social Security, welfare families, and outright transients who lived one place this week and another place the next.

Even in crowded urban areas where few people know anything for sure about their neighbors and usually care less, there is always someone who tends to be snoopy out of sheer boredom, or is at least normally curious when something out of the ordinary happens. The trick is to find that person.

The sleuths decided to check out residents in adjacent apartment buildings to see if anyone could provide relevant information. They got very lucky.

A man whose apartment overlooked the alley to the building of the crime scene hadn't been interviewed by officers yet, and he had plenty to tell.

Detective Murphy summarized the information: "He looked out his window the night of the homicide and saw a car about midway in the alley facing north. It appeared to have someone in the driver's seat. He left his room and went to the balcony area, and by the time he go there, the car was now close to the back door of the victim's apartment building.

"While he looked out there, he heard six or seven gunshots. He noticed an individual come from the building, get in the car, and then the car proceeded north in the alley. The car turned left on Tenth Street and went west.

"He gave a description of the car as being a dark vehicle, like a Camaro or Firebird. It appeared to him there might have been some kind of emblem on the hood of the car. He gave a description of clothing. He told detectives what the driver and passenger were wearing.

"After we spoke to him, we went back to the scene and, using our unit, posed our car in the area the best we could to his satisfaction and took photographs of it."

They had the witness look at the same police pictures Phillip Ruiz had looked at earlier. "He finally identified somebody who closely resembled Jesus Fernandez, but there was no positive identification of anybody," said Detective Murphy.

Dr. Valerie Rao reported on the autopsy findings. She said Perez had been shot five times, clarifying the initial impression caused by some clean through-and-through exit wounds. Some of the exit wounds were "shored" in appearance, which meant the body was against something like a wall or the floor, which made it difficult for those bullets to come out. None of the wounds were from close range.

The victim had a tattoo of a cross on his shoulder, with four dots on either side of the cross. There was also a tattoo of Saint Barbara, a

Santeria deity.

The toxicology report revealed the presence of Benzoylecgonine, a metabolite of cocaine, in his urine. But the medical examiner cautioned that studies show it is possible to have such metabolities in the urine up to 19 hours after ingesting cocaine, so that was not particularly significant.

Other lab reports came in. Swabs taken of the victim's hands did not show that he had fired a gun recently. That would eliminate any future suspect's claim that he was killed in self-defense. The surfaces at the crime scene had not been conducive to finding fingerprints, and even the 18 latents lifted from the outside of the front door proved useless for comparison purposes.

In the days that followed, the homicide office got numerous frantic calls from Phillip Ruiz, who always reported that he had just seen the suspects in the area, but the detectives could never reach the area in time to apprehend them.

Through patient digging, the lawmen learned that the victim told people he was a jewelry salesman, but they found no verification of that.

On June 17th, the sleuths traced receipts found in the victim's effects to a car-rental agency. They ascertained that Miguel Perez rented cars by the week, a different one each month, which wasn't a very economical way to rent cars. He clearly didn't support his odd lifestyle by peddling nonexistent jewelry.

Through an electric bill and a reference to a food-stamp office found in the dead man's apartment, the sleuths were finally able to locate the victim's estranged wife on July 1st. Through a translator, she told them that she and her husband had a fight and there was an arrest order on him for beating her up. She admitted there were two apartments, one in his name and one in hers. She claimed she knew nothing about any drug-dealing.

She mentioned that her husband was petrified with fear of someone named Ocana because of bad blood between them from Cuba. She said she'd heard Ocana was in New York or New Jersey—she didn't remember which. The last time she saw Miguel Perez was one week before his death.

By July 9th, the detectives decided to interview everyone all over again. They began with Phillip Ruiz, the victim's relative. He seemed terrified. He explained that his relation with Miguel Perez had been a strained one, because Pererz hadn't approved of his lifestyle. Philip Ruiz then admitted he was a homosexual.

That didn't explain his terror. The lawmen suspected he was afraid for his life. Ruiz told them he had located a woman and her boyfriend for them to talk to. He urged them to contact the couple.

They began looking for the pair, but before

they could be located, on July 13th, the woman was brought to them by Miami Beach Patrolman Armando Torres. The officer had handled a complaint for her previously on some matter, and she hailed him in the street. She asked Torres: "Who gets put in jail—the people who killed him, or the person that tells them to go out and kill him?"

She had information abut the murder of Miguel Perez, but for fear of reprisal, she wanted to be sure everyone responsible got arrested.

As soon as the officer knew it pertained to a homicide, he brought her to the station. He told her if there was enough evidence against a person, he would certainly be arrested. She decided to take the gamble. Detectives Murphy and Hanlon were off duty, but they arrived at 8:30 p.m. to question her.

"She was very nervous," recalled Murphy, "and there were certain things we wanted to hit on to make sure she actually knew what was going on, without giving her leading questions. It worked out fine."

Miami Beach detectives tape-record all interviews. Her story centered on a man nicknamed "El Chino," who was a boyfriend of a girl she knew. She related that a few days before the murder, she was at the home of El Chino. She heard him complain that he didn't want to pay Miguel Perez a debt he owed. El Chino mentioned that he'd told a man named Ocana and one nick-named "Jabao" to "take care of his problem with Perez." He'd told them they could split 50-50 any money and drugs they found.

At approximately 10:00 a.m. on the day of the murder, she related, Ocana came to her apartment while Jabao waited in the car. Ocana stated, "El Chino's problem is solved." He told her that the had severely beaten Perez, taken his gold chains, and left him for dead. Then Ocana left.

That night at about 11:15, Ocana and Jabao returned to her apartment. Ocana wanted her and her boyfriend to accompany him to El Chino's home to get a chain and a gun. He stated he'd learned that Miguel Perez was still alive and now he was going to kill him because he'd rather kill than be killed.

When they left her apartment, they drove in a black two-door Camaro. Ocana said he had just stolen it for the night's escapade because his own car was too well-known in the area.

At El Chino's house, her boyfriend was handed a gold chain to give to Ocana, who was waiting in the car. She told the officers she recognized that the chain belonged to Miguel Perez. She and her boyfriend returned with Ocana and Jabao to her apartment. Before she and the boyfriend exited the car, Ocana showed her a .38-caliber revolver and Jabao displayed a black semi-automatic pistol.

She then related to Detectives Murphy and Hanlon that at about 2:30 p.m. the following day, June 11th, El Chino came to her apartment. He told her Jabao and Ocana had killed Perez and solved his problem. "Now I don't have to pay him the money," El Chino gloated. "These people are leaving. But I can't be seen with them, so nobody will think I'm the one who sent them to kill him."

In a separate interview with the woman's boyfriend, Murphy and Hanlon were able to elicit another bit of information. He said that on June 10th at about 11:15 p.m., while they were in Ocana's stolen black Camaro, they pulled into a gas station. Ocana joked that he was going to fill his tank with gas and then fill up Miguel Perez with bullets.

Okay, the detectives wanted to know, do you know the real names of El Chino, Ocana, and Jabao? Sure, the pair said, they're Rolando Ocana and Jesus Fernandez. She showed them a picture of El Chino and said that was Felipe Beltran, the former manager of the victim's apartment building!

From prior arrest records for burglaries, the lawmen got mugshots of Fernandez and Ocana, which the pair quickly identified. The woman provided them with the name and address of Fernandez's girlfriend, who lived in Hialeah. The pair also provided Beltran's new address, where they said he had moved 72 hours before the murder.

Late on July 16th, the sleuths located Fernandez's girlfriend. She told them that Jesus Fernandez was in jail in New Jersey on a robbery charge. On July 17th, the detectives took her formal statement at headquarters.

"At first," recalled Detective Murphy, "she'd tell us bits and pieces, but wouldn't tell us the whole truth. She eventually disclosed to us that Ocana and Fernandez came to her place in Hialeah and took her for a long ride.

"They stopped for dinner and after that drove her someplace and put her out of the car. Fernandez pointed a gun at her and told her that he filled Miguel Perez with holes. He even said he shot him six times and had three bullets left.

"Then they left her someplace on U.S. 27 after ditching some guns and a sawed-off shotgun. They drove off and she had to hitchhike back home."

At 4:00 a.m., the detectives took her to the area off Okeechobee Road where she thought the guns had been discarded. They searched but couldn't find them.

On July 18th, they took the results of their investigation to the state attorney's office and obtained warrants for the arrest of Felipe Beltran, Jesus Fernandez, and Rolando Ocana on first-degree murder and conspiracy charges. They notified New Jersey authorities about the warrants for Fernandez and Ocana.

"We went to where Mr. Beltran supposedly lived," recalled Detective Murphy. "We found him at 5:30 p.m. in the alley one block away." Murphy approached him from one end, and detectives Hanlon and John Quiros came from the other direction and trapped the frightened suspect between them.

"We're police officers," Quiros shouted. "Relax. You're under arrest!"

Beltran was apprehended without incident. Apparently in his world, it was a relief to find himself trapped by men who were merely cops instead of other drug dealers intent on a vendetta.

The officers presented him a form which stated: "This is to certify, having been informed of my Constitutional Rights not to have a search made of the premises hereinafter mentioned without a search warrant, and of my rights to refuse to consent to this search, hereby authorize the representatives of the Police Department of the City of Miami Beach, Dade County, Florida, to conduct a complete search of my residence."

Beltran denied everything, even that he knew the victim. But he signed the consent form to search his rooms. They found a small quantity of drugs.

"We also found," Detective Murphy later reported, "a roll of clear plastic bags, a green plastic scale, a magnifying glass, plastic spoons, a small pair of pliers, nail clippers, two glass vials, a large plastic bag, a brown gun case, a black speed-loader, some .38 Special ammunition, and a .38-caliber three-inch Rossi revolver."

Phillip Ruiz would later tell them he thought that the gun belonged to Miguel Perez, the victim.

Beltran refused to talk, denying everything. When they showed him the gun, he began to make grudging admissions. He admitted knowing the victim, but said he moved out of the building several weeks prior to the murder. The lawmen had evidence to the contrary: he'd left only three days before.

When asked about the drug paraphernalia, Beltran had an explanation. "He stated," recalled Detective Robert Hanlon, "that Perez was selling drugs and that he wanted to hold some drugs for him, because the police were on to him. He said Perez accused him of informing the police about him. He denied that, of course.

"He said these were drugs Perez had given him, that it was all a mistake, he didn't owe him any money, and he'd heard on the street that Perez had put out a contract on his life for $10,000."

Sometimes the story changed. "We asked about the narcotics paraphernalia, which indicated he was dealing," added Murphy. "He said Detective Wonder gave the stuff to him so he would act as a go-between to get Miguel Perez. That didn't sound feasible to us at all."

When they asked Detective Lauri Wonder about it, she assured them: "He has no permission from me or from my unit to ever hold any drugs, if he was not working as a confidential informant. Even if he was, he would not be in possession of any drugs unless he was to deliver it to somebody.

"He never worked for us as a confidential informant," she emphasized. "It would be stupid for me to give him drugs from our narcotics locker and say it came from Miguel Perez. Then *I* could be put in jail. He wasn't thinking. He got caught in his own lie."

Beltran was jailed. The other two suspects were still at large.

In Newark, New Jersey, a robbery of patrons in a bar on Prospect Avenue had occurred back on June 26th. The perpetrators were described as two Hispanic males. Shortly after the robbery, a suspect was arrested on Bloomfield Avenue. He gave his name as Jesus Santiago.

A little later, a man ran into the police station at Belleville, New Jersey, and reported that a shooting had just occurred a block away, at Wil-

335

liam Street and Washington Avenue. At the scene, officers found a young man in a station wagon. He was bleeding slightly from a head wound. The back window had been shattered by a bullet, and the projectile could be seen lodged in the door post.

The small crowd which had gathered reported that the attacker, an unshaven Hispanic male — 5 feet 6 inches tall, thin build, with brown fuzzy hair, dressed in dark pants, a blue and white shirt, a leather jacket, and a baseball cap — had run east on William Street.

Squad cars immediately set up a perimeter. Two Belleville police officers, Charles Hood and Gregory MacDonald, began searching on foot from the Newark border back toward Belleville.

"There were a few garages with doors open," recalled Officer Hood, "and I went through a couple of them. Then I saw a man crouching behind a tarpaulin-covered pool in a back yard. Another man was in a back yard with a flashlight. I yelled to him, 'Who is that guy?' He said he didn't know.

"As I approached the suspect, he attempted to run through me, to get out of the yard, yelling and cursing at me. I tackled him to the ground and we struggled. Other officers heard the commotion and came to assist me and handcuff the suspect."

Officer MacDonald made a circular sweep of

the area. He noticed the tarp over the pool where the suspect had first been spotted. He lifted it and found a nine-millimeter gun.

"When we got back to the scene of the crime," recalled Hood, "there was a crowd on the corner. Everyone was saying, 'That's the guy who shot our friend.' It was unanimous."

The suspect gave his name as Jesus Jiminez. Unlike the Miami population of which every third person speaks Spanish, none of the Belleville police did. They had a severe communication problem with the suspect.

But Detective Jose Sanchez of the Newark, New Jersey police robbery squad, was born in Puerto Rico and had lived there until he was 18 years old. He spoke fluent Spanish.

"Miami Beach Detective John Murphy called me on July eighteenth," Sanchez recalled, "and through information received, he believed the people that I was working on the investigation of a robbery were involved in a homicide case in Florid. He supplied me with information as to what their real names were. He mentioned Rolando Ocana and Jesus Fernandez. He told me he was going to send me fingerprints and photographs on the late flight going to Newark."

Sanchez went to the Essex County Jail to interview "Jesus Jiminez," whom he now knew to be Jesus Fernandez, and "Jesus Santiago," who was really Rolando Ocana.

"I identified myself to Fernandez said Detective Sanchez, "and told him I was there to interview him about a robbery in Newark and certain other things I thought we had to talk about, like who he was and how he got to Newark, and everything else.

"He told me that he met this other fellow, Rolando Ocana, in Miami. He knew him for a couple of months and something happened there and they had to leave.

"I asked him to be specific about what happened. He told me he was on Miami Beach and Rolando Ocana came over and said, 'Let's go over to a house on the Beach. I got to do something, and then I am finished.' So he got in the car, which was a dark Camaro."

Fernandez told Detective Sanchez that he came to the U.S in 1980, and usually worked in Las Vegas restaurants. He spoke very rapidly and seemed to get very agitated at times during the conversation.

"At times when we were talking," recalled Sanchez, "he often went quiet. I had to ask the questions several times. He would tell me 'That's enough, I don't want to talk no more.' I'd just sit back and relax and wait until he pulled himself together and started talking to me again.

"He told me he was with Rolando Ocana, driving a dark Camaro to the beach. Ocana told him to wait in the car. He said, 'I was waiting, and suddenly I heard shots. I don't remember how many, but right after that I saw Rolando running back to the car, all nervous. He got in the car and drove off.' "

Fernandez claimed he couldn't identify a picture of Felipe Beltran.

When Sanchez tried to talk with Ocana, he got a different reception. "At that time," said Sanchez, "he wasn't talking to anybody. He chased me out of the cell, cursed me out, and didn't want to talk to me at all. He wanted to know where his lawyer was, and what he was doing there. As it turned out, Ocana wouldn't even talk to his New Jersey lawyer."

Miami Beach Detective Robert Hanlon flew to New Jersey. He got the authorities to test-fire the gun Fernandez had hidden under the tarpaulin just before he was apprehended. He took the projectiles back to Miami, where firearms experts determined that they were from the weapon that killed Miguel Perez.

The suspects were brought to Dade County, Florida, for trial. Fernandez's girlfriend said that he told her he shot Miguel Perez six times and had three bullets left. The prosecutor pointed out that the gun he had with him at the time of his arrest in New Jersey fired nine shots. Fernandez maintained that Ocana was the shooter. The suspects were tried separately and each was found guilty.

Jesus Fernandez and Rolando Ocana received life sentences. Felipe Beltran was sentenced to 10 years in prison.

On July 24th, Phillip Ruiz had returned to the Miami Beach police headquarters with information he said he had been afraid to give earlier. He said Miguel Perez had told him on the day he'd been assaulted that Beltran was going to kill him. He also said he'd seen Beltran wearing Miguel's medallion on July 4th.

He stated that Beltran had even approached him after the murder and said, "Listen, the problem is not with you, it was with Miguel." He also finally reluctantly admitted that his relative, the victim, had indeed been a drug dealer.

"Then Phillip Ruiz broke down crying," recalled Detective Murphy. "The reason he gave us was that he was afraid to tell us earlier about Perez dealing in drugs because he was afraid we wouldn't work on the case as hard if we knew he was a drug dealer.

"We told him we work each case the way it should be worked. They all get the same treatment."

"LOVING A NYMPHO DEVIL-WORSHIPER CAN BE FATAL!"

by John Dunning

It was a little after 12 noon of Monday, May 31, 1982 and the sun shown brightly on the city of Duesseldorf, West Germany. One of the most chic and expensive cities in the entire country, Duesseldorf, with a population of over 700,000 persons, is located on the Rhine River just to the south of the West Germany capital of Bonn. It is this location which makes it chic and expensive, for Bonn is not a city with very much to offer the hordes of politicians, bureaucrats and diplomats who find such a rich course of sustenance there where the contributions of the German taxpayers pour in a mighty stream into the national treasury. Duesseldorf offers everything that Bonn does not — exclusive shops, palatial homes and apartments, top level entertainment and air connections to anywhere in the world. The feeders at the trough of public funds, therefore, draw their money in Bonn, but they spend it in Duesseldorf.

Of course, not everyone in Duesseldorf is a diplomat or public servant. A good many are shopkeepers and still more are guest workers, the modern equivalent of colonialism under which, instead of taking the work to the colonies to be performed by cheap labor, the cheap labor is brought to the home country to perform the work there.

In West Germany, a great many of these cheap laborers are Turks, but the man who was walking down Metzer Street in the Derendorf sector of Duesseldorf on that spring afternoon was not a Turk. He was a 30-year-old Spaniard named Julio Esperanza, and he was using up some of his lunch hour to see why his friend, Jose Luis Mato Fernandez, one year younger than himself, had not come to work.

Julio Esperanza and Jose Luis Mato Fernandez both came from the village of Orense, far to the southwest in Spain and nearly on the Portuguese border. They had grown up together, they had come to Germany together and they had found work with the same construction company. That had been seven years earlier and now the economic climate had changed. Faced with two million unemployed among their own people, the Germans were rather desperately trying to divest themselves of the cheap labor which they had imported to keep local wages down. Losing your job usually meant being sent home, where there were no jobs, and staying away from work without a good excuse, such as being very sick, could easily result in losing your job. Julio Esperanza was hoping that his friend was good and sick.

He was more than sick. He was dead, and Esperanza realized it the instant that he pushed open the living room door and peered inside. Fernandez, usually known to his friends as Mato, was the tenant of a two room apartment on the second floor of the building at Metzer Street number 6. It was not a good residential district and the apartment was not a good one, but guest workers were supposed to keep themselves busy working and not spend too much time sitting around their apartments, anyway.

Mato Fernandez was sitting on the sofa in the living room of his and it was obvious that the question of losing his job was no longer pertinent. The handsome, dark haired young man sat with his head tipped back against the back of the sofa as if he were sleeping, but he was totally naked and the fingers of his right hand were still hooked over the wooden handle of a knife which had apparently been driven to the hilt in his chest. There was not very much blood around the knife wound itself, but blood had gushed out of the corners of the dead man's mouth and had run over his shoulders, down his arms and had saturated a large patch on the back and seat of the sofa on either side of his body.

Julio Esperanza, who had been born a peasant in Spain and had frequently assisted at the butchering of pigs, took one look at the knife handle and then turned to run out of the apartment. He did not approach the corpse, because he knew that it was just that. If there were any similarities in the anatomies of pigs and human beings, the blade of the knife was planted in Mato's heart.

There are quite a few similarities in the anatomies of pigs and humans, and Julio Esperanza's estimate was entirely correct. Having completed the autopsy of the body, Dr. Friedrich Koppler, the tall, distinguished, white haired and gold-spectacled senior expert in forensic medicine attached to the Criminal Investigations Department of the Duesseldorf police, reported that the murder weapon, an ordinary butcher knife with an eight-inch, single-edged blade, had passed completely through the right chamber of the heart. Before doing so, it had cut through the third rib on the left side and had partly severed the second rib as well. It had been delivered with great force. There were no other injuries on the body or any indications of a struggle. The fingerprints on the handle of the knife were those of Fernandez himself. It was, therefore, tentatively established as an act of suicide. It had taken place at approximately nine o'clock on the morning of Monday, May 31st, with a possibility of error of

20 minutes in either direction.

"If I had to live like this, I'd commit suicide too," said Inspector Karl Bart. He was a tall, muscular, blond man with a clean shaven, squarish face and a neat haircut. The appearance of the apartment horrified him almost as much as the corpse.

At the time that Inspector Bart, chief of Homicide Four at the Department of Criminal Investigations, made this remark, the corpse was still there, sitting on the sofa. The inspector and the man to whom he had addressed the remark, his assistant in charge, Detective Sergeant Max Leinauer, had been brought out by Julio Esperanza's telephone call to the emergency police number. Esperanza was now at police headquarters making a tearful statement about his discovery of the body and the inspector and sergeant were waiting for a report from the detachment of technicians going over the apartment as to whether there was any reason to suspect that this was anything other than the suicide which everyone believed.

As the apartment was an incredible mass of filth and trash; not all of it from Fernandez, but from a whole series of predecessors, it took the technicians most of the rest of the day. Like everyone else, they believed that this was merely suicide of another despondent guest worker. Such things were not uncommon. By the standards of his own country, the guest worker was very well paid, but he paid himself a heavy price in return. At best despised, and at worst hated, by a large segment of the local population, he was isolated by custom, education and language from the society around him and lived in a sort of ghetto composed of his fellow guest workers. The fact that he was sometimes found sexually attracted by the often totally promiscuous young German girls, who had something of the same ideas about sleeping with guest workers as the rich who had gone slumming in the 1920s had had, only made things worse. What the guest worker, almost invariably an unsophisticated peasant, took for a human relationship, turned out to be a purely sexual relationship or, worse yet, merely a desire to be modern and "in."

When such situations arose, it was not uncommon for a guest worker to put an end to his own life, and the indications were that this was what had befallen Jose Luis Mato Fernandez. The apartment was filled with traces of female presence, and it had not been platonic. The sheets of the bed, unchanged for weeks, perhaps, months, were stiff with semen and the lubricating secretions discharged by the human female in a state of sexual excitement. Whatever problems he might have had, Mato Fernandez had obviously had no cause to feel lonely in West Germany.

Nonetheless, despite these clear indications, the

technicians did a very thorough job and took literally thousands of bits of potential evidence off to the police laboratory. The only thing found that was in any way exceptional was a small diary, presumably the property of one of the girls who had stayed in the apartment at one time or another, not, necessarily, during Fernandez' tenancy. The girl had not noted her name anywhere in the book nor had she given an indication of the year, but as there was some duplication of dates, the diary had apparently been kept off and on for several years.

It was not the diary itself, but some of the entries which were of interest. According to these, the young lady was a worshiper of the devil. The first entry was framed by two upside-down crosses and read, "He who reads this book shall be damned for all eternity."

This warning did not discourage the police technicians, who read every word in the book including such comments as, "Lucifer. Lord of Darkness. I would sell you my soul; I would bring with you evil to the world. I wait your sign."

And later, in an entry dated April 30th, but without the year, "Lucifer. Lord of Darkness. Give me a sign. I believe in you. I want to belong to you wholly. Come to me when Mato is sleeping."

Whether this was the Mato who presumably

had stabbed himself through the heart or not could not be determined. Lucifer had, apparently, also not heeded the call, for there was no mention of a visit in any other entry in the diary. There was a great deal about black masses and some extremely graphic descriptions of orgies from which it appeared that the author had been not only bisexual, but a good deal besides.

The diary was not thought to be connected with Fernandez' death, despite the reference to Mato and the only thing that could be determined from it was that the author was a person whose mother tongue was German, but who had been rather sketchily educated. German is a language with a complex and precise grammar and it requires a certain level of education to avoid grammatical errors in composition. The young lady had made quite a number.

In the meantime, the police were engaged in trying to locate the next of kin of the dead man so that the body could be returned to Spain or, failing this, buried in Germany at the family's expense. They did not have much success in this, as Fernandez had either had no relatives or they were unwilling to come forward and accept the expense of his burial.

It was during the course of this search that Inspector Bart had Sergeant Leinauer bring Julio Esperanza, Fernandez' friend who had discovered his body, to his office at police headquarters. As

Esperanza came from the same town in Spain, the inspector thought that he might be able to identify some of the relatives who, up till now, had been dodging their financial responsibility.

Unfortunately, Esperanza did not speak German very well and understood even less. Apparently assuming that the inspector was trying to stick him with the burial expenses, he became very excited, lost what little German he did have and burst into such a flood of Spanish that the inspector was forced to summon an interpreter.

What his remarks actually boiled down to was that it was unusual, illegal and an outrage that the friends of a murder victim be required too bear the expense of his funeral. If Germany was such a dangerous place that even simple construction workers got murdered, then the German government should bear the expense of it. Neither he nor Jose Luis Mato Fernandez had come to Germany to be murdered. They had come to build houses.

"Murdered?" said the inspector, smiling tolerantly. "Your friend was not murdered. His death has been investigated and has been declared officially a suicide."

The interpreter started to interpret, but Esperanza, who had apparently understood what the inspector said, stopped him. "He is not suicide," he said. "What for suicide? He have job, good money, plenty girl. What for suicide?"

349

"Probably because of the 'plenty girl,' " the inspector replied. He had, however, stopped smiling. "Your friend was in love with some German girl, wasn't he?"

Esperanza shook his head vigorously. "He beautiful man. He (using such a vulgar term for the sex act that it made the inspector wince) plenty girl," he said. "German girl like very much. He plenty, plenty. Don't know name even. Every night different. Sometime, girl stay one month, two months. Mato no kill self for (here he used such a savagely pejorative term for German gutter slang for a female that it made the interpreter start and look anxiously at the inspector)."

The inspector did not, however, react to this insulting description of German womanhood; not, necessarily because he found it accurate, but because his professional instincts were setting off alarm bells all over his nervous system. It appeared that the investigation into the death of Jose Luis Mato Fernandez had not been as thorough as could be expected from the Criminal Investigations Department of a large city. He saw now that the motive for Fernandez' supposed suicide had merely been assumed on the basis of the autopsy and on the supposition that no one would have any particular reason for carrying out a concealed murder on a Spanish guest worker. It was not that there were no homicides among the

350

guest workers. There were a great many, but they were nearly always clear cut and represented a fight between guest workers, frequently over a woman, or the act of some local German who objected to guest workers on general principle. The murder of a guest worker where motive and identity of murderer was not almost immediately clear was rare.

Was this one of these cases? After Esperanza had gone, the inspector got out the Fernandez file and sat leafing through it. He had questioned Esperanza at length on his suspicion concerning what he believed to be Fernandez' murder, but all that the Spaniard had been able to provide was negative information. He had no idea who might have wanted to kill Fernandez, actually knew a great deal less about his personal affairs that he had pretended and was only convinced that he had not committed suicide because he had no reason to do so.

After a time, the inspector who had been staring for some minutes at the official photograph of the corpse taken as it had been found, took the picture out of the folder and stood it on the top of the desk, supporting it with his fingers resting on the top edge.

"What does this look like to you?" he called to Sergeant Leinauer.

The sergeant, a tall thin man with a long face and a fringe of blond beard running along the line of his jaw, came over and looked at the photograph carefully. The inspector was not given to asking questions for no reason.

"It looks like a dead Spaniard who has committed suicide by stabbing himself in the heart," said the sergeant finally, raising his eyes from the photograph to look inquiringly at his chief.

"Where's his hand?"

"On the hilt of the knife," said the sergeant. "If you mean the right hand."

"It shouldn't be," said the inspector. "His muscles would have relaxed at the moment of death and his hand would have fallen into his lap."

"Are you certain of that?"

"No," said the inspector. "Call Koppler and ask his opinion on it."

"And if Koppler agrees?" asked the sergeant, reaching for the telephone.

"If Koppler agrees, then somebody clasped Fernandez' hand around the handle of that knife after he was dead," said the inspector flatly.

Dr. Koppler did agree, and expressed himself as highly embarrassed over the matter. "I should have caught that when I made the initial examination of the body at the scene," he said. "An unforgivable oversight, I'm afraid, inspector."

"Everything is forgivable except tax evasion," said the inspector, quoting a remark popular with taxpayers. "The main thing is: You agree now that it was homicide?"

The doctor agreed and the investigation into the murder of Jose Luis Mato Fernandez began immediately.

Fernandez having had nothing worth stealing nor any relatives who had benefited by his death, it could be assumed that his murder had been the result of his contacts with the opposite sex. Although the young German girls who were running around Duesseldorf, democratically spending their nights in the beds of the guest workers, were sexually liberated beyond all belief, their male relatives frequently were not, and sometimes took violent exceptions to their activities. If an outraged father, brother, boyfriend or even husband had murdered the handsome Spaniard, there would be nothing very exceptional about him. All that was necessary was to find out who it had been.

Who it had been would, presumably be a relative or intimate friend of Fernandez' latest conquest and the investigation, therefore, concentrated on identifying the lady in question.

This did not take very long. Although Fernandez had had an almost startling number of interludes on the side, he had been more or less living with 22-year-old Sylvia Brakel since the end of August of 1981.

Although Miss Brakel had regarded the apartment at 6 Metzer Street as her official residence, she had rarely been home. Much of her time had been spent with her 19-year-old friend Susi, who was a self-proclaimed lesbian and who referred to Sylvia as "my wife."

Miss Brakel, it seemed, had not regarded herself as anyone's wife or, at least, she had not believed in monogamy and had been remarkably even-handed in devoting herself to homosexual affairs, heterosexual affairs and group enterprises in which it was difficult to assign specific sexes to all of the participants. A very pretty girl with a round, childish face, thick, blonde hair and brown eyes, Sylvia looked as innocent as a mouse but carried on a sex life which would have exhausted a nymphymaniacal mink.

When she was not engaged in sex and in a great deal of time when she was, Sylvia went in for more serious things such as witchcraft, black magic and worship of the devil. Through a combination of energy and talent she was already famous within the pertinent circles as the star performer in countless black masses which had been celebrated in Duesseldorf. Among the "in" crowd, no black mass was considered to be really first class without Sylvia serving as the altar.

The police did not even have to investigate to find all this out. They already knew it or, at least, it was in the memory of the police computers, for Sylvia Brakel had a criminal record. She had received an 18-month sentence, suspended, on August 18, 1981 for stabbing, not fatally, a 20-year-old baker's apprentice named Christian Kon. She was not entirely clear as to why she had stabbed Mr. Kon, with whom she had been living for the past three years, but having heard some of the circumstances, the court apparently came to the conclusion that Mr. Kon had deserved it, hence the 18-month suspended sentence.

At the time, a complete file had been assembled on Sylvia Brakel and formed one of the unsavory records in the police files.

According to Sylvia, she had been introduced to sex at the age of eight by her grandfather, with whom she had practiced mutual masturbation.

She had quickly extended her field of activity to outside the family so that, when she was 16 years old and subjected to a 24-hour prolonged multiple rape—vaginally, anally and orally—by the nine members of a gang of rockers, she suffered no ill effects other than a feeling of exhaustion.

A few weeks after her encounter with the rocker gang, she was sufficiently recovered that she was caught shoplifting in a department store and sent to an education center for juvenile delinquents. There she was retained, against her will and against the will of the whole administration, for two years until reaching the legal age of 18, whereupon she was released, to the relief and satisfaction of all parties concerned.

Never having learned anything which might be of value to an employer, Sylvia had never had a job nor looked very seriously for one. As a consequence, she never had any money. Had she chosen to sell her sexual services, she could have been rich, but she never did. Whatever else there might be wrong with Sylvia Brakel, she was never a prostitute.

Not long after leaving the reform school, Sylvia had met Christian Kon who was, despite his tender age, already active in Satanist circles in the city. He was, in fact, quite popular at the black masses and general orgies of the devil worshipers; he was so handsome as to be almost pretty and totally bisexual. He and Sylvia had formed a team the combined sexual experience of which would have made the madam of a Central American whorehouse turn crimson with shame. Rarely had sexual liberation achieved such heights.

What precisely had gone wrong in this meaningful relationship between two young, modern people was not made completely clear during the course of the trial, but it could have been a dispute over something to eat. Christian was technically a baker's apprentice, but he did not work very often. Sylvia did not work at all, and as Christian was no more disposed to sell his body than she, they were often very short on cash.

The discovery that Sylvia Brakel had been Jose Luis Mato Fernandez' recent, if not exclusive, companion was of the greatest interest to Inspector Bart, for Sylvia had already stabbed one of her companions previously and it now seemed more than probable that the diary found in Fernandez' apartment in which a certain Mata was mentioned was her property.

Taken into custody, Sylvia admitted that the diary was hers and, as a matter of fact, could scarcely deny it, as the handwriting in it corresponded precisely to her own. She also admitted that she had been living more or less continuously with Fernandez since the time of her trial in 1981. She had not, however, murdered him, she said, and, indeed, had had no reason to do so.

The inspector pointed out that she had not had any very good reasons for stabbing Christian Kon, either, but he was forced to admit that the financial basis that was presumed to be at the root of the Kon stabbing was not present in the case of Fernandez. The Spaniard had been a city worker, had been able to pay the rent on the apartment and had kept the refrigerator stocked with food. It had, as a matter of fact, been well stocked when his body was discovered.

As Sylvia Brakel, despite her denials, appeared to be the best suspect in the case, the inspector ordered the arrest of her friends and a number of her fellow devil worshippers. If Sylvia Brakel had murdered Fernandez, then there was some kind of a motive, and it was possibly known to the others. The inspector wanted to know what it was, and he did not think that the kind of friends that Sylvia Brakel had would accept very much inconvenience in order to protect her. After all, betrayal was one of the devil worshipper's higher virtues.

The devil worshippers were apparently, by their own standards, virtuous, for they practically clamored to accuse their friend and altar of the crime and to provide motives for it.

In this respect, they were, perhaps, a trifle too enthusiastic, as they provided more motives than Sylvia would have been able to remember. One of the witnesses, however, was able to offer something more than suppositions.

Twenty-nine-year-old Detlef Kraft, a truck driver when he was working, told investigators that he knew for a fact that Sylvia had committed the murder, because she had confessed it to him only four hours after it had taken place. The motive, it seemed, had not been tender love or mad passion, but a simple matter of dignity.

Being a lower class Spaniard, Fernandez had been a firm believer in the double standard. Sexual liberation was fine when it meant that practically any teenage girl he encountered would go to bed with him immediately upon simple request and ask nothing in return. Sexual liberation was, however, completely out of the question when it concerned his female relatives or any woman with whom he had a formal relationship. In such cases, the woman's behavior reflected on him personally and his honor was besmirched.

Sylvia, it seemed, had been living with him long enough that he was beginning to look upon her as an official mistress or he had, at least, believed that his fellow guest workers did. He had, therefore, reprimanded her for having sex relations with everyone she met, male or female, and other excesses which he considered not to be in keeping with her position as his consort.

There had been a long and bitter quarrel from around midnight on when Sylvia had come home, and the exhausted Fernandez had eventually fallen asleep on the sofa with the arrival of morning.

Sylvia, who did not believe in the double standard at all, had gone to the kitchen and got the largest butcher knife. Returning to the living room, she had taken a real roundhouse swing and slammed the knife into her companion's chest to the hilt, aiming, as she would later tell the court, for the heart.

She had then left the apartment and gone to visit her friend Susi, who comforted her in the manner which might be expected. She had told

Susi that she regretted killing Fernandez very much, because he had been capable of making love five times a day and such men were rare.

After leaving Susi, she had gone to visit Detlef Kraft, where she had also told the whole story. Detlef was, however, a devil worshipper, so it was only logical that he would betray her.

Susi, who was also a devil worshipper, did not, but her finer sensibilities were, perhaps, involved.

Confronted with Detlef Kraft's statement and formally charged with the murder, Sylvia Brakel admitted rather indifferently that it was true and repeated essentially the same confession that she had made to Kraft. The impression which she made was that she did not care very much what happened to her and, considering what her life had been up until then, this was, perhaps, an understandable attitude.

The court did not show very much understanding, however. After four days of deliberations and testimony, she was found guilty of intentional homicide without extenuating circumstances and on March 25, 1983 sentenced to life imprisonment.

She did not appear to be very upset over the sentence nor did she have any reason to be. A life sentence is only a polite fiction in Germany today, and the actual time served seldom exceeds seven years. Sylvia should be out of prison well before she is 30 years old.

"THE HEINOUS CRIME OF SATAN'S HIGH PRIESTESS OF DEATH!"

by Harry Hildebrand

The story which follows is definitely not for the squeamish. It contains several elements considered reprehensive and loathsome to most who have knowledge of the case that this story details, elements such as religious fanatacism, satanic worship and, perhaps the worst and most serious of all offenses, the coldblooded murder of an innocent, trusting and unsuspecting child.

Because of the bizarre and unusual elements of the case, which include child sexual abuse in addition to murder, this case is likely one of the most, if not the most, shocking and shameless cases ever to come out of Clark County, Washington, perhaps out of the entire Northwest. It is a case that will not soon be forgotten.

Although the death or murder aspect of the case did not occur until Monday, March 19, 1984, the case actually opened the day before, on Sunday, March 18th, when deputies from the Clark

County Sheriff's Department, located in the southwestern Washington community of Vancouver, were sent out to investigate a report of suspicious circumstances involving a young child.

That evening, according to sheriff's department records, deputies were dispatched to the home of Dr. Harold Becker, a local chiropractor, located in the 17800 block of Northeast 29th Avenue, after a concerned person called and asked the department to check on the well-being of a six-year-old girl who was staying at the Becker residence with her mother.

According to sheriff's department records, a male teenager who had been at the Becker home told another family member that he had been told that the six-year-old girl, Gail Vert, referred to by detectives as Little Gail, "was going to die and God was going to take her."

The teenager also reportedly said he had seen the girl's mother and Dr. Becker praying over the little girl. However, the two deputies who responded that Sunday evening to attempt to do a welfare check on the young girl didn't see any unhealthy conditions. There were several adults there, young kids were playing and Little Gail seemed fine. In short, there were no indications that anything was wrong in the household, definitely no signs of foul play.

At approximately 1:00 p.m. the following afternoon, however, paramedics were called to the Becker home via that 9-1-1 emergency dispatch number. When they arrived they discovered Little Gail in the downstairs part of the house, her skin blue in color. She was not breathing, and there was no sign of a heartbeat. Following CPR (cardiopulmonary resuscitation), she was transferred to a local hospital, where she died a short time later. Her death was listed as death from natural causes. No police officer responded to the scene, either at the Becker home or at the hospital, because there was no evidence and no indication of foul play at that time. It was later learned that those present at the Becker home at the time paramedics were called included Dr. Becker, his son, and Little Gail's mother, Gail Ray.

"There was no on-scene investigation due to the fact that the girl's body had been transported," said Clark County Sheriff's Detective Pat St. John, who worked the case with his partner, Detective Tim McVicker and their supervisor, Sergeant Mike Davidson. "The case was handled like so many cases where somebody is found at home not breathing and is rushed off to a hospital. In this case the person rushed to the hospital died."

According to Sergeant Davidson and Detective St. John, the Clark County Coroner, Dr. Archie Hamilton, happened to be at the emergency ward of the hospital at the time Little Gail was brought in by the paramedics. According to Davidson and St. John, Hamilton said that the young girl was treated and examined by her own physician at the hospital. Little Gail was said to have had a history of certain types of medical problems but, other than the fact she died the day after sheriff's deputies were dispatched to check on her welfare, everything seemed basically "on the up-and-up."

It wasn't until the following day that the case began to take some really bizarre turns, such as a telephone call received by Detective McVicker from a woman to be known here as Marcia Miller, not her real name. As it turned out, Ms. Miller told McVicker that she had been at the Becker residence on Sunday, March 18th, the day before Little Gail died, where she had been greeted by the six-year-old.

"She (Marcia Miller) said she was greeted by Little Gail, who was rather boisterous, exuberant and in good physical shape," said Detective St. John, relating the telephone call received by his partner. "Little Gail said to Ms. Miller, 'Guess what! I'm going to go see God. I'm gonna die and go be with my daddy in Heaven. But it's all right, because that's a good place. I'm gonna see God.' "

It was at that point that Marcia Miller became extremely concerned for the well-being of the child. Even with the vivid imaginations that six-year-olds are known for, it seemed highly doubtful that Little Gail would have, or could have, made all that up on her own. Shortly after being greeted by Little Gail, Ms. Miller said she was ushered into a sewing room at the residency by Dr. Becker.

While in the sewing room, Marcia Miller told Detective McVicker, she was told by Dr. Becker that he was going to be the new prophet of the Reorganized Church of the Latter Day Saints and that he and Gail Ray, Little Gail's mother, were going to be the leaders of a Zionic community based in nearby Battle Ground, Washington.

For those not familiar with the beliefs of the doctrine of the Reorganized Church of the Latter Day Saints (RLDS), the formation of the Zionic community is actually based on RLDS scriptures, which teach that Christ will come again to earth. According to the RLDS scriptures, a Zionic community will be built under the direction of Christ at Independence, Missouri. The community will be only for RLDS believers, who proclaim that it will be a community of eternal love and happiness, free of sickness and disease, and will be basically a "Heaven on Earth." However, as can readily be seen from the case at hand, the RLDS doctrine, like any other, is not exempt from zealots and fanatics capable of distorting and perverting the guidelines to satisfy their own inclinations.

Returning to the sewing room scene, where Marcia Miller was being told about a new Zionic community and prophets by Dr. Becker, Gail Ray entered and complained of having chest pains and of generally not feeling well. In what was determined to be a "performance" for the benefit of

Marcia Miller, Dr. Becker then laid his hands upon Gail Ray, professing his healing power. Gail Ray immediately, miraculously, began to feel better. At that point, according to Detective St. John, Dr. Becker and Gail Ray "attempted to determine" if Marcia Miller "had the power," if she could in fact be a chosen one and become a member of the planned Zionic Community in Battle Ground.

Dr. Becker then moved to stand behind Ms. Miller, placed his hands at the side of her head and asked, "Do you feel anything?" "No," replied Ms. Miller, after which Dr. Becker reached down to her neck and began to pinch off her carotid arteries with his fingers. At that point, Ms. Miller said, she began to feel faint, as if she would pass out.

"Don't drain her," said Gail Ray to Dr. Becker.

"Did you feel my power?" asked Becker.

"Yes, I felt the power," replied Marcia Miller, feeling as if she had nearly passed out and knowing full well that "the power" was merely the slowing of her blood flow to her brain because of the pinched-off arteries in her neck but nonetheless playing along with them until she could find an opportune time to excuse herself and leave.

"Let's see if *you* have the power," Becker said to Ms. Miller, and instructed the somewhat confused and frightened woman to place one of her hands on Gail Ray's chest and the other hand on Gail

Ray's back. The room was suddenly very quiet.

"Oh, yes, she has the power," said Gail Ray. "I can feel it. She's going to be a chosen one." At that point Marcia Miller really became scared, and she immediately left the residence, taking with her her young son who had stayed overnight Saturday, with one of the Becker children.

Concerned and frightened about some of the strange and bizarre goings-on at the Becker home, including the fact that this apparently healthy little girl said she was gong to die and see God, prompted Marcia Miller to relate what had occurred at the home to one of her relatives, who in turn spoke with a police officer in Oregon where they lived. The police officer strongly suggested that the strange situation be reported to the Clark County Sheriff's Department as suspicious circumstances. The report, as previously mentioned, was received via telephone on Tuesday, March 20th, the day after Little Gail had died.

Although a well-being check had been conducted prior to Little Gail's death, the telephone call from Marcia Miller on Tuesday was the first indication that possible foul play had occurred in the death of Little Gail Vert. Admittedly, although strange and suspicious, Ms. Miller's story wasn't enough for the detectives to be able to bring charges against anyone connected with the case. Without doubt, further investigation would become necessary.

Background investigation revealed that Gail Ray, Little Gail's mother, first met Dr. Becker in the autumn of 1983 when she went to him as a patient for treatment of back pain.

"During this time," said Sergeant Mike Davidson, "she started revealing her depression to him and the fact that she had been involved in satanic worship." According to Davidson, it was on this basis that Dr. Becker decided to befriend her and soon persuaded her to begin attending his church.

From Becker's point of view as a priest in the RLDS Church, according to detectives, he saw the ideal chance in his lifetime to convert a member of Satan's Church (Gail Ray) over to the RLDS Church. On the other hand, others, particularly members of the RLDS Church, believe that Gail Ray was actually a disciple of Satan sent to seek out people like Dr. Harold Becker, enter into their lives, then utterly destroy them. In any case, Dr. Becker invited Gail Ray and her three children to move into his home in February, 1984 after Ray began experiencing water and/or plumbing problems in her own home in Vancouver. She readily accepted the invitation and moved in almost immediately.

It should be pointed out that although the details surrounding the meeting of Dr. Becker and Gail Ray, as well as their growing relationship, was indeed unusual, even bizarre, they weren't, by themselves, a motive for murder.

In addition to her religious benefits as a Satanic worshipper, detectives revealed that Gail Ray was no stranger to local law enforcement agencies. According to Detective McVicker, Ray had a "history of telling stories" to police, and some law officers felt that she derived a peculiar sense of enjoyment out of contacting the police and telling yarns which didn't always turn out to be the complete truth. At best, anything she reported to police was usually greatly exaggerated, but often commonly outright lies.

When Clark County Coroner Dr. Archie Hamilton performed the autopsy on Little Gail's body, he was initially unable to come up with anything which suggested a criminal death, in spite of the fact that certain things just "did not compute." As a result of his findings, or rather lack of findings, Dr. Hamilton had certain organs of Little Gail's including her heart, sent to the Orthopedic Hospital in Seattle for additional pathological examination.

"But at the same time," said Detective St. John, "the autopsy really didn't come up with anything showing why she should have died in the first place. That's why the coroner sent tissues, including her heart, up to Seattle for some further testing, where a slight amount of infection, called 'viral myocarditis,' was found in the heart tissue." St. John pointed out that the bacterial infection is often a fatal disease of the heart. However, in

Little Gail's case, the infection was very slight, probably not enough to cause death.

In addition to the myocarditis, it was revealed that little Gail also sustained a prolapsed valve in her heart which, St. John pointed out, is not all that uncommon in females. Even with the viral myocarditis and the prolapsed valve, said St. John, the pathologists who examined the tissue felt that neither condition, while very serious, probably had not caused Little Gail's death. Because of the pathologists' findings, results in the case of Little Gail were still inconclusive and detectives still had no physical evidence of foul play.

As a result of the additional testing, the coroner's report initially stated that Little Gail died a natural death as a result of the viral myocarditis and/or the prolapsed valve in the heart, but the report suggested that Little Gail's demise was an unexpected, unexplained death. With nothing to go on medically, the homicide investigation was naturally suspended indefinitely until something of substance could be turned up.

"There were some things that were a little unusual about the death (of Little Gail)," said Sergeant Mike Davidson. "For example, when Little Gail was buried she was not embalmed, at her mother's request . . . which is a little out of the ordinary because decomposition sets in relatively quickly. As a matter of fact," he continued, "we sent photographers out to take pictures of the body two days after her death and she was already starting to decompose. Probably (the reason Little Gail's body was not embalmed at her mother's request), and you can only speculate (about that), is that maybe there was physical evidence present that they felt uncomfortable about, but that's only speculation," he concluded.

Little progress was made in the case until May, more than two months after the death of Little Gail, and that progress came about in a rather unusual manner, like so many other aspects of this very bizarre case. As it turned out Gail Ray, Little Gail's mother, made a report to Clark County road Deputy Peyton Backus that Dr. Harold Becker had sexually molested her deceased daughter prior to her death, and had, in fact, sexually molested his own children.

Deputy Backus' report was turned over to Detective Roger Kessel of the department's sex crimes unit, and Kessel in turn initiated an investigation into the alleged incidents of sexual abuse.

In following up the Backus report, Detective Kessel went out and conducted an interview with a young relative of Dr. Becker's, a male teenager, in which he confronted the youth with the allegations of sexual abuse committed by Dr. Becker. However, the boy denied being the victim of any sexual abuse.

Next Detective Kessel arranged an interview with Dr. Becker himself, in which Detective Kessel confronted him with the sexual abuse allegations made against him by Gail Ray. At that point Dr. Becker denied any such contact with his own children and with Little Gail. Instead, Dr. Becker proceeded to describe how Gail Ray allegedly murdered Little Gay by straddling her chest and placing a plastic bag over her head. It was indeed a shocking and unexpected revelation made by Dr. Becker but, said detectives, it proved to be the "straw that broke the camel's back."

"One of the things . . . that caused (Gail Ray) to come forward with that information (to Deputy Backus)," said Sergeant Davidson, "was that Dr. Becker had asked Gail Ray to leave his residence . . . that he didn't want to have anything else to do with this woman . . . so what in essence happened is that she got mad at Becker and blew the whistle on the sexual abuse, and by doing so made the classic screw-up. Instead of letting it go (Becker's avoidance of her and the alleged sexual abuse), she chose to snitch . . . had she kept quiet, the details surrounding Little Gail's death probably never would have come out."

Subsequent interviews with Dr. Becker, conducted by Detective Kessel, revealed that Little Gail's death had been "prophesized" by Gail Ray and Dr. Becker, and that the supposed prophecy was to be the signaling of the coming of Zion. According to what Becker told Detective Kessel, he and Gail Ray had been telling people that

Little Gail's death was to occur on Monday, March 19, 1984, that God was going to take her as revealed in the prophecy claimed to have been experienced by Becker and Ray.

Others, too, were going to die in fulfillment of prophecies made by Becker and Ray. Other non-believers would also die, according to the predictions Becker said he and Ray had made. Detective Kessel relayed the information he learned from Becker to homicide Detectives St. John and Mc-Vicker.

As a result of the unexpected break in the case, Detectives St. John and McVicker immediately re-opened the investigation into the death of Little Gail. They interviewed Dr. Becker's teenage male relative who, after several attempts at getting him to talk, laid out the details involving Little Gail's death, details which implicated not only Gail Ray but himself as well.

According to the youth, he stayed home from school on the day of Little Gail's death. The teen-ager told detectives that Gail Ray told him that it now looked like Little Gail wasn't going to die on March 19th as she was supposed to, according to the prophesies, and that God had now instructed Gail Ray to help bring about the death in order that the prophesies would be fulfilled. The teen-ager then said that Gail Ray tried to lure her six-year-old daughter into a large plastic bag by placing pepperoni inside, and had instructed the

374

young girl to go inside the bag and get it. However, the boy said, Little Gail refused to go inside.

Because Little Gail refused to go inside the bag to get the pepperoni, the boy told detectives, Gail Ray then sat astride Little Gail's chest as the defenseless six-year-old struggled against the tremendous weight of her mother (more than 200 pounds). The young boy told the cops that, while standing in the doorway to the basement room, he witnessed the girl's mother place the plastic bag over her daughter's head. He told the cops that the actions and the inevitable result made him sick, and that he went outside the house and walked around the pool in the backyard at least 14 times, until such time that Gail Ray came outside and told him that Little Gail was now with God, that she was dead.

Following the interview with Detectives St. John and McVicker, the teenager was taken to Portland where he was administered a polygraphs test regarding the alleged homicide he told the detectives about. He passed.

A child psychologist who administered the polygraph test to the young boy told detectives that he attempted to question him about the alleged sexual abuse, but that the youngster refused to answer his questions. However, the psychologist told Detective St. John that he felt the boy was being sexually abused, a conclusion based largely on the youngster's reactions to the questions he refused to answer.

When the boy was returned to the sheriff's office, detective St. John attempted to interview him regarding the alleged sexual abuse but, again, the lad refused to talk about it. Sex crimes Investigators Sharon Krause, known for achieving positive results with victims of sexual abuse, also failed in her attempts to get the teenager to talk about it. It wasn't until Sergeant Mike Davidson interviewed the youth that he broke down and admitted that Dr. Harold Becker had been sexually molesting him for quite some time.

Following the young man's admission to having been sexually abused, Dr. Becker was called into headquarters that same afternoon. The detectives told Becker what his young relative had told them about the incidents of sexual abuse, after which Dr. Becker broke down and confessed that he had, in fact, been sexually abusing the young boy. Becker was subsequently arrested and charged with the crime.

However, it should be noted that during that same interview, Becker also admitted and laid out for the detectives how he and the young boy had been involved in sexually molesting Little Gail before her death. According to what Dr. Becker told the investigators, there were two incidents of sexual abuse involving Little Gail, one in which Becker alone was involved, and another in which Becker, the young boy and the girl's mother, Gail

Ray, were involved. The second incident, involving all three abusers, occurred at Ray's Watson Street residence in Vancouver and was, according to Dr. Becker, a religious act known as "burden taking."

"Burden-taking," according to Dr. Becker's statements to detectives, involved talking with the victims of sexual abuse and bringing the abuse out into the open. If that were done, said Becker, all the guilt and fear would vanish and all those involved would be "cleansed." According to Becker, it is necessary that all of one's "burdens" be given up to God in order for that person to enter into the Zionic community. However, Dr. Becker told the detectives that if the victims failed to remember what had been done to them during the sexual abuse, the subject of the so-called burden-taking here, the abuse would have to be reenacted. And since Little Gail had been a victim of sexual abuse two years earlier at age 3 or 4 by a relative, Becker told the cops, it was necessary that they perform burden-taking on Little Gail since she was "going to be dying and going to God."

That's how, he said, that he and Gail Ray came up with the idea that Becker would attempt to have sexual intercourse with the little six-year-old girl. According to what Becker told the detectives, sexual intercourse with Little Gail was attempted on two occasions, the most recent occurring four days prior to her death at the Watson Street residence, involving Becker and the teenage boy in the presence of the young girl's mother.

When Dr. Harold Becker was talking about his attempted rape of Little Gail, he told the detectives that the act "was disgusting and that I didn't want to do it."

"Why did you do it, then?" asked Detective St. John.

"It was my duty based on revelation from God," replied Becker.

While attempting to clear up the sexual abuse portion of the case, the Clark County detectives talked to members of Harold Becker's family and ultimately discovered that he had been sexually abusing every one of his children. Some of his children, in their upper teens and early twenties, revealed that they had been sexually abused for as long as 17 or 18 years.

"It came out at trial that he began sexually abusing his daughters at one or two years of age, and was having complete sexual intercourse with them when they were about ten years old," said Detective St. John.

As a matter of fact," said Sergeant Davidson, "one of his daughters, who's married, revealed that Dr. Becker engaged in sexual intercourse with her in his office on Valentine's Day (1984) as part of the belief of 'Burdentaking,' all done under the guise of religion." It was revealed that when the

378

victim was asked if she had been worried about becoming pregnant, she replied that the intercourse had occurred anally.

When Gail Ray was brought in and questioned by detectives about the death of her daughter, she denied any involvement. She was asked to take a polygraph, to which she agreed because, she said, she wanted to clear the matter up. However, she changed her mind and decided not to take the polygraph, then, after wavering back and forth about taking the test, finally agreed. On June 13, 1984, Gail Ray took a polygraph that was administered by Sergeant Davidson.

"As a result of the polygraph," said Davidson, "deception was indicated and she ultimately failed the test. I proceeded to do an interview with her, at which time she confessed to me the entire sequence of events . . . She started out using the excuse that her daughter was dying as a result of some serious asthma . . . review of Little Gail's medical records later failed to substantiate Gail Ray's claims of severe asthma whatsoever."

"She didn't have *any* severe conditions," said Detective St. John.

"In any case, Big Gail (Gail Ray) had kept Little Gail home from school (on the day of her death)," said Sergeant Davidson. "Dr. Becker left home for work that day around 9 a.m. (The young boy), Big Gail and Little Gail were the only ones home at the time . . . She instructed her daughter, Little Gail, to go down to the basement and lay down on the bed on the floor, which is where Little Gail normally slept. Little Gail stayed there until about 10 or 10:30 a.m., at which time Big Gail went downstairs after having decided it was time that Little Gail should go to God. Big Gail said she placed a plastic bag over her daughter's face while straddling her daughter's chest. Big Gail is over 200 pounds, and she said she sat in this position holding a plastic bag over Little Gail's head for one to two minutes. Although (the young boy) said that he'd only watched from the doorway, I asked Big Gail where he was while the death occurred. She said that he was with her the whole time that he handed her the bag and held Little Gail's arm," said Sergeant Davidson.

"Big Gail said she went back upstairs after the killing," continued Sergeant Davidson, "and called Dr. Becker, who came home. Big Gail had him delay the phone call to 9-1-1 for a period of time. When the call was placed, she told Dr. Becker to make it sound urgent and excited, as if they had just found Little Gail . . .

"What ultimately happened then was that we brought (the young boy) back over here, re-interviewed him, and he then admitted that he had in fact held the little girl's arm and provided the plastic bag that was used to suffocate her, corroborating Gail Ray's story.

"It was also then that he admitted there had ac-

380

tually been two attempts to kill Little Gail," continued Davidson, "the first being when Big Gail placed pepperoni in a plastic sack and tried to persuade Little Gail to crawl inside the bag where she would naturally suffocate. When that attempt failed, she, Gail Ray, held the bag over her daughter's head."

When confronted with the question of why he helped kill Little Gail when he knew that killing another human being was wrong, the young boy said that Gail Ray told him that by helping with the act he would attain "celestial glory."

What did "celestial glory" mean to him? the boy was asked.

"He said his understanding was that it meant that he would be guaranteed a place in Heaven," said Detective St. John.

As mentioned earlier, Gail Ray was supposedly involved in satanism and was, in fact, described as a "high priestess" of a satanic cult. During the course of the investigation, Sergeant Davidson and Detectives McVicker and St. John had the opportunity to interview a 15-year-old boy who had resided with Gail Ray at one time and had attended a satanic ceremony, known in some circles as a "Black Mass."

"When Tim (Detective McVicker) and I had the opportunity to interview him (the 15-year-old boy)," said Sergeant Davidson, "he was currently residing in a mental ward in a Portland, Oregon hospital because of the bizarre chain of events, largely attributable to what had gone on . . . at one point in time he'd even engaged in sexual intercourse with Gail Ray . . . They'd had a satanic ceremony in Gail Ray's house."

According to what the 15-year-old told the detectives, he was at one point blindfolded after which he, accompanied by several other people, attended a satanic church. The youth told the detectives that the cermony was held in a large, airy building and that lots of candles were burning. People were smoking marijuana during the devil worship, he said, and at one point he fell into a trance he believed was caused by Gail Ray. The boy told the detectives that he acquired some knife marks on his legs, apparently inflicted while he was in the trance.

Additional investigation into the background of Dr. Harold Becker revealed that one of his aspirations was to establish a chiropractic clinic for "adjusting" children, "obviously because he is a pervert," said one of the detectives. It was pointed out that it was well-documented during the course of the investigation that Dr. Becker had been a pedophile for years, but wasn't restricted to just that type of deviate behavior. "He's just your basic pervert," said one of the detectives. "He doesn't care whether you're four or forty."

During an interview after his arrest, one of the detectives asked Dr. Becker if he ever masturbated. "Oh, God, yes," he purportedly replied. "It's like a scourge." Investigators said that Becker told them he would wait until his wife had gone to sleep at night, after which he said he would get up and masturbate. He even convinced his wife, he told detectives, that he suffered from a prostate problem, and that the recommended therapy was rectal massage. He said he convinced his wife to insert a vibrator deep into his rectum to carry out the treatment. (It should be pointed out that prostate massage is a legitimate treatment for certain types of prostate ailments, but it is not done with a vibrator.)

"The bottom line is," said one of the detectives who worked on the case," Becker is nothing but a Bible-toting pervert who hid behind the Bible and used religion to justify his sexual perversions."

On August 21, 1984, the 13-year-old boy involved in the death of Little Gail pleaded guilty of conspiracy to commit murder before Clark County Superior Court Judge James Ladley. He was sentenced to a juvenile institution, and will remain under the jurisdiction of the institution until his 18th birthday.

On September 11, 1984, Dr. Harold Becker pleaded guilty to one count of first-degree incest in connection with admitted intercourse with his sons and daughters. He also pleaded guilty to one count of second-degree statutory rape, involving numerous incidents since 1982, with his teenage son, and pleaded guilty to one count of statutory rape involving 6-year-old Gail Vert. He was sentenced by Superior Court Judge Robert Harris to 25 years in prison for his sex crimes.

In November, 1984, Gail Lorraine Ray, also known as Gail Lorraine Vert, was tried and convicted by a jury in Clark County Superior Court on charges of first-degree murder in connection with the asphyxiation death of her daughter, Gail Vert. Ray stared forward and showed no emotion as the four-woman, eight-man jury returned its verdict. On Thursday, December 20th, Judge Harris sentenced Ray to life in prison and recommended that the State Board of Prison Terms and paroles set a minimum sentence of 25 years for the 37-year-old mother of three.

"NEBRASKA'S WEIRD TORTURE CULT!"

by Bruce Stockdale

The morning of Tuesday, June 25, 1985, found Cory McNabb, sheriff of Richardson County, Nebraska — a 550-square-mile county with 11,000 people situated in the very southeast corner of the state — on routine patrol on Route 7. The 45-year-old lawman could see that the day was shaping up into a nice one; the warm sun ascending into the eastern sky was pouring its radiance onto the cornfields stretching as far as the eye could see from each side of the two-lane blacktop road. Indeed, the lawman mused, it was the sort of day that must have inspired the song "June Is Bustin' Out All Over."

As Sheriff McNabb steered his patrol car west along the narrow winding road, his musings were suddenly interrupted by the sight of a pickup truck heading in the opposite direction at a high rate of speed. When the vehicle sped by, Sheriff McNabb could see that it was towing a piece of farm equipment which looked to be a new spray rig.

The alert lawman remembered that just that morning a bulletin had come over the teletype from the Nehema County Sheriff's Office in Seneca, Kansas, advising that a new spray rig valued at $3600 had been stolen overnight from a Seneca farm equipment dealer.

Cory McNabb wasted no time in making a quick U-turn, turned on the cruiser's flashers, and sped off in pursuit of the pickup truck.

The chase was on. Instead of stopping, the driver of the pickup accelerated. The pursuit continued for two miles until the village of Salem appeared and the pickup slowed and came to a stop.

Sheriff McNabb ordered the two men in the truck to get out and to keep their hands where he could see them. When quick patdowns disclosed that each was carrying a .25 caliber automatic in his pocket, the two were placed under arrest, handcuffed, and placed in the patrol car for safe-keeping. And, when inspection of the spray rig confirmed that it was indeed the one stolen in Seneca, Kansas, the two suspected thieves were locked up in the Richardson County Jail on the fourth floor of the depression decor courthouse located in Falls City, the county seat of Richardson County, Nebraska.

The suspects had readily identified themselves

as James Haverkamp, 26, and John David Andreas, 32, both residents of the farm located just north of the village of Rulo, Nebraska, nine miles east of Falls City. They admitted that they had been headed for the Rulo farm with the stolen spray rig at the time of their apprehension by police.

Cory McNabb's eyebrow lifted when he heard this, because for the past several months, stories had been circulating around Richardson County about the strange group of people living on the 80-acre farm along the Missouri River just north of Rulo. The group was reportedly engaged in military training. As one concerned Rulo resident put it: "Sometimes you would swear the National Guard was up there because of all the shooting."

Still, it seemed that nobody knew for sure what the 20 or so inhabitants of the formerly quiet and peaceful hog farm were doing. But there was one term that kept cropping up regularly whenever the Rulo farm situation was discussed—"The Posse Commitatis."

Curious, Sheriff McNabb had decided to do some research on radical extremist groups in general and the Posse Commitatis in particular.

Hw learned that, according to the Posse Commitatis philosophy, the county sheriff, not the President of the U.S., should be the highest elected official in the land. Therefore, the federal government represented illegal tyrannical power which must be opposed and nullified—by force if necessary. The Posse's major political targets were the federal reserve system, believed controlled by a conspiracy of bankers, and the Internal Revenue Service, which administers what was believed to be an oppressive and unjust tax system. Interspersed with the political extremism were strains of religious fanatacism and racism. Posse followers were supposed to be anti-black and anti-Semitic, in addition to being anti-federalist.

Still, despite the rumors rife about the "strange goings-on" at the Rulo farm, county authorities did not feel that they had legally sufficient cause to take action against the people of the farm—so long as their activities did not infringe on the rights of others. Their political beliefs were protected, as in the case of every citizen, by the First Amendment.

But now, two members of the Rulo farm group had been caught red-handed attempting to steal a valuable piece of farm equipment. With the line between thought and deed now having been crossed, it was decided that the time had come to take direct action in the matter of the Rulo farm.

Cory McNabb did not know it then, but his seemingly routine arrest of two thieves was about to balloon into the biggest case of his career.

The next day, Wednesday, June 26, 1986, saw the Rulo farm raided by a combined force of the

Nebraska State Patrol (NSP) and Richardson County Sheriff's Office deputies, 30 men in all. The officers split into two forces: one to check out all the people found on the premises; the other to execute the search warrant.

The latter force's effort quickly yielded paydirt. The lawmen found five truckloads of stolen farm equipment, 30 automatic and assault rifles, 13 fully automatic pistols and rifles, 150,000 rounds of ammunition, and a survivalist bunker containing food, water, and ammunition.

Thirty-seven-year-old Terry Becker, an investigator with the NSP, was leading the detail of lawmen assigned to round up the group's members. He found the leader of the group Michael Ryan, aged 37, in the bedroom of the farmhouse. When a search of the room turned up a machine gun hidden under a blanket, Ryan was arrested and charged with a violation of the state firearms law. Also found at the farmhouse was a woman wanted by Kansas authorities on a warrant charging her with interfering with parental custody; and her four children, the subject of a bitter custody fight.

Ryan and the Kansas woman were taken to the Richardson County Jail to be held for appropriate court action while the children were turned over to the Department of Social Services and eventually returned to Kansas.

Three other women and a number of children

were checked for identity and dismissed when it was found that they were clear of entanglements with the law.

Somehow Michael Ryan was able to raise his bail money, posted it, was released and returned to the Rulo farm. However, fellow radicals John David Andreas and James Haverkamp were unable to do so. They continued to cool their heels in the Richardson County Jail.

In addition to providing police services to Richardson County, the county sheriff is in charge of the county jail. It soon became apparent to Cory McNabb that Andreas and Haverkamp had far weightier matters on their minds than a theft of farm equipment.

Eventually, they sent word that there was something really important that they wanted to discuss with the sheriff. And, when Sheriff McNabb heard the incredible story they had to tell, he made a beeline to the office of County Attorney Doug Merz.

It was decided that the time had come to advise the federal authorities of the Rulo farm situation in order to get the assistance of the Federal Bureau of Investigation and the Bureau of Alcohol, Tobacco and Firearms. As a result, the next several weeks were to see a flurry of activity on the part of the interested governmental agencies as they made preparations for a showdown with the Rulo radicals.

Finally, on Saturday, August 16, 1986, a combined force of 80 lawmen representing local, state, and federal law enforcement agencies assembled at the National Guard armory located on northwest edge of Falls City. At 7:30 a.m., the force moved out and headed west on the narrow winding country road leading to Rulo, nine miles away. Curiously, the convoy of lawmen included a bulldozer being carried on a flatbed rig.

It took the convoy only 20 minutes to reach the farm's location—a ridge overlooking the Missouri river just north of Rulo. The farm's residents enjoyed excellent views to the south, east, and west.

But the lawmen weren't there to enjoy the scenery. Quickly, the FBI SWAT team heading the raid swept the dirt road leading onto the property, for booby traps. Then, the raiding party quickly spread out to secure the area and commence the search for contraband. Meanwhile, the operator of the bulldozer started to excavate in a grassy, weeded area about a quarter-mile south of the farmhouse. Accompanying reporters wondered why the lawmen had picked this particular area for excavation; it was as if they knew beforehand precisely where to dig.

Upon the removal of a layer of earth by the blade of the bulldozer, officers began to probe the soil by hand. About three feet down, they found what they had been looking for—a corpse.

The body of a man lay shrouded in a sleeping bag.

Twenty-five feet away, another detail of lawmen discovered the body of a little boy wrapped in a blanket.

Both corpses were in advanced states of decomposition, indicating that they had been dead for some time. Moreover, due to the state of decomposition, it was obvious that positive identification of the bodies would have to be made by means of forensic pathology.

With the discovery of the bodies, the only two people found on the farm that morning, Michael Ryan, and 22-year-old Timothy Haverkamp, a cousin of James Haverkamp, were arrested on a charge of suspicion of murder. By nightfall, County Attorney Merz had filed formal charges of first-degree murder against both men. FBI agents transported them to Omaha area jails so that they could be held separately from John David Andreas and James Haverkamp, who obviously had become informants for the authorities.

While the results of the autopsies were pending, Investigator Becker, a 10-year veteran of the NSP, was assigned the task of making an extensive background investigation of the six-foot, two-inch, 220-pound bearded patriarch of the radical group, Michael Wayne Ryan. Realizing that if they were going to deal effectively with this bizarre individual, they would have to get answers to the questions: Who is Mike Ryan and what makes this man tick?

Terry Becker's investigation disclosed that Ryan was born in Anthony, Kansas, a small town of 2,000 people in south central Kansas. Even in his youth he had displayed an anti-authority streak; at the age of 15 he had been expelled from high school for assaulting the principal. He had been rejected for military service after refusing to submit to the induction physical (it had taken six MP's to subdue him when he had become violent at the examining station). He had worked at a variety of jobs, including truck driver, construction laborer, and agricultural worker until he had become involved with the Posse Commitatis. Prior to moving to the Rulo farm in 1984, Michael Ryan lived with his family in Whiting, Kansas, a village about 25 miles south of Falls City. After getting the feeling that his neighbors resented what they regarded as his radical activities, he had moved to the Rulo farm with his family and a group of about 20 followers. With his commanding physical presence and the fierce zealotry of his beliefs, he had become the undisputed leader of the group. Indeed, he claimed that God—whom he referred to by the Old Testament Hebrew name of Yahweh—spoke directly through him. Thus, to disagree with Mike Ryan meant disagreeing with The Almighty Himself.

The radical group had quickly become an object of curiosity and a subject of gossip around Richardson County to a certain extent, it seemed that the expressions of concern and sympathy by the Posse for the plight of the Midwestern farmer struck somewhat of a sympathetic cord.

It seemed to Terry Becker that Mike Ryan had created a sort of paradise for himself in that little corner of the world where Nebraska, Kansas, and Missouri come together. According to John Andreas and James Haverkamp, (whose stock as informants had risen by virtue of their having demonstrated that they knew where the bodies were buried) Ryan had treated the women on the farm as his personal harem, marrying three of them in mock marriage ceremonies. To support his regal life-style on the farm (he called himself the "King"), he had ordered the male members of the cult to steal farm equipment and rustle livestock. Anyone who disobeyed him was subjected to physical abuse and demoted to the status of "slaves." Ryan spent much of his time smoking marijuana and sitting in his easy chair watching movies on the VCR.

Andreas and James Haverkamp claimed that the body of the man was that of James Thimm; the boy, Luke Stice, son of cult member Ora Stice.

When the autopsy report confirmed that the victims' identities were indeed those claimed by the informants, Investigator Becker did some checking on the background of James Thimm, aged 26, formerly of Beatrice, Nebraska. He learned that Thimm had been a respectable citizen before becoming involved with the Rulo group. He had worked steadily at one job for five years before evidencing a change of attitude towards life.

As his former employer explained to the sleuth: "Before Jim got tangled up with them (the cult group), he was the best P.R. person we had. He could talk with or to anybody. He was one of the nicest kids you ever saw. But six to nine months before we let him go, he began to change. He didn't care if he showed up for work anymore. He said he had better things to do than work for a living."

Probers learned that five-year-old Luke Stice had been living on the Rulo farm with the cult members, ever since his mother died of Hodgkin's Disease on April 4, 1983. At that time, the farm was owned by his father, Rick Stice. The hog farming operation went bankrupt in late 1983 and the farm was taken over by the bank. In 1984, two members of the radical group, Tom Baker and James Haverkamp, had somehow come up with the $10,000 down payment necessary to take title to the farm which by now had become the base of operations for the radicals' activities.

Dr. George Gammell, who conducted the

autopsies, reported that Luke Stice had died from a fracture of the skull caused by a blow to the head. James Thimm had died as a result of "multiple traumatic injuries." No single cause of death could be pinpointed, explained Dr. Gammell, because of the advanced state of decomposition of the body although it did appear that James Thimm had been whipped and beaten. In addition, the victim had been shot in the head but it was impossible to say whether the wound had been inflicted before or after death. Finally, the body had had no genitals when he had examined it; it was impossible to determine, however, whether they had been cut off or had simply decomposed.

Now that probers had established who the victims were, they sought next to determine the how and why of their deaths.

Anxious to cut the best possible deal for themselves in court, John Andreas and James Haverkamp proved most cooperative.

They related how Thimm had fallen out of favor with Michael Ryan because he had become disillusioned with life on the farm and had begun to question the cult's beliefs. To discipline him, Ryan had demoted Thimm to the status of "slave."

Matters came to a head on April 25, 1985, after Rick Stice had disappeared from the farm. In an apparent attempt to make an example of

396

Thimm and thereby scare any other disaffected cult member out of the idea of fleeing the farm, Michael Ryan ordered the torture and murder of this one-time devoted follower.

For a hellish five days, James Thimm was subjected to a variety of tortures. He was taken to the hog shed where he had his arms chained to an overhead beam. Then he was whipped unmercifully with a cattle prod. The next day, he was spread-eagled over a piece of farm equipment to have his rectum probed with a shovel handle.

By the time he mercifully died on April 20th, the tips of his fingers had been shot off, his leg skinned with a razor, and another leg broken by a blow from a lead pipe.

During the final hours of his life, the torture victim screamed and begged for forgiveness.

John Andreas and James Haverkamp identified the perpetrators of these crimes as themselves, Tim Haverkamp, Michael Ryan, and Ryan's 16-year-old son, Dennis.

Finally, on March 30th, Michael Ryan ordered John Andreas to take a tractor and disc an area where Thimm's grave was to be located. Andreas said goodbye to Thimm and left the hog shed to disc the field. When he returned Thimm was dead. Andreas, Dennis Ryan and Tim Haverkamp dug a grave and placed the sleeping bag containing the victim's body into the ground. At the gravesite, Michael Ryan told Tim

Haverkamp to shoot the corpse in the head to make the death look like the result of a shooting, in case the body was ever discovered.

Faced with a charge of first-degree murder in the death of James Thimm, Tim Haverkamp also decided to jump on the deal bandwagon. He gave authorities the following account of the death of little Luke Stice:

"On March 25, 1985, I walked into the south trailer where I encountered James Thimm, Michael Ryan, Dennis Ryan and Rick Stice. Michael Ryan said, 'You just missed something.' Luke Stice, who had been lying on the floor, got up and Ryan said, 'Well you didn't see it, so here.' Then Ryan, using both his hands, pushed Luke Stice, causing him to stumble backwards and hit his head on a stand. Michael Ryan then started to holler at Rick Stice and James Thimm about their bad thoughts. After Michael Ryan finished hollering at Rick Stice and James Thimm, he again pushed Luke Stice causing him to fall backwards and hit his head on the same stand. Michael Ryan then left the south trailer. Luke Stice stood up and then started to shake and collapsed. His breathing was rough and he was unconscious. Rick Stice then went over to Luke Stice to see what he could do. Michael Ryan then came into the south trailer and told Rick Stice to stand back so he could take care of it. Michael Ryan then stated that he was going over to the north house to talk to Yahweh (God). Michael Ryan returned to the south trailer in approximately five minutes and stated there wasn't anything he could do and he told Rick Stice to wrap Luke in a blanket and place him in a bedroom. At this time, Luke Stice was still unconscious. I then left and returned the next morning. Mike Ryan told me that Luke Stice had died and would have to be buried. He was buried in the land south of the trailer in the presence of John Andreas, James Thimm, Rick Stice, Michael Ryan, Dennis Ryan, and me."

In addition to describing the manner of Luke Stice's death, Tim Haverkamp provided details of the cruel abuse inflicted on the little kid that even shocked the case-hardened lawmen investigating the case. These details were corroborated by Andreas and James Haverkamp. According to these informants, the various members of the cult had used the boy's mouth as an ashtray, spit in his mouth, rolled him in the snow while clad only in his underwear, whipped him severely, an banged his head against the wall.

On more than one occasion, he had been forced to perform fellatio on an adult cult member.

The reason given by Michael Ryan for inflicting this sort of treatment on a five-year-old boy was that Yahweh had told him that Yahweh had told him that Luke Stice was "possessed by Satan" and needed to be exorcized of his devil possession by having it beaten out of him.

It was because they felt Luke was possessed by the Devil that on occasion he had been painted with the number "666"—the Biblical number which stands for Satan.

With Dennis Ryan now implicated in James Thimm's murder, investigators swore out a warrant for his arrest. The 16-year-old son of the cult leader had not been found at the Rulo farm but he was quickly located living on a survivalist farm near Norton, Kansas. Terry Becker took an NSP plane to Norton, served the warrant on the fugitive, and returned with him upon completion of extradition proceedings. Like his father, he elected to stand on his right to remain silent when advised of his constitutional rights under Miranda. He joined his father in pre-trial detention since, under Nebraska law, jurisdiction is waived by the Juvenile Courts in the case of juveniles charged with serious crimes.

Shortly after Luke Stice's death on the Rulo farm, Rick Stice had disappeared and did not surface in Richardson County until September 18, 1985, when he showed up for Luke's funeral in Falls City. On a placard in front of the small coffin was a color photograph of Luke Stice, smiling.

Although Rick Stice was to join the parade of witnesses turning states evidence against Michael and Dennis Ryan, he was still to find himself charged by U.S. Attorney Ron Lahners with the Interstate Transportation of Stolen Livestock as a result of his part in the cult's rustling operations. On January 10, 1986, he was sentenced to five years in prison on the charge.

Based on information received from informants John Andreas and James Haverkamp, Tom Baker, co-owner of the Rulo farm with James Haverkamp, found himself charged with burglary and theft in Decatur County, Kansas. He was convicted after a jury trial and sentenced from one to five years on these charges.

With four eyewitnesses to the death and burial of Luke Stice (James Haverkamp, and Rick Stice) and three (James Haverkamp, John Andreas, Tim Haverkamp) in the shocking case of the torture-slaying of James Thimm, Richardson County attorney Doug Merz, 31, was confident that he had a strong case to take to court. He filed charges of first-degree murder against Michael and Dennis Ryan in the James Thimm case; a first-degree murder charge against Michael Ryan in the Luke Stice case; a first-degree murder charge against Tim Haverkamp in the James Thimm case; and charges of assault, receiving stolen property, and carrying a concealed weapon against John Andreas and James Haverkamp with regard to all the crimes they committed in Richardson County.

With the Thimm-Stice homicide case the first murder prosecution to be handled by the young prosecutor, District Court Judge Robert Finn deemed it advisable to appoint a more experienced prosecutor, Otoe County Attorney Randall Rehmeier, to assist with the prosecution of the Ryans.

And with what had been dubbed by the press as "The Rulo Farm Murders" the most sensational news story in the history of Richardson County, Nebraska, defense attorneys sought and were granted a change of venue to Omaha, on the grounds that all the publicity about the case had rendered it impossible for the Ryans to get a fair trial in Richardson county.

Pre-trial legal maneuvering continued throughout the winter of 1985-86 until trial commenced in the case of the State vs. Michael and Dennis Ryan. The James Thimm case was to be tried first.

Veteran courthouse observers knew that by virtue of the eyewitnesses to the Thimm torture-slaying that were in the prosecution camp, the state would have no problem proving that the two defendants actually did the deeds alleged in the indictment. The real question that the jury of ten women and two men had to decide was: Did the Ryans know the nature and quality of their acts with which they were charged? And did they know the acts were wrong when they did them?

Were the Ryans bad or insane?

What the contest would actually boil down to was a battle of the psychiatrists, with the prosecution and defense each putting psychiatrists and psychologists on the stand whose testimony would prove their respective contentions.

The smart money around the Douglas County courthouse was betting on the prosecution, because, in conservative Nebraska, insanity defenses have usually proved difficult to sell to a jury.

After a seven-week trial during which a total of 50 witnesses testified, the jury returned its verdicts on April 10, 1986, after 22 hours of deliberation. Michael Ryan was found guilty of first-degree murder; Dennis Ryan, guilty of second-degree, each for their part in the death of James Thimm.

Judge Finn postponed the sentencing of Michael Ryan since the Luke Stice prosecution was still pending against him. However, sentencing of Dennis Ryan took place on May 9, 1986.

The apparently remorseful teenager put his head in his hands and wept when he heard the sentence pronounced—life imprisonment. He cried for two or three minutes before looking at Judge Finn and saying, "I'm sorry for what happened, Your Honor."

Judge Finn quoted a newspaper reporter who wrote that the Rulo case contained elements of "every horrible thing from every horrible story" he'd ever covered in his years as a reporter. The judge said that possibly nothing as horrible as the Rulo farm torture-slaying had been recorded in the history of the Nebraska judiciary.

Apparently, Mike Ryan could not take the ordeal of another trial so he entered "no contest" plea to a charge of second-degree murder in the case of Luke Stice. On August 28, 1985, he was sentenced to life imprisonment for the crime.

This life sentence became what lawyers term "moot" when on October ??? 1986, Judge Finn sentenced Michael Ryan to death in the electric chair for the murder of James Thimm. In sentencing the defendant, Judge Finn noted that the aggravating circumstances and the heinous nature of the crime against James Thimm coupled with the prior crime of Luke Stice's murder, far outweighed the mitigating circumstances that there must be something wrong with Mike Ryan's mind for him to do such things in the first place.

Timothy Haverkamp negotiated a plea bargain which spared him from a trial on the first-degree murder charge for his part in the crimes against James Thimm. He was sentenced to life imprisonment after pleading guilty to second-degree murder.

John David Andreas and James Haverkamp received their reward for turning state's evidence when they were each sentenced to 30 years in prison on all the charges lodged against them.

Since no minimum sentence was specified, they are both eligible for parole.

Dennis Ryan is now serving his sentence in the Nebraska Penal Complex. Michael Ryan is now lodged on Death Row in the same prison. Michael Ryan's attorneys indicated after sentence was pronounced that they will file an appeal with the Nebraska Supreme Court.

EDITOR'S NOTE:

Tom Baker is not the real name of the person so named in the foregoing story. A fictitious name has been used because there is no reason for public interest in the identity of this person.

"SATAN'S DISCIPLES DEMANDED HUMAN SACRIFICES!"

by Bill G. Cox

Every spring it happens: Hundreds of thousands of college students descend on coastal resorts such as Fort Lauderdale, Florida; Galveston, Texas; and South Padre Island at the far southern tip of Texas. Spring break, it's called—the annual ritual of youth on a fling.

In 1988, college pre-med student Mark Kilroy had a ball during his springtime visit to South Padre and the nearby Mexican border city of Matamoros, Mexico. He had so much fun that he told fellow frolickers that he would be back in 1989, especially to visit the colorful Matamoros. No one had any idea at the time that he had thus doomed himself to a hideous death.

South Padre Island, at one time a retreat for swashbuckling pirates and today a tropical resort known for its beautiful beaches, runs along the coastline in the vicinity of Brownsville. Just across the Rio Grande River that separates the

United States and Mexico is the city of Matamoros. The two cities are connected by an international bridge over which tourists flow by the thousands.

The border cities of the United States and Mexico are stepchildren of their respective counties, a sort of no-man's land dependent on each other for their primary economic activity — tourism. Yet, the border is a strange paradox of American tourists seeking fun and adventure and Mexican drug smugglers seeking northern markets. It can be a deadly, deadly mixture, as law enforcement agencies on both sides have known for a very long time.

Mix with this atmosphere the occult, weird and devil-worshiping rituals that have migrated from the Caribbean and Africa, from remote lands where voodooism, black magic and superstitions run rife, and there exists a blatant evil waiting to erupt.

Evil unimagined and unparalleled in border history began to unfold amid the fun-loving, drinking and shouting crowds that jammed the streets of Matamoros early in the morning of Tuesday, March 14, 1989.

True to his promise of one year earlier, 21-year-old Mark Kilroy, a University of Texas pre-med student from the little Texas town of Santa Fe, was back for 1989 spring break festivities. He and three buddies from other Texas schools had come to Matamoros from South Padre Island. The spring night had been one of bar-jumping in the Mexican city, of loud talk and laughing, of blaring music from the street cantinas, flashing-eyed senoritas and purveyors offering for sale anything under the sun.

But shortly before 2:00 a.m., Mark, a handsome youth with blond hair and an athletic build that had made him a basketball star in high school and college, was heading for the international bridge with his three friends. They were jostled by the hundreds of celebrants milling along the busy street and bound for the bridge to return to Brownsville and American soil.

Somewhere along the way, Mark became separated from his companions. When they looked around for him, he was nowhere to be seen.

None of them had the remotest idea where he might have gone. They thought he would show up shortly, probably to report embellishments to the night of fun and games.

But as the sobering effect of the next few hours set in, the seriousness of the situation became apparent. The worried college friends sought the help of U.S. Customs authorities after crossing the Gateway International Bridge into Brownsville. There, they spoke with Oran Neck, special agent in charge of the U.S. Customs Service investigations office.

After he listened to their story of Kilroy's disappearance from the Matamoros street, Neck launched a hunt for the missing youth. Customs Service agents accompanied the three youths back to the Mexican border city to retrace their steps.

It was highly possible, the officers knew, that the American college youth had somehow ended up in a Mexican jail, not an uncommon occurrence for festive-minded tourists. The investigators combed the city's jails and police stations seeking the vanished Texan. Mexican authorities cooperated in the search, but nothing turned up on Kilroy's whereabouts.

Kilroy's friends notified his parents in Santa Fe, who said they would come to Brownsville and Matamoros to aid in the search. They soon made it clear to American and Mexican officials heading the hunt that Mark would not have voluntarily absented himself for long.

Fear of foul play involved in the youth's disappearance was now uppermost in the minds of the searchers. They wondered if Mark had somehow fallen victim to border violence precipitated by drug-trafficking.

Such happenings had been rife in recent weeks along the 1,960-mile border between the two nations. Lately there had been a steady outpouring of violence and death, much of it drug-related.

In November 1989, a Texas man and his wife were fired on by snipers on the Mexican Side of The Rio Grande as the couple rafted down the river. The man had been killed and his wife, though badly wounded, escaped to notify authorities. The snipers were eventually caught and admitted they had been high on drugs when they shot at the Texans.

On March 29th, and April 1st, the bodies of 12 persons—nine men and three women—had been found in a well and sewage pit tank at an abandoned ranch near Agua Prieta, Mexico. The town is just over the border from Douglas, Arizona, 130 miles southeast of Tucson. The victims had been tied up, tortured and shot to death, investigators said. All were Mexican nationals. The dozen murders were thought to be connected to the slayings, two days earlier, of five men whose bound and stabbed bodies were found stacked in a shed in a rented home in Tucson. Arizona officers said that the five murders also were drug-related.

On April 27, 1989, the prime suspect in the drug murders, a Mexican national who owned the ranch where the bodies were found in Mexico, was arrested about 30 miles southwest of Tucson. He was turned over to Mexican authorities.

Mexican officials said he was charged with first-degree murder, concealment of accomplices, criminal association and violation of burial laws. Still another body possibly linked to the Agua Prieta and Tucson drug murders had been found several days earlier by judicial police in Sonora, Mexico. The corpse identified as that of a reputed Mexican drug dealer was found five miles south of Agua Prieta. He had been shot twice in the back of the head. His arms were tied behind his back, and lime had been tossed on the body, as was the case in the other killings on the nearby ranch, officers said.

Besides the series of murders growing from drug-trafficking, ordinary—if they can be so described—robbery killings are a frequent thing in the border cities. Said one U.S. Border Patrol official, "Someone sees a group coming down a trail, shoots one of them from behind a bush and then starts going through the others' pockets. The violence along the border is getting out of hand."

Most of the robbery-killings were illegal aliens crossing or trying to cross the Rio Grande into the U.S. But it wasn't remotely possible that such a fate could have befallen an innocent tourist such as Mark Kilroy, the investigators realized.

As the search for the missing youth continued, his hometown went all out to help in every possible way.

Everyone in Santa Fe knew and liked Mark. He had been an honor student in high school and excelled in basketball and golf. He wanted to be a doctor. For that reason, he had transferred the previous fall to the University of Texas in Austin, from another college he was attending on a bas-

411

ketball scholarship.

The community rallied behind the Kilroy family. Townspeople held bake sales and garage sales to help fund the hunt for Mark. Someone suggested local residents should tie yellow ribbons to trees and display them everywhere to symbolize the faith the town had that Mark would be found alive.

The student's relatives and friends walked the streets in Matamoros, posting flyers that offered a reward for information leading to the youth's safe return. Mark's disappearance was even dramatized on a nationally televised program in hopes that someone would provide a clue.

But days, then weeks, passed with no results.

As a last resort, investigators arranged to have one of the friends who was with Mark on the fateful night placed under hypnosis. They hoped that a clue might be jarred from his subconscious that way.

The hypnosis produced the first tangible bit of information on the mysterious disappearance. While under, Mark's college friend remembered an incident that happened before the group noticed Mark was no longer with them.

The youth recalled he had glimpsed a man, an Hispanic, motion to Mark and say something. This had happened near a cafe just a few yards from the international bridge. From his deep subconscious, the friend recalled for officers that the man was wearing a blue plaid shirt and had a cut or a scar on one cheek and had spoken to Mark in English.

As best the friend could recall, the man had said to Mark, "Hey, don't I know you from somewhere?"

Mark had stopped, apparently to talk with the stranger. After that, the friend remembered nothing else, except it was the last time they had seen their longtime friend.

From this story, the officers deduced that Mark had been abducted for purposes of robbery or ransom.

The first theory was more probable. No ransom demands had been made since his disappearance. If he had been abducted and robbed, it was possible, lawmen feared, that he had been slain and dumped in some remote place.

Though more than 100 persons were quizzed by the American and Mexican authorities on both sides of the Rio Grande, no leads developed on the youth's disappearance.

In Brownsville, Cameron County Sheriff Alex Perez placed Lieutenant George Gavito in charge of the investigation. Gavito was convinced that the college student had met with foul play and was probably dead. He enlisted the help of the Border Patrol to comb the Rio Grande and its banks for the missing youth. Helicopters and four-wheel-drive vehicles that could plow through the deep sand of the area were summoned, but they failed to find anything.

As the hunt for the American went on, Mexican Federal Judicial Police were also busy on the continuing battle with drug smugglers. No one, even the veteran officers who had seen all kinds of violence and death in their border work could have anticipated the stark horror that would be uncovered during what was thought to be a routine drug-trafficking investigation.

On Sunday, April 9th, the driver of a truck crashed through a roadblock for drug smugglers that was being manned by Mexican Federal police. The driver seemed oblivious to the blockade as he drove through at high speed.

Pursuit of the pickup led the Mexican officers to a small ranch about 16 miles west of Matamoros along Highway 2, which runs between Matamoros and Reynosa. The highway follows the route of the Rio Grande River through desolate farm and ranch country.

When investigators searched the pickup, they found a quantity of marijuana inside. Thinking that the ranch and its scattered assortment of rundown shacks and buildings might be the base for a border drug smuggling operation, the federal police obtained a search warrant to go over the premises. When they descended on the site, the lawmen arrested two suspects.

Their search turned up about 100 pounds of

marijuana, some cocaine and a cache of arms including machineguns.

They also saw evidence that members of the group practiced voodoo or black magic rites inside a dilapidated and dirty shack. Among the suspects rounded up after the Sunday raid was a man identified as the caretaker of the ranch.

During interrogation, the caretaker began talking about the strange happenings in the shack near the main ranch house and how he was once ordered not to come close. On a hunch, one investigator showed him a photograph of the missing American student, Mark Kilroy.

The caretaker glanced at the picture and said that he had seen the man handcuffed in a vehicle at the ranch a few weeks earlier. He said he had wondered about the strange activities on the ranch, especially in and around the large shack, but he had kept his distance.

The Mexican federals arrested two more men the next day, and questioned all four suspects at length. In the long hours of grilling, the investigators took the lid off a Pandora's box of horrors. Directing the Mexican "federales" was Commandante Juan Benitez Ayala, who had been cracking down hard on Mexican drug operations since he was assigned to the border post.

It was 1:30 in the morning, Tuesday, when the Mexican authorities notified the Cameron County Sheriff's Department in Brownsville of the big break in the Kilroy's disappearance. At daybreak, the Mexican and Cameron County officers, along with U.S. Customs agents headed by Neck, converged on the site known as Rancho Santa Elena.

They had with them the suspects, who the Mexican federal police said had confessed to being involved in two killings at the ranch—one of them the missing Mark Kilroy.

When they arrived at the ranch, the contingent of officers expected to find two bodies. The suspects in custody had admitted killing Kilroy after abducting him from the Matamoros street. They also told about the murder of one other victim.

Their motives reeked of fire and brimstone. They said they were devil worshipper, members of a cult who believed they would have lasting immunity from detection and arrest for their drug-smuggling operations if they offered up human sacrifices. They claimed to have performed these sickening and otherworldly rituals in the weathered shack on the Rancho Santa Elena.

The cult members believed so strongly in the black magic they practiced that they were sure that they were invisible to the human eye. It was no wonder the man who drove through the police blockade on Sunday had been unabashedly confident. He had been sure the lawmen couldn't even see him or his truck!

The excavation of hellish evidence started on the lonely ranch at 6:00 a.m. One suspect first directed the officers to a spot he said concealed the remains of Mark Kilroy. Customs Agent Neck saw a chain sticking from the ground.

And when the gravesite was dug up, little doubt remained that the search for the American student had come to a chilling end. The horror grew when investigators realized that the chain partly protruding from the ground was attached to the spinal cord of the victim. The suspects said they planned to pull out the spinal cord after decomposition was complete, to use the vertebra to make necklaces.

Instead of finding two graves, the lawmen looked on in amazement as the suspects guided them to other graves containing bodies of young males.

"There, and there, and over there," said one of the suspects, gesturing with his hands.

As the brassy sunlight replaced the dawn's grayness, the air grew fetid as the mass disinterments continued. Four of the graves were within a rough, wooden-fence corral, about 40 feet southeast of the shack where the victims were said to have been slain. The other burial sites were scattered around the corral area.

One grave contained two bodies, another grave held three bodies, and seven bodies were in single graves. The graves were about six feet apart. They weren't visible, but the suspects located them easily.

417

Agent Neck described the burial ground as "the killing field."

Sheriff Perez said: "It was horrible. It was like a human slaughterhouse."

It was an apt description. More gruesome details of the sacrificial murders came to light as the lawmen scoured the corn and sorghum ranch and listened to the suspects in custody.

The bodies removed from the shallow graves showed evidence of torture and mutilation. Some victims had been shot in the head, others had apparently been struck in the head with a sharp instrument. The ritualistic killings had been done in the large shack about a half-mile from the main ranch house, the officers were told.

On the ground in front of the shack was graphic and sickening evidence of some of the things that had taken place. The contents of four cauldrons or pots repulsed the investigators as they examined them. The three smaller ones contained a drying chicken head, gold-colored beads in oil, and a goat's head. Wooden sticks had been jammed into a sickening mixture in the larger vessel, a two-foot-wide pot. Investigators identified the evil-smelling contents as animal bones, human blood and human brain matter.

Inside the shack, the air was foul with strange odors.

The building contained the remains of some kind of altar. It was littered with candles, broken glass, cigar butts, chilis and bottles of cane liquor. The suspects said the items were used as satanic offerings to their devil-gods. As exhumation of the decomposing bodies and gathering of the grisly evidence continued, the officers listened in shocked silence to four Mexican suspects calmly relating their activities.

Two of the suspects admitted they had taken part in the killing of Mark Kilroy and one other person as yet unidentified after Lieutenant George Gavito, the head investigator assigned to the case in the Cameron County Sheriff's Department, brought the pre-med student's dental records to Matamoros. Comparisons of the dental charts and the teeth of the body taken from one of the graves, matched.

One of the suspects talked freely about the abduction and killing of Kilroy, making a full statement to the Mexican authorities who had grilled him.

Agent Neck later told reporters: "A truck pulled up next to him (Kilroy) and an individual motioned to him and spoke to him in English like, 'You need a ride?' or something like that. Mark Kilroy came close . . . and they threw him into a pickup truck. There was another car directly behind the pickup that had two or three individuals in it.

"They went around the corner about three or four blocks to a vacant lot. Mark Kilroy jumped out, ran, and the others behind him cut him off. They drew guns on him and tied him up. They took him to the ranch and ultimately killed him."

The probe revealed that the young student had been a prisoner in another building, a barn, for about 12 hours before he was slain. It was also learned that Mark Kilroy had been picked at random. Most of the other victims were also randomly selected, except two who were killed because they had ripped off the devil-worshipers.

While held captive in the barn, Kilroy was fed raw eggs. His arms were bound behind him and his mouth was taped. He had been killed by a blow from a machete to the back of his head, according to the suspects. His brains had been removed and the chain was attached to his spinal cord before the body was dumped into the grave. One suspect said the youth's legs had been severed so the body would fit into the grave.

The full horror of the devil-worshiping rituals came to light when investigators learned that the victim had been boiled alive, and the other been decapitated and castrated.

Victims had apparently been killed on a blood-stained tarpaulin found on the earthen floor of the shack. Pennies were found in one of the cauldrons. The suspects told investigators that they worshiped over the pennies, hoping to make a lot of money in their drug operations.

As Neck explained to reporters who quickly

thronged the site, "They went out there every morning. They smoked cigars. They drank whiskey and they prayed." According to the officers, the cult members had been conducting human sacrifices for about nine months.

Investigator Gavito said, "They prayed to the devil so the police would not arrest them, so bullets would not kill them, and so they would make more money."

The Mexican authorities ordered autopsies to be conducted on the victims. With the exception of Kilroy and one Mexican man who had come from Texas, the other murder victims were Mexican nationals, all young men. The cult suspects in custody said that they did not kill females.

The suspects provided the lawmen with the names of some half-dozen other gang members. They also disclosed the identity of two of the cult's ringleaders.

The cultists identified a Cuban-born U.S. citizen named Adolfo de Jesus Constanzo, 26, as the spiritual leader and chief executioner for the devil cult. He was known as the padrino, the godfather. He was aided in running the organization and the life-taking rituals by a tall young woman named Sara Maria Aldrete, 24, who was known to the cult members as the bruja, or the witch. Though a native of Mexico, the tall and striking "witch woman" was a co-ed at Texas Southmost College in Brownsville. As the investigation progressed, it was learned that she had a puzzling dual personality and led a hauntingly Jekyll-and-Hyde existence that, when unraveled in the next few days, would shock her family, friends and college instructors.

The godfather and witch woman had taken it on the lam at about the time that the federales raided the devil-cult ranch. Constanzo, the officers soon learned, was a strangely charismatic mystery figure who had homes in Miami and Mexico City, and who moved in high-roller circles that took in celebrities, high political figures and the elite of the drug-trafficking underworld on both sides of the border.

It had been the godfather who killed Mark Kilroy with a blow from a machete, the cult suspects told the officers. Earlier, he had ordered them to randomly abduct an American student from among the spring-break revelers. His sacrificial death would protect the smugglers from American police, the godfather had said.

In Brownsville, the Cameron County Sheriff's Department issued an all-points bulletin for Constanzo and Aldrete on charges of aggravated kidnapping in the snatching of Kilroy from the Matamoros street. The search was intense on both sides of the Rio Grande. It was reported that the couple might be headed for Miami, and authorities there were alerted. Pickup orders were also issued for the other cult members named by the men in custody.

Meanwhile, Mexican police moved fast to search the Matamoros residence of Sara Aldrete, where she lived in an upstairs apartment in the home of relatives. When the police gained access to the apartment, they found an altar, assorted cult objects including candles, and blood spattered on the wall. Was it possible, the amazed sleuths wondered, that the tall and bewitching coed had performed killing rituals in the apartment in the fashionable Matamoros neighborhood?

Relatives at the home were shocked by the findings. They professed no knowledge that the young woman was involved in any devilworshiping rites and crimes.

As the manhunt for the two cult leaders spread over Mexico and the United States, developments were breaking fast on the murder ranch. One of the suspects was taken back to the site to dig up still another body that he said was buried in the killing field.

The suspect was handed a pick and shovel and told to unearth the body. He proceeded to work in the broiling midday sun. After a while, a portion of the buried corpse came into view, and the stench of rotting flesh hung over the area, prompting the suspect to request a face mask while he completed the job.

"You didn't need one when you buried him," a

Mexican officer growled.

Finally, the man dug until the body of a man thought to be in his 30s was recovered. It became quickly apparent that like other corpses found on the death ranch, this body had been cut open and the heart had been removed. With the disinterment of the 13th body Mexican and Texas authorities arranged for two bulldozers and other equipment to start excavating the ranch in a search for other possible victims.

Police revealed at this time that blood-spattered clothing belonging to children had been found in Sara Aldrete's apartment. They feared that some children might have also been victims of the satanic rituals.

But the suspect who had dug up the latest body said no children had been slain. He said the bloody clothes found in the woman's apartment belonged to a relative of the woman. The blood must have come from another source because the boy who owned the clothes was alive and uninjured, he said. This was verified by police.

The investigators learned that Constanzo and Sara Aldrete had last been seen together in a silver or blue Mercedes-Benz. No one was sure whether they were still traveling together. The woman's car, a blue Ford station wagon, was found in Brownsville on Thursday night, but it contained few clues and no leads to her whereabouts.

In a cooperative probe between the U.S. and Mexican law enforcement agencies, a profile of the handsome Constanzo began to take shape. A Cuban-American born and raised in Miami, where his Cuban refugee family had settled, he left that city in the mid-1980s to live in Mexico City. He was said to travel from Mexico City to Matamoros at least once a week to oversee the profitable drug-smuggling operations and the necessary hokus-pocus that the cult members believed made then invincible. In fact, the authorities learned, the so-called godfather had performed his weird and devilish work in return for one-half of the gang's profits.

Lieutenant Gavito said that Constanzo was extremely wealthy. The fact that he had bought the brand-new Mercedes for cash said it all. He also paid cash for all sorts of luxury items, clothing, jewelry and even fur coats that he sometimes wore, the officers were told.

Adolfo really was an out-of-this-world young man, said those who knew him well.

"He had out-of-body experiences, healing the sick and predicting the future," relatives who had known the cult leader as a boy claimed. Although he had dropped out of school, Adolfo had two things going for him—his uncanny psychic talents and the good looks of a male model.

This combination of looks, psychic abilities and boyish charm coupled with unmatched sophistication put him in touch with Mexico City's high society. People paid him thousands of dollars a session for his fortune-telling and ritualistic "cleansings."

It was reported that this mystery man's customers included top-ranking government officials and some of Mexico's most popular entertainers—all of whom would later deny any link at all with Constanzo when grilled by Mexican investigators.

It is not yet known how Adolfo Constanzo met Sara Aldrete. But somewhere along the way, their paths crossed, setting the stage for drug-smuggling and devil-cult rituals.

Sarah drew stares wherever she went. She was 6 feet 1 inch tall, had light brown hair and striking features. She was bright and sparkling and popular at the college in Brownsville where she was a physical education major. She was an Honor Roll student. Born in Matamoros, she grew up in a middle-class neighborhood. She had been enrolled at the Brownsville college since January 1986.

She was among 30 people added to the school's "Who's Who" list in 1988 and had been chosen outstanding physical education student. She had also won a national physical education award and was president of the college soccer club.

A professor at the college who had taught Sara anthropology, said, "This is totally unbelievable.

She never showed any signs of unusual behavior. She was always cheerful, always well-groomed and dressed, a perfect model student and a striking woman."

But Lieutenant Gavito said, "It looks to us like she was leading a double life. She had one life in Matamoros . . . The friends here didn't know what her life was in Mexico." Investigators quizzed other students, perhaps closer to Sara, who had seen a darker side to her personality. One college student recalled that she and Sara once watched a videotape of a TV documentary about Caribbean voodoo rites known a Santeria. The coed remembered that while they talked about the videotape, Sara had asked, "Do you want to know what Santeria is?"

"Then she told us about the rituals they had—she told us they covered themselves in blood to purify themselves. By the time she was finished, we knew she knew what she was talking about and we were scared. She kind of hinted that she was one of very few chosen ones who lead such cults."

One student said Sara had never mentioned human sacrifices. But the Cameron County Sheriff's Department investigators had a theory that Sara, as the high priestess of the drug cult, had lured men across the Rio Grande so that the gang could abduct and murder them. At least one of the suspects in custody had told investigators that it was Sara who used her charms to induce him to join the group.

Long before the devil cult's killing activities came to light, drug agents on both sides of the border were aware of the marijuana-smuggling operations by gangs whose members once had been poor farmers. It wasn't surprising that the farmers came to the conclusion that there was a bonanza in smuggling marijuana up north. There seemed to be an unlimited demand.

The operations of one particular family was considered small-time by the authorities. It was within this gang, a family that suffered a violent split wrought by rivalry over pot profits, that the devil cult rituals had their demonic birth.

It was this feud that led some family members to turn to black magic which they believed was offered by the strange homosexual godfather, Constanzo. Things began to fall apart for the dope-smuggling gang when its 38-year-old chieftan was gunned down on a Matamoros street in January 1987. After that, the survivors didn't have the connections, the power and the money that the slain boss had held.

In the spring of 1988, one family member who had heard about a shadowy figure in Mexico City named Adolfo Constanzo, a man with powerful underworld connections in more ways than one, went to Mexico City and pitched Constanzo a deal — 50 percent of all profits if he could come

428

through with supernatural protection.

Constanzo was more than willing to trade his devilish influence for dope dollars. Psychic powers were one thing, but the big bucks were the hook. Sara Aldrete became the priestess of the outfit, using her intelligence and charm to recruit gang members and lure potential victims into the web, according to statements given to Mexican authorities by the suspects under arrest.

Though she apparently didn't take part in the sacrificial rites, she helped set the stage for violent ceremonies by showing a videotape of a movie titled *The Believers,* a 1987 American film that depicted wealthy Americans resorting to human sacrifices to protect their prominence.

As the authorities continued to amass a thick file on the dope smugglers, the body count rose again. Investigators followed up a tip by children who said they had seen a hand sticking from the ground on another ranch, the Rancho Los Leones, belonging to other members of the family.

When the Mexican federal police dug in a clearing in an orchard, they discovered a common grave containing two bodies of unidentified males. Later, the remains were identified as those of two suspected drug-traffickers, one a 52-year-old Hispanic who had lived in Houston, Texas, and the other, a Mexican national who lived on a small farm near Matamoros. Neither appeared to have been tortured or mutilated.

The investigators believed the two victims had somehow been involved in the operations of the drug-cult gang led by Constanzo. In Brownsville, Sheriff Perez told newsmen that the two newly discovered killings were "drug-related, revenge type killings." Relatives of the two victims, however, denied the men had been implicated in any drug dealing.

Meanwhile, eight of the 13 murder victims on the other ranch had been identified, police said. The other five were buried in paupers' graves, their identities unknown. In a Catholic church near the town of Santa Fe, Texas, Mark Kilroy was laid to rest. An estimated 1,000 mourners attended the service, tearful and grieving.

In Matamoros, families of missing relatives seeking to identify the victims filed through a funeral home where the bodies were taken.

It was unlikely that the bodies would be identified because of the advanced state of decomposition, police said. A forensic specialist had performed autopsies on seven of the bodies. He reported that in addition to the castrations, the men's lungs, hearts and brains had been removed. In several cases, the skin had been peeled from their faces. More horrible, some of the mutilation had been done while they were alive, according to the pathologist's report.

In addition to Kilroy, victims said to have been

identified included Gilberto Garza Soa, about 36; Victor Saul Sauceda-Galvan, a 22-year-old former policeman; and Valente Del Fierro. Additional victims included Jose Garcia, 14; Ezequiel Rodriguez Lana, 27; Ruben Vela Garza, 30; and Ernesto Rivas Diaz, 23 — all from Mexico.

Police told newsmen that three of the victims whom they identified as drug-traffickers — Luna, Garza and Diaz — had been machine-gunned to death by cult leader Constanzo.

The two bodies found on the other ranch were identified by authorities as Moises Castillo, of Houston, and Hector de la Fuente, 39, who lived near Matamoros.

Meanwhile, in Mexico City, several hundred miles from the border city where the mass murders had been unearthed, police were hot on the trail of Constanzo and his towering priestess, Sara Aldrete.

Federal police swept down on two residences where Constanzo was known to have lived. One was an apartment that the cult leader maintained in the Roma District of the capital city. The other was a large white stucco house 11 miles northeast of the center of the city.

The apartment yielded names and addresses of other cult members, as well as a photograph of Adolfo Constanzo that had been taken in Mexico City. Inside the heavily guarded stucco house, police discovered the cult leader's version of a Santeria altar. Federal agents armed with submachineguns raided the large house but found that Constanzo had left earlier. Neighbors grilled by the agents said that several young men who said they were university students had moved into the house two years before.

Inside the house, the officers found remains of goats and chickens. The animals apparently had been used for sacrifices, they said. According to neighbors, the men usually dressed in black and drove large luxury cars, including a Mercedes-Benz, with foreign licenses.

As the manhunt continued, agents learned that Constanzo had ties in Houston, Texas, and had purchased luxury cars there.

Mexican officials speculated that the tall cult priestess, Aldrete, might be dead, a murder victim herself. There were reports that her passport and purse had been found in the white stucco house in Mexico City. There was one theory that she had been slain by Constanzo to keep her quiet about the scope of the drug-smuggling operations. Authorities did learn that Constanzo and three other men had boarded a flight from Brownsville to Mexico City on April 11th, the same day the bodies were discovered on the Matamorous ranch.

Address books found in the big stucco hideaway prompted police to question men in Mexico City's homosexual community, where the cult leader was said to be well known.

"They are men who knew him from parties and gay bars," one Mexican investigator said. He added that pornographic magazines showing men engaged in sex acts were found in Constanzo's apartment. Investigators also turned up a photo of Constanzo with a man they said was his lover.

The suspects in custody continued to spill what they knew about the devilish cult leader: he drank alcoholic beverages, he didn't use drugs and he forbade their use by any of the gang. Police confirmed that Constanzo had slain one of his gang members, one of the men found in the ranch killing field, because he used cocaine.

Authorities were deluged with scores of tips about "sightings" of the fugitives Constanzo and Aldrete and other cult members. A convenience store clerk in Clovis, New Mexico, reported that a couple answering the description of the two had stopped to make a purchase. But no trace of the suspect was found in the area.

Customs Agent Oran Neck told newsmen, "We've been inundated with leads that have not paid off yet. But we encourage people to keep looking. That's how we will find them. We've got lawmen looking for them throughout North and South America."

And as it turned out, Neck's words were prophetic.

In the central part of Mexico City, residents of

433

one neighborhood wondered about the occupants of an old apartment building. The people who lived in the building seemed to be preoccupied with keeping their activities from any public scrutiny.

When they bought large supplies of groceries, they made it a point to lug home the groceries themselves and not allow any delivery people into their apartment, the neighbors noted. And there was the strange-acting, tall young woman with the men, who honed the curiosity of the area's residents. Finally, somebody went to the police and told them of his suspicions.

As a result, On Saturday, May 6, 1989, a large contingent of police combed a five-block area around a supermarket looking for suspects.

A detail of officers spotted a black Chrysler that was thought to belong to the elusive cult leader. They were looking at the car when a burst of gunfire broke out from a fourth-floor window of a nearby apartment building.

As the armed officers scurried for cover and began returning the gunfire, someone threw numerous bills of paper currency from the apartment window. A man who scuttled about trying to gather some of the money was wounded in the blaze of shots being fired from the building.

Some 45 minutes later, after reinforcements wearing bulletproof vests swarmed into the area, the heavily armed officers stormed the apartment. As they burst through the door, the people inside quickly raised their hands and surrendered.

Sweeping through the apartment, the officers looked into a closet and discovered the bullet-riddled bodies of two men.

The survivors of the gun battle told police that the bodies were those of Adolfo Constanzo and his male lover, Martin Quintana Rodriguez, who was said to have been the godfather's right-hand man. Unbelievable as the story sounded, the suspects claimed that Constanzo had ordered them to kill him and Rodriguez after the gunfight with the police broke out.

Among those nabbed in the apartment was Sara Aldrete. She had cut and dyed her hair to avoid identification. She told the police that one of the gang members, Alvaro de Leon Valdez, had been ordered by Constanzo to kill him and his companion, Rodriguez. This was confirmed by de Leon Valdez in his statements to police and reporters.

He said that he was asleep in the apartment when Constanzo spotted the officers on the street outside and mistakenly thought their hideout had been pinpointed.

The suspect said that after one member shouted that the police are here, Constanzo went bersek. He said, according to Valdez, "Why run? Don't hide." "Then he grabbed a bundle of money and threw it out the window. He said if he could not enjoy the money, no one else could, either."

As police ringed he apartment, the cult leader begged de Leon Valdez to kill him and his male lover, the suspect said. As de Leon Valdez balked, Constanzo told him it would be hard on him in hell if he didn't comply with the order.

The suspect said, "He slapped me twice in the face. We could hear the cops outside shooting. A lot of shots could be heard. They sat down in a closet, Constanzo on a stool and Martin beside him. I just stood there in front of them and pressed the trigger. That was it."

He had riddled them with a Uzi machinegun, according to his story. The suspect said he then continued shooting out the window at the police until his ammunition ran out.

The priestess told police, "He (Constanzo) ordered him to kill him because he wanted to die with Martin."

Valdez also admitted having taken part in several of the killings on the Matamoros ranch and said that he and others had sat around a table watching Constanzo mutilate the victims. Also arrested in the apartment were a man and a woman identified by police as Omar Ochoa and Maria Rofillo Gomez. Police said two others escaped during the battle.

At first, U.S. authorities were suspicious that Constanzo might have faked his death and had someone else slain by the machine gunner. But the cult leader was positively identified through a fingerprint analysis.

Mexican authorities booked the five suspects on charges of homicide, criminal association and wounding a police agent during the arrest and damage to property.

The suspects arrested earlier at Matamoros and charged with murder, kidnapping, narcotics, trafficking, clandestine burial and weapons charges in the ritual deaths, were identified as Serafin Hernandez Garcia, 22; his uncle, Elio Hernandez Rivera, 22; Sergio Martinez, 23; and David Serna Valdez, 21.

On May 9th, Mexican officials announced that the drug-cult gang was apparently implicated in eight other slayings that had occurred in 1987 in Mexico City and were similar to the Matamoros ritual killings.

Police said the victims included five men and three women whose mutilated bodies were found at the bottom of a lake. The bodies were found after a tip that a housekeeper—whose body could be found in the lake, according to the informant—had disappeared after telling friends she planned to attend a "black mass."

The chests had been cut open and their bodies had been mutilated, said police. The bodies were bound to cement blocks with wire.

"These cases were very definitely linked to

437

Constanzo," said Rodrigo Martinez, chief of the investigating team probing the slayings.

One of the men nabbed in the apartment-building shootout with the gang also blamed the murder and dismemberment of a man said to be a transvestite on Adolfo Constanzo, police disclosed. The victim was identified as Ramon Baez, also known as Edgar N. Or Claudia Ivette.

The five nabbed in the apartment shootout were later indicted in a Mexican court on charges of murder and other related charges in the slaying of Constanzo and Rodriguez. The Mexico City suspects were not charged in the Matamoros ranch killings, police said.

Sara Aldrete denied implication in any of the killings, though Mexican prosecutors said she had given statements deeply implicating her in the gang's operations. The cult members were also charged in Texas with drug-smuggling, but U.S. authorities said the Mexican government would have priority over prosecuting the group.

APPENDIX

"Skinheads' 'Boot Party' Bloodbath!"
True Detective, December, 1990
"Six Lovely Girls for Satan's Flesh Eaters!"
True Detective, September, 1985
" 'Disciples' Strangled the Teenage Sex Kitten!"
Front Page Detective, June, 1984
"Satanic Mutilations in the Graveyard!"
Inside Detective, January, 1987
"Murder Wasn't Enough for the Killer-Cultists!"
True Detective, January, 1985
"Three Slain Because They Were Witches!"
True Detective, May, 1985
"A Human Sacrifice to Satan!"
Official Detective, February, 1989
"Murdered at the Foot of a Voodoo Altar!"
Official Detective, March, 1988
'Loving a Nympho Devil-Worshipper Can
Be Fatal!"
True Detective, May, 1984
"The Heinous Crime of Satan's High Priestess
of Death!"
Official Detective, October, 1985
"Nebraska's Weird Torture Cult!"
Inside Detective, March, 1987
"Satan's Disciples Demanded Human Sacrifices!"
Official Detective, January, 1990

THEY'RE NOT FOR THE FAINT-HEARTED — TRUE CRIME FROM PINNACLE BOOKS!

THE BEST IN CONTEMPORARY SUSPENSE

WHERE'S MOMMY NOW? (366, $4.50)
by Rochelle Majer Krich

Kate Bauers couldn't be a Superwoman any more. Her job, her demanding husband, and her two children were too much to manage on her own. Kate did what she swore she'd never do: let a stranger into her home to care for her children. *Enter Janine.*

Suddenly Kate's world began to fall apart. Her energy and health were slipping away, and the pills her husband gave her and the cocoa Janine gave her made her feel worse. Kate was so sleepy she couldn't concentrate on the little things—like a missing photo, a pair of broken glasses, a nightgown that smelled of a perfume she never wore. Nobody could blame Janine. Everyone loved her. Who could suspect a loving, generous, jewel of a mother's helper?

COME NIGHTFALL (340, $3.95)
by Gary Amo

Kathryn liked her life as a successful prosecuting attorney. She was a perfect professional and never got personally involved with her cases. Until now. As she viewed the bloody devastation at a rape victim's home, Kathryn swore to the victim to put the rapist behind bars. But she faced an agonizing decision: insist her client testify or to allow her to forget the shattering nightmare.

Soon it was too late for decisions: one of the killers was out on bail, and he knew where Kathryn lived. . . .

FAMILY REUNION (375, $3.95)
by Nicholas Sarazen

Investigative reporter Stephanie Kenyon loved her job, her apartment, her career. Then she met a homeless drifter with a story to tell. Suddenly, Stephanie knew more than she should, but she was determined to get this story on the front page. She ignored her editor's misgivings, her lover's concerns, even her own sense of danger, and began to piece together a hideous crime that had been committed twenty years ago.

Then the chilling phone calls began. And the threatening letters were delivered. And the box of red roses . . . dyed black. Stephanie began to fear that she would not live to see her story in print.

Available wherever paperbacks are sold, or order direct from the Publisher. Send cover price plus 50¢ per copy for mailing and handling to Pinnacle Books, Dept. 17- 528, 475 Park Avenue South, New York, N.Y. 10016. Residents of New York, New Jersey and Pennsylvania must include sales tax. DO NOT SEND CASH.

ED MCBAIN'S MYSTERIES

JACK AND THE BEANSTALK (17-083, $3.95)
Jack's dead, stabbed fourteen times. And thirty-six thousand's missing in cash. Matthew's questions are turning up some long-buried pasts, a second dead body, and some beautiful suspects. Like Sunny, Jack's sister, a surfer boy's fantasy, a delicious girl with some unsavory secrets.

BEAUTY AND THE BEAST (17-134, $3.95)
She was spectacular—an unforgettable beauty with exquisite features. On Monday, the same woman appeared in Hope's law office to file a complaint. She had been badly beaten—a mass of purple bruises with one eye swollen completely shut. And she wanted her husband put away before something worse happened. Her body was discovered on Tuesday, bound with wire coat hangers and burned to a crisp. But her husband—big, and monstrously ugly—denies the charge.